OSF DISTRIBUTED COMPUTING ENVIRONMENT

# *Understanding* DCE

OSF DISTRIBUTED COMPUTING ENVIRONMENT

# *Understanding* DCE

## WARD ROSENBERRY
## DAVID KENNEY
## GERRY FISHER
*Digital Equipment Corporation*

O'Reilly & Associates, Inc.
103 Morris Street, Suite A
Sebastopol CA 95472

*Understanding DCE*

by  Ward Rosenberry,  David Kenney, and Gerry Fisher

Cover design by Edie Freedman
Cover illustration by Chris Reilley

Copyright © 1992 O'Reilly & Associates, Inc.  All rights reserved.
Printed in the United States of America.

*Editor:*  Andy Oram

*Printing History:*

| | |
|---|---|
| September 1992: | First Edition. |
| May 1993: | Minor corrections. |

Nutshell Handbook and the Nutshell Handbook logo are registered trademarks of O'Reilly & Associates, Inc.

Many of the designations used by manufacturers and sellers to distinguish their products are claimed as trademarks.  Where those designations appear in this book, and O'Reilly and Associates, Inc. was aware of a trademark claim, the designations have been printed in caps or initial caps.

While every precaution has been taken in the preparation of this book, the publisher assumes no responsibility for errors or omissions, or for damages resulting from the use of the information contained herein.

This book is printed on acid-free paper with 85% recycled content, 15% post-consumer waste.  O'Reilly & Associates is committed to using paper with the highest recycled content available consistent with high quality.

ISBN: 1-56592-005-8

[2/96]

04418784

# Table of Contents

## Chapter 2: Cells: The Domain of the Distributed Environment     *23*

## Chapter 3: Remote Procedure Call: The Foundation of Distributed Computing     *39*

## *Chapter 6: DCE Directory Service: Locating Resources*     *71*

## *Chapter 7: DCE Time Service: Synchronizing Network Time*     *87*

## Chapter 8: DCE Distributed File Service:
##           Providing Cellwide Access to Files                    *93*

## Chapter 9: A Look at Writing DCE Applications                    *101*

# *Figures*

# *Examples*

# *Tables*

# *Preface*

*Understanding DCE* fills a serious information gap that has emerged in the field of networked computing. On one side is the Distributed Computing Environment (DCE), an enormous software system from the Open Software Foundation (OSF) embodying some novel and complex concepts. On the other side stand potential purchasers, system administrators, application programmers, and end users, many of whom have little previous exposure to distributed computing. Before studying and mastering the various daemons, utilities, and programming libraries that make up DCE, newcomers must answer the basic questions "What are all these things?" and "What do they mean for me?"

In this book we try to answer those questions. We try to bypass the steep slopes of novelty and complexity by returning to the basic reasons that DCE was created. We talk about how typical organizations are set up, and how their work-flow and information needs are satisfied (or hampered) by their computing environments. We fit each component of DCE carefully into its proper place—not just within the rest of DCE, but within the larger context of user needs and organizational structures. The final chapters of the book offer some guidelines to help you plan your move to DCE even before you make a purchase decision.

DCE is meant to link people together and provide them with a shared system for running their computer applications, irrespective of the number of different computers they use and where the computers are located. When DCE is installed and maintained well, users don't deal directly with it. In fact, the critical achievement lies precisely in what users don't have to deal with: they don't have to log in to different computers to do different tasks, or send each other files over e-mail in order to share information, or ask for special user accounts on every system they have to use on occasion.

To produce this illusion of seamless, one-system computing, DCE puts a certain burden on administrators, and on programmers who write applications that are meant to run on more than one system at once. Administrators have to install a lot of daemon processes, register users, and assign security attributes. Programmers have to put new wrappers and error-handling functions in their programs, at the very least. Some of the burdens are absorbed by DCE's sophisticated utilities and services. But you still need a sense of what each service does and what is left for you to do.

The authors of this book have been studying the how's and why's of DCE for several years. We all work at Digital Equipment Corporation in the Distributed Processing Engineering group that designed and developed many core components of DCE. Before the idea of DCE was born at OSF, our group collaborated with Apollo Computer to develop a remote procedure call product based on Apollo's Network Computing System (NCS), one of DCE's chief predecessors. While DCE was still just a buzzword in most of the computing world, our group was running prototype versions and learning what it is like to live with the environment. This book benefits not only from our thoughts on the subject, but especially from the many engineers who designed DCE components, made applications work on DCE, and then told us what they learned in the process.

There are many angles from which you can approach DCE—that is one reason why three of us collaborated on this book—but we think there is something special here for everybody. For system and network administrators who have to do resource planning and configuration, we say what the major components of DCE are for, and discuss alternative strategies for managing them. For programmers who need to make their applications run over DCE, we show the major tasks they have to carry out, warn them about problems to watch for, and suggest a variety of ways to use DCE creatively.

## Document Structure

This book is organized into three parts; it includes 14 chapters and five appendices.

**Part I**, *Components*, gives you the facts—and also a little interpretation. It talks about all the files you see streaming by when you install DCE: libraries, utilities, and daemon services. When you get through with this part, you should have some idea of why they are there and how they fit together.

Chapter 1, *DCE: The Network as Computer*, describes the problems involved in getting applications and people to work across networked hosts. It gives you a sense of DCE's scope, but only hints at solutions and design decisions. These appear in the chapters that follow.

Chapter 2, *Cells: The Domain of the Distributed Environment*, jumps into the architecture of DCE. This chapter lies mostly at the level of system and network administration, with some discussion of effects on users. One of the essential trade-offs in distributed computing is how large to make your domain or administrative unit: you want it big enough so that users can reach resources easily, but small enough to avoid drowning in administrative overhead. The term used in DCE for an administrative unit is a cell. DCE tries to balance the needs of access and overhead by offering a variety of naming conventions tied to different DCE services, and by running a sophisticated daemon called the Cell Directory Service (CDS) that helps programs find resources.

Chapter 3, *Remote Procedure Call: The Foundation of Distributed Computing*, continues the general discussion of DCE architecture by explaining the glue that holds everything together at the programming level. DCE RPC is far more than a programming interface: in addition to calls used by application programmers, it embodies a descriptive language that ensures compatibility between clients and servers, and a set of automatically-generated routines to take the burden of communications off of programmers' shoulders. Aside from general concepts, this chapter discusses utilities and tasks that are of interest to programmers.

Chapter 4, *Threads: Improving Program Performance*, discusses another programming feature, one that is less fundamental to the whole DCE concept. DCE Threads are mostly POSIX pthreads, but offer some extensions to make programming a little easier. We'll see more about threads (and RPC, too) in Chapter 9.

Chapter 5, *DCE Security Service: Protecting Resources*, is the first of a set of four chapters describing the services that are part of DCE. Most computer users think of security as more of a headache and an imposition than a valuable service, but it is absolutely critical in a networked environment. The solution found in DCE is actually quite intriguing and clever, and we expect this chapter to persuade you that your data will stay safe and private.

Chapter 6, *DCE Directory Service: Locating Resources*, winds its way through one of the more complex collections of servers designed to hide the network from users. This chapter revisits the Cell Directory Service (CDS), which was mentioned in Chapter 2. Here we delve into more detail about how this service works, so that programs can continue to operate even when systems go down and servers are moved around. A lot of the factors in the structure and operation of CDS actually affect performance, so it is worth your while to understand what CDS does to improve response time, and how you can organize your directories to help. By the way, the "directories" in this chapter contain pointers to servers and other DCE objects, not files; files are discussed in Chapter 8.

Chapter 7, *DCE Time Service: Synchronizing Network Time*, briefly covers one of the most intellectually satisfying of the DCE services. In modern life, seconds can make a difference. When computers share files and tasks, it is important for hosts to stay in step, and the DCE Time Service uses some interesting techniques to keep them that way.

Chapter 8, *DCE Distributed File Service: Providing Cellwide Access to Files*, discusses the last of the DCE services, and the one that has the most direct effect on users. DFS makes filenames completely independent of the systems on which files are located. Ultimately, after it undergoes some more development and becomes more stable, DFS will allow file replication, so that users can keep working even when some systems go down.

Chapter 9, *A Look at Writing DCE Applications*, gives you a glimpse of what it is like to work with DCE. While it discusses application programming, it makes valuable reading for everyone at the site where DCE is installed, because many of the questions deal with the purpose of an application and what people want to do with it. The chapter includes design steps, debugging tips, and programming language issues. As an exercise, it applies the design steps to the small program in Appendix A.

**Part II**, *Configuration and Management Considerations*, moves away from the technical issues and toward problem-solving. We hope that this part of the book will be useful to system and network administrators long before they install DCE. At the very least, these chapters should help people get a feel for what life with DCE is like.

Chapter 10, *Getting Started with DCE*, is a brief introduction meant to put you in the proper frame of mind. DCE installation and management is a gradual, continuous process, not a frantic one-time activity.

Chapter 11, *Determining Your Cell's Boundaries*, lays out a few important criteria for the first decision you'll have to make (after the decision to install DCE at all, which might not be under your control). This chapter talks about very general matters, such as the work flow and the needs of users at your site, so you can apply the ideas before DCE even arrives.

Chapter 12, *Initial Cell Configuration Guidelines*, discusses the first things to do after DCE arrives. It suggests how to choose a name for the cell, describes what you need to install in order to get DCE started, and offers some reasons for putting DCE services on one host or on several.

Chapter 13, *Setting Up Security in a New Cell*, discusses the question of who manages each resource and service in DCE. Security policies are rather complicated, even at the beginning of your cell's existence, when DCE offers you a default set of access rights. A concern running throughout this chapter, is how to find a set of people to whom you can appropriately delegate some management tasks.

Chapter 14, *Distributing and Replicating Core DCE Services*, discusses the trade-offs in breaking up or replicating key data used by DCE, such as directories within CDS and the Registry within the Security Service.

**Part III**, the *Appendices*, provides some useful side discussions that could add another dimension to your understanding of DCE.

Appendix A, *DCE Client/Server Examples*, lists the complete code of some very simple but functional programs (a "hello world" application) that give you the flavor of programming with RPC, threads, and security. These programs are the basis for a sample discussion of design considerations in Chapter 9.

Appendix B, *Common DCE Questions . . . and Some Answers*, is like a Notes group or Frequently Asked Questions list. It contains lots of interesting tidbits for purchasers, system administrators, and programmers. Browse any time.

Appendix C, *External Time Providers and Services*, summarizes where to find an accurate time source to tap into.

Appendix D, *Registering a Name: GDS and DNS*, tells you how to register your cell names so that they can be used consistently by organizations outside of your own.

## *Conventions*

Throughout the book we use the following typographic conventions:

Constant width
> indicates a code example, system output, or user input.

**Bold**  introduces new terms or concepts. Words in bold also represent system elements such as filenames and directory names, and literal portions of command syntax. DCE-specific routines, data types, and constants are in bold.

*Italic*  words or characters in command syntax or examples indicate variables for which the user supplies a value.

[]  enclose attributes in interface definitions and Attribute Configuration Files (ACFs) and are part of the syntax. Note that this is different from the common convention where brackets enclose optional items in format and syntax descriptions.

>  represents system prompts.

S>    represents a server system prompt to distinguish it from a client system prompt.

C>    represents a client system prompt to distinguish it from a server system prompt.

In order to execute commands, you must press the Return key. The Return key is assumed (not shown) in examples.

## Related Documentation

Sudama, Ram. *Distributed Application Methods.* Digital Equipment Corporation: June 14, 1991.

Birrell, Andrew D. *An Introduction to Programming with Threads.* Digital Equipment Corporation: 1989.

Open Software Foundation. *DCE Administration Guide.* Cambridge, MA: 1992.

———. *DCE Administration Reference.* Cambridge, MA: 1992.

———. *DCE Application Development Guide.* Cambridge, MA: 1992.

———. *DCE Application Development Reference.* Cambridge, MA: 1992.

———. *Introduction to DCE.* Cambridge, MA: 1992.

Shirley, John. *Guide to Writing DCE Applications.* Cambridge, MA: O'Reilly and Associates, Inc., 1992.

## Acknowledgments

Writing about DCE has been a challenging and gratifying experience. Much of what appears was culled directly from many of the engineers who designed and developed DCE. Thus we owe our thanks to a great many people in Digital and at other companies, without whom this book would not have been possible.

First, our heartfelt thanks go to Andy Oram at Hitachi Computer Products. His exhaustive reviews and many suggestions for keeping our audience in focus were a major force in determining the shape of this book. We're still trying to figure out how he knows so much about DCE.

Much of the research for this book was conducted with Digital engineers who designed and developed major DCE components. We would like to thank Digital Equipment Corporation and all of these people, including Danny Cobb, Joe Comuzzi, Paul Curtin, Mark Fox, Brian Keane, Peter Keegan, Howard Mayberry, Janet McCann, Wick Nichols, Ken Ouellette, and Ram Sudama.

Equally important in refining the technical accuracy of the book were many iterations and review cycles involving those already mentioned and the following people at Digital and at other companies: Larry Augustus, Michael Blackstock, Alex Chen, Judy Egan, Andy Ferris, Tonie Franz, Jean Fullerton, Fred Glover, Jerry Harrow, Wei Hu, Peter Hurley, Darrell Icenogle, Vicky Janicki, Tim Mann, Linda Marshall, Laura McCauley, Marll McDonald, Brian Schimpf, John Shirley, Jeff Kaminski at Transarc Corporation, Inc., Stephan Katz at IBM, and Mike Mason at Sequent Computers.

DCE documents written by technical writers at Digital Equipment Corporation formed the basis for some information we've provided in this book. For their work on these documents we'd like to thank Sally Hehir, Eric Jendrock, Kathleen Johnson, Suzanne Lipsky, Craig McGowan, Mary Orcutt, Mary Beth Raven, Gary Schmitt, Diane Sherman, Margie Showman, and Ellen Vliet. We also want to thank Susan Hunziker for her editorial help and indexing expertise.

The production staff at O'Reilly and Associates has done a wonderful job of putting the finishing touches on this book. Special thanks goes to Kismet McDonough, who copyedited the manuscript and integrated countless last-minute changes from three authors. Our gratitude also goes to artist Jeff Robbins, who masterfully instilled life into our flat sketches and drawings, and to Ellie Cutler for polishing up the final index. For all of their work, we thank the entire O'Reilly staff, including Edie Freedman for the cover design and Chris Reilly for his inital work on our illustrations.

Finally, we want to thank Frank Willison at Digital Equipment Corporation and Steve Talbott at O'Reilly and Associates for their vision and efforts in getting this project off the ground in the first place.

# PART I
## Components

1

# DCE: The Network as Computer

Every day, computer networks continue to grow in both size and complexity. Network managers everywhere are connecting more computers to networks and connecting networks to other networks. The single purpose behind such explosive growth in networks is to enable computers to work together efficiently, to simplify sharing resources such as files, applications, printers, and even special computers.

Many networks contain computers from different manufacturers, which complicates the task of getting computers to work together efficiently. Computers in such "multivendor" networks are usually difficult to operate together because they do not use common data formats. For instance, some hosts use 32-bit data while others use data of other lengths such as 16-bit or 64-bit. Byte ordering within these data constructs can vary as well, requiring special converters to enable data sharing between differing hosts. The lack of a common network naming scheme also limits the degree to which computers can share information.

Such obstacles promote continued dependence on applications that run only on individual computers. People who work in organizations that depend on computers must cope daily with the limitations imposed by poorly integrated computing environments.

The following scenarios show computing environments at varying levels of development. Each scenario is slightly further along in the development of true distributed computing. But in each case, users still suffer because of large areas of inefficiency and potential for error.

- **Level 1. Collaborative Work.** A nutritionist and a statistician decide to write a joint paper about field data collected by their organization. Each has analytical information to contribute and wants to weave a particular point of view into the paper. In many organizations, these users would have to send floppy disks through the mail in order to share work on the project. In a more sophisticated setting, they can exchange files through electronic mail or file-transfer programs like FTP. But even these solutions, while they can cut down the time lag in transferring data, still require the users to take turns working on each file. Even more frustrating, each user spends a lot of time reintegrating the changes made by the other. An alternative way to work on shared projects—logging in remotely to the system with the data—is cumbersome too, because a user has to move into an unfamiliar environment and leave behind some favorite tools.

- **Level 2. Individual Computers.** A financial analyst runs a sophisticated modeling program on a low-powered workstation, making long-term projections for various groups in her department. Although each projection is based on changing only one or two data points, each one takes about a half an hour to complete. She has tried to speed up the compute time by simplifying the model but this has also made the projections less dependable.

Today's processor-hungry, stand-alone applications are frequently confined by a computer's ability. More and more users are finding themselves stranded on islands of limited computing power.

- **Level 3. Local Data Storage.** New personal workstations are distributed to an excited group of users, who have become tired of the poor response time of their old multiuser system. When they bring up the new systems, though, they are surprised to find that there is not enough disk space for their files. The bitmapped fonts alone take up more than four megabytes. Ultimately, the users have to keep most of their work files on the old system.

This scenario is a dramatic instance of the increasing size of a typical user's data. Databases, programming libraries, and graphics packages are all burgeoning. It is critical, therefore, to make secondary storage (disks) available across systems seamlessly, while preserving the response time of the personal workstations.

- **Level 4. Tendency of Data and Programs to Move Around.** A Management Information Systems (MIS) group maintains a large database on one of their systems and distributes several applications throughout the company so that other employees can feed data into and query the database. Once every few years, the database has to be moved to a different host because of a system upgrade or a department reorganization. Because the host name and file name are hard-coded in the application, each change requires the MIS group to rewrite the source code, recompile the application, redistribute it to all users, and follow up to make sure the new version is being used. Now the MIS group is shifting to smaller systems and splitting the database into independent sections that will be relocated frequently. The resulting logistics of changing and redistributing applications two or three times a month become totally unfeasible.

This scenario could be improved if the programmers kept volatile configuration information out of their executable files. Many organizations set up a convention such as "whenever the program starts, look in a particular file on the system to find the available service and database." But even this solution becomes a maintenance headache, as is known to anyone who has maintained a mail alias file or a list of local systems in **/etc/hosts**. There is usually a time lag before any change is reflected at each site. If system administrators use an automated procedure to maintain the file, it can easily be corrupted. For continuously running applications, the users must terminate and restart the program so it can reread the file.

- **Level 5. Maintaining Distributed Applications.** A programmer has written a distributed form-based application, in which the portion retrieving the forms runs on the server system containing the database, and the portion displaying the form runs on each user's workstation. In almost every quarter of the fiscal year, users ask for new fields or for changes in existing fields. And each time, the programmer has to change both the program that manages the database and the program that displays the fields. The functions that transmit the data across the network must also be changed. Any inconsistencies among these modules can cause the program to crash or display incoherent information.

  Despite far-sighted attempts to make the program modular, the interrelationships and data structures are so complicated that the programmer must spend a good deal of time updating the program during each three-month cycle, and only the person who wrote the program is capable of maintaining it.

Some vendors have done a good job of interconnecting computers for specific applications such as the Network File System (NFS) from Sun Microsystems® and e-mail. But in many cases, networks have become electronic Frankenstein monsters, hodge-podges of devices, wires, and software patches that are too expensive to abandon or overhaul, trapping their owners in an endless cycle of disappointment and upgrade.

The Distributed Computing Environment (DCE) software provides an enormous opportunity to transform a group of networked computers into a single, coherent computing engine. As a layer of software that masks differences among different kinds of computers, DCE enables you to develop and execute distributed applications that can tap into your network's latent power, using widespread resources such as storage devices, CPUs, and memory. Because distributed parts of these applications can execute concurrently, they can be much more powerful than single-processor applications that must act on data sequentially.

Of course, distributed computing raises issues of its own. How do you protect data that must be shared among multiple computers? How do you synchronize events on separate computers? How do computers with differing data formats and file-naming schemes work cooperatively? DCE software provides an integrated set of tools and services to address these and other distributed computing issues.

# 1.1 DCE Addresses Many Distributed Computing Issues

DCE software includes the tools and services you need to develop and execute distributed applications. Development involves a set of standardized, portable library routines, and a preprocessor that automates many DCE functions. Execution involves a set of daemons that provide everything the applications need at runtime. Once you install and configure DCE on computers in your network, your environment is ready to run distributed applications. Each host computer contains the necessary software to run both clients and servers.

Now let's look at some of the issues of distributed computing and the ways that you can address them using DCE.

## 1.1.1 DCE Harnesses Latent Computing Power

Most organizations have networked computers that spend most of their time simply unused or waiting for input and relatively little time actually processing data. Word-processing applications behave in this manner. Similarly, many high-powered workstations are underused because they run only a graphical interface while their users log in to some other host where the application actually executes. All of this leads to enormous network inefficiency; some experts estimate that about two-thirds of a network's available power is unused.

Despite so much idle computing power, users on overcrowded hosts are frustrated by their hosts' slow response time. Slow response time also affects single-user computers. While today's industrial-strength applications often run workstations at or near capacity, they bring low-powered workstations to their knees.

Furthermore, attempts to tap into the vast power sitting idle on other machines in the network have been hindered by incompatible machine architectures and network limitations.

DCE Remote Procedure Call (RPC) software helps solve these problems by allowing you to distribute applications across multiple computers—even computers of different types. Distribution enables applications to tap into latent computing power wherever it exists in a network, and it can free applications from the confines of stand-alone operation.

DCE can focus even more compute power onto applications through the use of DCE Threads. Using threads, programs can execute multiple remote procedures simultaneously on multiple host computers in the network, greatly speeding up these applications. In short, DCE can help you use the resources you already have without purchasing additional resources.

## 1.1.2 DCE Increases Availability

When applications are located on just a few systems, critical work can be held up for hours if one of these systems goes down. By locating critical application servers on multiple hosts and replicating (copying) important files onto other systems, you can keep critical work in progress even when some systems fail.

## 1.1.3 DCE Facilitates Collaborative Work and Minimizes Storage Limitations

We talked earlier about the difficulties of collaborative work across systems and about limitations of local data storage. Users need a "distributed" or "remote" file system, in which to read or edit files that are physically located on other hosts in the network. Many UNIX system users have encountered a partial solution in the form of Sun's NFS, which makes remote file systems look the same as local ones. DCE goes even further with the Distributed File Service (DFS), which provides a single view of all the files in an organization—on both UNIX and non-UNIX systems—to all users.

## 1.1.4 DCE Services Track Data and Programs that Move Around

When data or programs move from one computer to another, DCE services keep track of their locations, relieving users from having to worry about this low-level detail. The DCE Distributed File Service (DFS) has a database that stores the location of all files in the file service. When files move, DFS automatically updates the database with the new location.

Similarly, distributed application clients can use the DCE Directory Service to locate their associated servers. The Directory Service is comparable to Sun's Network Information Service (NIS) (formerly called "Yellow Pages") but maps host addresses to attributes such as interface name and version

7

number instead of host names. In addition to location information, the Directory Service has generalized support for other resources besides servers, and allows you to specify alternate resources and to set priorities among resources. Moreover, the DCE Directory Service is not limited to operating in a UNIX environment.

When DCE application servers start, they can write their location into the Directory Service. Clients look in the Directory Service for location information, caching it to expedite future uses of the same service. Furthermore, if a server fails in the middle of the application, its clients can find a new server without interrupting users. Using RPC development tools, you can automatically generate the client and server code that uses the DCE Directory Service in this manner.

## 1.1.5 DCE Accommodates Heterogeneous Data

The bit stream that represents a floating-point number or a character string on one computer system may be unintelligible on another. More and more organizations are mixing computers with different architectures and compilers, leading to differences in byte ordering, data formats, and padding between data items. Even character sets have become extremely heterogeneous, as the software tries to accommodate different natural languages.

DCE RPC hides differences in data requirements by converting data to the appropriate forms needed by clients and servers.

## 1.1.6 DCE Helps You Maintain Distributed Applications

Maintaining distributed applications can mean painstaking work to ensure consistency between a server and its clients. DCE RPC uses formal interface definitions that allow programmers to define exactly what data passes between a client and a server. A lot of the programming details in managing and transmitting data—including the conversion of data formats between heterogeneous systems—reside in the interface definition and the code automatically generated from it, freeing programmers to concentrate on higher levels of the application.

Any number of programmers can write servers and clients that communicate correctly, as long as they use the same interface definition. Moreover, programmers can maintain libraries of interfaces in the same way they maintain routines in a runtime library. When it becomes necessary to support new features of the application, programmers can change the interface definition, assign a different version number, and recompile the clients and servers. The version number ensures that each client finds a compatible server.

## *1.1.7 DCE Helps Synchronize Events*

Process control mechanisms frequently depend on timestamps to coordinate interdependent events. A secure computer might allow login and use during a short period of time each morning. If the computer's clock is not synchronized with real time, it might disable logins before employees have even arrived at work.

When host clocks in a network are not synchronized, the age of a shared file cannot be determined accurately or consistently by all hosts that share the file. When copies of shared files exist on multiple hosts, no one can truly determine which file is the most recent, leaving users to rely on possibly outdated versions of data.

The DCE Time Service (DTS) runs on every host in the distributed computing environment, keeping host clocks closely synchronized. You can also synchronize your distributed environment with others by connecting external time signals.

## *1.1.8 DCE Protects Distributed Resources*

Highly publicized network break-ins have alerted everyone to the vulnerability of distributed systems. Different kinds of networked computers use different security mechanisms that often don't operate together seamlessly or, more frequently, don't operate together at all. Such a patchwork of security mechanisms often leaves security holes that attract network snoopers and eavesdroppers.

The DCE Security Service authenticates all DCE users and servers, making certain that people and programs using DCE are who they claim to be. Furthermore, resource administrators can protect distributed resources from unauthorized access using the authorization capabilities of the DCE Security Service.

# *1.2 DCE Is Based on the Client/Server Model*

A typical application contains a number of subroutines or procedures executed from the main program. You can view the procedures as providing services for the main program—say, multiplying two vectors or retrieving a weathermap from a database. Client/server computing results when you establish a set of such procedures as an independent program (server) on one machine and make it possible for client programs on other machines to invoke the procedures, much as if they were local to the client programs. Let's look at a general nondistributed computing model, then we'll talk about some simple client/server models with several variations.

## 1.2.1  A General Nondistributed Computing Model

Most end-user applications consist of three basic parts: a user interface, a computational function, and information storage. In the general computing model for nondistributed applications (see Figure 1-1), these components are often integrated so that they seem indistinguishable. Even in this case, however, using good design principles such as modularity is important. By designing a clearly defined interface between components, you can simplify the task of modifying or maintaining applications later on. Furthermore, such principles allow reuse of these application "building blocks" by other programs or people.

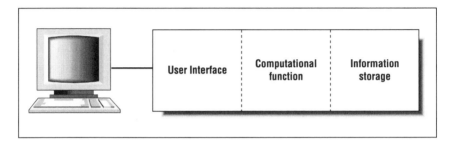

*Figure 1-1: Nondistributed computing model*

## 1.2.2  Distributed Computing Models

To distribute an application across computer systems, the simplest approach is to break it down along the lines of the components shown in Figure 1-1. Each component can then be developed on top of the resources and system services of the computer where it will run.

For example, a user interface can be remote from the computational function, as you find in remote terminal access (see Figure 1-2). In this case, a display function, such as one that draws curves on a screen, might communicate with a remote function that computes the points of an arc.

Likewise, information storage may be remote, as in a distributed file system; routines that process the information in the files are remote from the functions that manage the physical storage media. These simple forms of distribution are extremely useful, primarily because they preserve well-defined interfaces that are already included in many applications, such as the terminal interface and the file system interface. In other words, you can distribute an application by reworking function invocations in the application so that they invoke remote functions. The application makes the same call as it would for a local function, but the interface invokes a remote function.

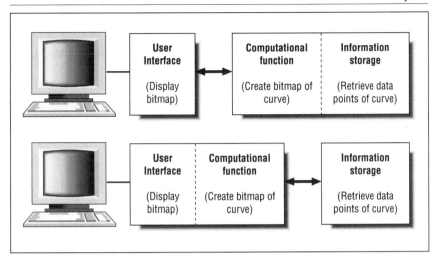

*Figure 1-2: Simple models of distribution*

Often, however, it is desirable to distribute a component itself among multiple machines (see Figure 1-3), rather than distributing a component intact. This approach introduces a level of concurrency not possible in nondistributed applications. Note, though, that concurrency also requires a level of control not required in nondistributed applications.

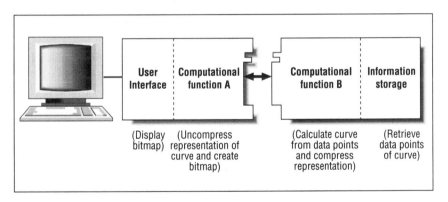

*Figure 1-3: Distribution within an application component*

## 1.2.3 The Client/Server Computing Model

The client/server model is one of the most popular forms of distribution in use today. In this model, a *client* initiates a distributed activity and the *server* carries out that activity. For example, a distributed file service is typically based on the client/server model. One or more systems (the servers) provide access to a set of files for many clients that actually use the files (see Figure 1-4).

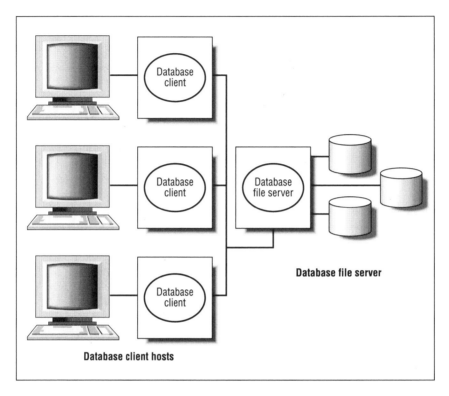

*Figure 1-4: Typical client/server application*

## 1.2.4    Client and Server Are Relative Terms

The terms client and server refer to software rather than to hardware, such as a host computer. This distinction allows a host computer to run multiple applications, some of which can be servers and others of which can be clients. For instance, a host computer can be running editors that are clients of another system's file server, while simultaneously offering a math server that provides special computing power to other systems' clients. Figure 1-5 shows another such configuration, in which one host is both the file server and a print client.

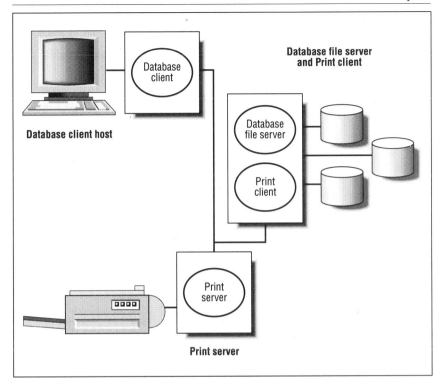

*Figure 1-5: A host can be a client and a server*

## 1.2.5   Client/Server Communications

The foundation of distributed computing is the communication among the distributed components of an application. In a traditional network, distributed applications need to manage many aspects of communication. For instance, an application may need to perform operations such as reverse byte ordering and padding to accommodate differing data requirements between client and server hosts. Applications need to make calls to lower layers of networking software to control communications between client and server, as well as handle recovery from network or server failures.

In a distributed computing environment based on DCE, applications need interact only with high-level DCE software. The RPC component of the DCE software automatically searches the DCE Directory Service for a compatible server. RPC also converts data to and from forms required by different kinds of hosts. Furthermore, RPC manages all of the lower-level aspects of communications, providing network transport independence, connection management, and in some cases, automatic recovery from network or server failure.

# 1.3  DCE: A Model for Distribution

The Distributed Computing Environment provides a set of integrated services that work across multiple systems and remain independent of any single system. The DCE software creates the distributed environment by relying on its own design principles. By incorporating DCE design principles into your design, you can impart similar characteristics to your distributed application.

DCE services are protected from a single point of failure by replicating (copying) the services and important files to additional hosts in the network. Replication ensures that critical services and data are available even after some failures. Distributed user applications can also include replication to improve availability.

Though many interdependencies exist among the DCE components, decentralized control allows you to manage each component independently of the others. For example, the DCE Directory Service information can be divided with parts located close to where they're needed rather than being kept in one central location. Each part of the Directory Service can be independently managed, with the Directory Service automatically updating the other parts with the correct information. This decentralized control allows the distributed environment to expand across LANs and WANs, accommodating potentially thousands of systems. To facilitate management of such large environments, you can divide them into independently manageable subenvironments called **cells**, with each cell providing the DCE services required for a distributed environment.

Such decentralization minimizes bottlenecks. The work load is distributed across multiple hosts rather than being concentrated on a single host. Decentralization promotes flexibility. You can change, add, or reconfigure hardware or software without impacting the surrounding environment. Decentralization is also cost efficient. You can add just the equipment or software that you need to address a particular problem. Distributed applications can use decentralization to improve cost efficiency and to ease application use and management.

DCE is closely integrated, yet its modular structure allows you to tailor DCE configurations by installing DCE servers on computers with appropriate resources. For instance, the DCE Distributed File Service might manage many files, so you are likely to install this service on a computer with a lot of disk space. On the other hand, the DCE Distributed Time Service does not store a lot of data, so you can install these servers on computers that don't have much disk space.

Modularity helps you keep distributed applications more flexible and reuse code for a variety of purposes. An example is a large, multipurpose database in a hospital where admissions has read-only access to certain fields within certain database records. Doctors have read/write access to medical fields in only their own patient's records, and accounts payable has read/write access to patients' financial information fields in all records. Each client application used by admissions, doctors, and accounts payable could be custom tailored to the needs of its user.

# 1.4 A Look at DCE Application Programming Interfaces

As we mentioned earlier, DCE is a layer of software that masks differences between various kinds of hosts. As a layer, it sits on top of the host operating system and networking services, and offers its services to applications above. Figure 1-6, one conceptual model of DCE, shows the relationship of the DCE distributed services (Security, Directory, and Time) to RPC and Threads services. RPC and Threads are base DCE services that are available on every system on which DCE is installed. The figure also shows how the DCE File Service is similar to an application that uses the underlying DCE services for distribution. Notice that the DCE Directory Service consists of the Cell Directory Service (CDS) and the X.500 Global Directory Service (GDS), which programs use by calling the X.500 Directory Service (XDS) application programming interface (API).

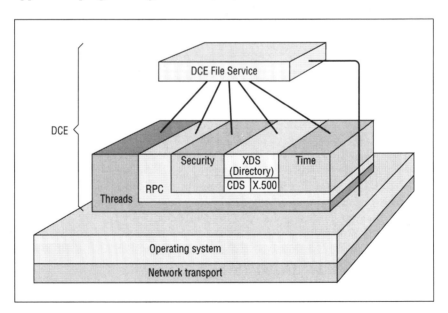

*Figure 1-6: DCE application programming interfaces*

Figure 1-7 shows how an application can use DCE APIs. Notice that the application uses only the APIs it requires. A distributed application does not have to use all DCE APIs. In this example, the application uses the RPC, Security, XDS, and operating system APIs.

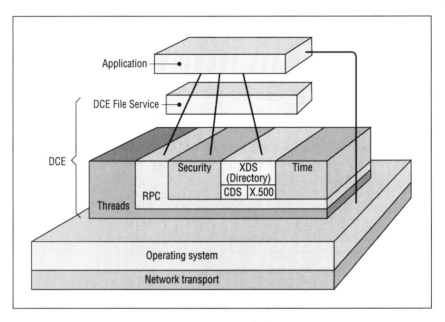

*Figure 1-7: A distributed application uses DCE APIs*

## 1.5 DCE Is a Good Start

DCE, as provided by the Open Software Foundation (OSF), forms a basis for a powerful computing environment. Composed of widely used and well-tested technologies, DCE has the raw ingredients necessary for success. But like any Version 1 product, DCE has areas where improvements can be made. OSF plans to deliver subsequent versions of DCE that will introduce various improvements. In the meantime, we'll tell you where to expect some limitations so that you can write better DCE distributed applications.

### 1.5.1 Component Availability

Although this book treats DCE as though all components are being used, some DCE components are not as mature as others. Consequently, some DCE components or features are not included with DCE version 1.0. At this writing, DFS is not fully functional and the Security Service server replication feature is not yet available. OSF plans to deliver these features in subsequent releases.

## 1.5.2  Administration

DCE components that require administration have individual management interfaces, which you must invoke and use separately. Administrators cannot control all DCE components from within a single management interface.

Some DCE components have succeeded more than others in distributing their own management interfaces. For example, you can control some DCE Security Service features from any host that runs DCE Security Service software. Other DCE components provide distributed management for some operations. To control components or operations that have nondistributed management, you must log in to the host system on which the applicable server resides.

OSF is developing a Distributed Management Environment (DME) that will offer distributed management of all DCE components from within one administrative interface.

## 1.5.3  Documentation

The OSF DCE documentation describes the components of DCE, the routines and commands offered by the system, and some basic guidelines for installing, configuring, and developing applications in DCE. As vendors port DCE to other hardware and software platforms, they will likely need to supply customers with tutorial and practical information for running a distributed computing environment.

## 1.5.4  Performance

DCE performance determines the speed at which distributed applications execute in DCE. Remote procedure calls, security operations, caching, and use of threads affect DCE performance.

### Remote Procedure Calls Affect Performance

Because remote procedure calls involve data conversion and transmission over a network, a remote procedure call usually takes longer to complete than a local procedure call. How much longer depends on factors such as argument length, the network transport used, and the network implementation. On the other hand, a server suited for a particular purpose may process a remote procedure faster than the local client system.

Programmers can reduce the time a program spends on remote calls by making multiple remote procedure calls to different servers simultaneously. Programmers can further offset the effects of remote procedure calls by using local procedure calls wherever practical. Programs that contain a mix of local and remote procedure calls can run faster than programs that use remote procedure calls exclusively.

Because remoteness is a factor, server proximity can affect performance. Response from a server on the client's LAN is likely to be faster than from a server across a WAN link.

### Security Operations Affect Performance

Security operations are time-consuming because they rely on CPU-intensive data encryption and decryption functions. Security operations can occur during connection establishment, preparation of data for transfer, and file or program access, so users may notice delays at any of these points.

Many applications that use security will rely only on authentication and authorization without using the special features that promote data integrity and privacy. Using encryption to ensure the integrity or privacy of all data exchanged with RPC increases the time it takes for all remote procedure calls to complete. For applications that require this level of security, programmers must allow for the added time.

### Caching and DCE Threads Improve Performance

Several DCE services use caching to store expensive information locally. Cached information can be reused, avoiding the need to look it up each time it is needed. The DCE Directory Service caches name and location information, the DCE Security Service caches authentication and authorization information, and the DCE DFS caches information from the files being used. Programmers can use caching to improve the performance of their own DCE applications.

Some programs that use DCE Threads can execute faster than nonthreaded programs because several functions can execute concurrently. Threaded programs on single-processor computers usually interleave fast operations with slower ones. In a DCE environment, threads on a client can control separate remote procedure calls to various server hosts on the network. Threads on a server enable the server to handle multiple client requests concurrently.

## 1.5.5  Support for Object-oriented Programming

Various application development methods referred to as object-oriented programming have rapidly grown in importance in recent years. Although DCE does not provide the tools needed for object-oriented programming, RPC has some features built in to make it easier to implement object-oriented systems. For example, a remote procedure call can be dispatched directly to an object. Similarly, complete object-oriented distribution mechanisms can coexist with DCE RPC, in effect bypassing DCE entirely. Furthermore, programmers can use the Interface Definition Language (a C-like language for developing distributed applications that use DCE RPC) to create objects and define the methods on objects of that class.

However, there is more to distributed object-oriented programming that DCE RPC doesn't do. For example, there is no concept of class hierarchy or inheritance in RPC itself. Also, the definition of objects is static. It's defined in the source code, so a programmer who adds new object definitions to the system must recompile the application.

## *1.5.6 Support for Message Queueing*

Message queueing is an asynchronous programming method wherein a calling program sends data to another process—usually a remote one. When a program sends a message, it just continues executing without waiting for a response.

DCE uses remote procedure calls that are inherently synchronous. Consequently, the calling program always waits for a response from the destination of the remote procedure call before continuing to execute.

Although RPC does not currently support asynchronous semantics necessary for message queueing, application programmers can use other means to include message queueing functions in programs.

## *1.5.7 Support for Transaction Processing Applications*

Many commercial applications depend on individual transactions that either succeed or fail. Automatic Teller Machines (ATMs) use this model called **transaction processing** to guarantee that transactions (electronic deposits or withdrawals) are made correctly. Each transaction depends on the successful completion of a specific sequence of events. A client (the ATM) and server (the computer at the bank) use messages to notify each other as each event completes, committing to the transaction only when both agree that all events have transpired successfully. If any event in the sequence does not transpire, both client and server use the messages to back out of the transaction, restoring the original state, as though the transaction had never been attempted.

Even though DCE does not handle transaction semantics directly (because RPC does not currently support individual management of multiple messages), you can build transaction semantics into a DCE application.

## 1.5.8  Compatibility with Standards

One of DCE's design goals is to conform to standards where they exist. Thus DCE Version 1.0 is compatible with certain standards such as with the Domain Name System, as implemented in Berkeley Internet Name Domain (BIND) and the International Telegraph and Telephone Consultative Committee (CCITT) X.500 Directory Services. In regard to X.500, DCE is close to the International Standards Organization's (ISO) model for Open Systems Interconnection. DCE Threads is an implementation based on the POSIX 1003.4a (Draft 4) standard.

This design goal also applies to future releases of DCE. Thus we anticipate that DCE will continue to track and conform to applicable standards as they mature and emerge.

## 1.5.9  Internationalization

DCE is poised to become a standard for distributed computing and as such, has provisions for accommodating the language needs of many cultures. Currently, DCE supports alphabets that use 8-bit character sets. OSF has set complete internationalization as a goal for DCE Version 1.1. When fully internationalized, DCE will include support for alphabets that use multibyte character sets.

The DCE command interface, error messages, and documentation currently exist only in English. Vendors reselling DCE into non-English-speaking countries may need to translate these DCE components.

# 1.6  Who Will Use DCE?

DCE is not an application in itself, but rather a set of tools and services that helps you create and run distributed applications. In a way, DCE is like an operating system that has application development tools but, as yet, no applications.

At first, application developers will be using DCE tools to create distributed applications. They will be installing DCE and using its tools to create DCE applications. Programmers can develop these applications from the ground up, or they can retrofit existing applications to run in a DCE environment.

Once commercial applications are available, corporate network managers will begin purchasing DCE software and applications to run on their networks. They will assign people to administer the distributed computing environment, and users will begin working with DCE applications. As more applications become available, DCE administrators will install DCE software on more hosts and add more users to the environment until everyone in a company is a member of the distributed environment.

Users who are registered in the distributed computing environment will log in to the environment similarly to the way they log in to their host computer now. Regardless of where they log in from, users will always view their directories and files in one consistent way, and they will always invoke applications in the same way.

# 1.7   What Next?

Now that you have a general idea of how DCE can help consolidate your network into a consistent distributed computing environment, we can look at the ways you can use each service to control your distributed environment. The remaining chapters in Part I provide more detail on each service and the role it plays in DCE.

# 2

# *Cells: The Domain of the Distributed Environment*

The Distributed Computing Environment is extremely scalable. Small environments can consist of several host systems and their users. Even smaller environments are possible, but are likely to be impractical. At the other end of the scale, large environments can include thousands of host systems and many thousands of users spread over a worldwide geographic area.

Smaller environments frequently consist of a single group of users who share common goals. These users frequently work on related projects and are likely to depend on common resources such as files, services, and printers or other devices. Because these users must share resources to reach their goals, they must implicitly trust one another. Such small environments can be managed quite effectively by one or two administrators.

Large environments, on the other hand, can consist of many diverse groups of users, with each group having its own pool of shared resources. Members of one group may have little need to establish trust with members of other groups with different goals. Large environments might require numerous administrators, with perhaps one or more administrators managing each group in the environment.

To accommodate such a wide scale, DCE allows you to divide large environments into independently manageable units called cells.

# 2.1   What Is a Cell?

A **cell** is the basic unit of operation and administration in DCE. Understanding cells is the first step in understanding many DCE concepts.

A cell is a group of users, systems, and resources that typically have a common purpose and share common DCE services. At a minimum, the cell configuration includes the Cell Directory Service, the Security Service, and the Time Service.

A cell usually consists of nodes in a common geographic area—for example, on the same local area network (LAN)—but geography does not necessarily determine its boundaries. It can include one system or as many as several thousand. A small organization may have only one cell, but a large corporation can have many cells. Factors that can determine the configuration of cells include an organization's size, its network topology, and its needs and preferences.

The boundaries of a cell, in terms of the number of systems and users, are influenced by four basic considerations: purpose, administration, security, and overhead.

## 2.1.1   Purpose

Because the concept of a cell revolves around shared resources and shared DCE services, a useful step in determining the boundaries of a cell is to identify a group of users who need easy access to a common set of resources or who will likely share common administrative resources. For example, the people involved in developing a product may all want to share the same cell. Depending on an organization's preferences, the marketing, manufacturing, and support groups associated with that product might also participate in the same cell. Alternatively, if the company is more function-oriented than product-oriented, the development, marketing, manufacturing, and support groups might each have their own cells.

Because the emphasis is on purpose or function, geographical considerations can, but do not have to, play a part in cell design. For example, if a product is being developed partially in New York and partially in California, the New York and California engineering groups can participate in the same cell. However, across long distances additional considerations become important, such as the reliability of connections and security across a Wide Area Network (WAN). Administration and security considerations, discussed next, are likely to be a natural part of the process of identifying a cell's overall purpose.

## 2.1.2 Administration

A cell should contain at least one cell directory server, one security server, and three time servers, as well as the databases that these servers use. These servers can be on separate hosts or on one host. The scope of administrative tasks involving the DCE services and their databases, and the availability of people to do those tasks, can help to determine the scope of the cell. Not all services in a cell need to be managed by the same person or group. An organization can delegate cell administrative tasks in whatever way is most practical and reasonable.

## 2.1.3 Security

In an authenticated environment, users and servers, known as **principals**, must prove their identities before being allowed to accomplish a task. This proof is in the form of a special kind of password. When a user enters a password at login, an authentication server verifies it against the data stored for that user in the authentication database. Principals within a cell share a common authentication server and database.

Security issues that help to determine the scope of a cell include:

- What are the trust boundaries of users in the network? Because all principals in a cell share a common authentication server and database, authentication within a cell is generally less complicated and thus less prone to attack than authentication across cells. Therefore, a cell should contain a set of users that are more likely to establish trust with each other than with principals outside their cell.

- How much work is necessary to repair damage if the security of a cell is compromised? If the security of a cell's authentication server is compromised, all passwords in that cell must be changed because they can no longer be considered secure. The larger a cell, the more work it can be to repair the damage resulting from a breach of security.

- How many cells will operate together? When clients use servers in other cells, the cooperating cells must share a password. Thus a DCE environment with 5 cells that cooperate with each other cell must maintain 20 passwords for complete intercell operation. Each cell administrator maintains a separate account and password for the other 4 cells, exchanging replacement passwords with other cells' administrators when they expire or if the security of a cell's authentication server is compromised. This may not be a problem in DCE environments with 5, 10, or even 20 cells, but it may be a problem if 100 cells (sharing 9,801 passwords) must get new passwords.

## 2.1.4 Overhead

Name resolution and authentication operations incur more software interaction and network traffic between cells than they do within the same cell. The boundary of a cell, therefore, is partially determined by the kinds of resources that users need to access and how often users need to access them.

# 2.2 Each Cell Has a Set of DCE Services

Distributed applications that execute in a DCE cell require a minimum of three DCE services to ensure that the distributed pieces interact properly. Distributed application clients find their application servers by looking up information posted in the DCE Cell Directory Service (CDS). Application servers determine the authenticity and authorization level of clients by using highly protected information from the DCE Security Service. The Security Service uses time information from the cellwide DCE Distributed Time Service (DTS) to limit the lifespan of security information. These and other DCE services rely on base communication services provided by DCE RPC software.

Other DCE services facilitate distribution of information within a cell and help extend the distributed environment to various hardware platforms. But the DCE Directory Service, the DCE Security Service, and the DCE Time Service, supported by DCE RPC, provide the minimum functions that enable distribution within a cell.

## 2.2.1 DCE Services Enable Distributed Operation

To see how required services support distributed computing, let's look at a simple model of how a distributed application runs in DCE. Figure 2-1 shows the client and server parts of a distributed application running on Host 1 and Host 2. We'll assume the application server is an inventory database and the application client is a graphical user interface to the database. Hosts 1 and 2 have DCE client software, including the CDS and DTS clerk software that enables these hosts to interact with DCE server software running on Host 3. All communication between hosts uses DCE RPC.

The simple model in the figure omits some details and is more schematic than an actual implementation. However, it demonstrates the basic interaction among participants in the distributed computing environment.

Though the DCE Time Service is not explicitly mentioned, this service synchronizes time on all DCE hosts so that applications dependent on time for things like event sequencing can function correctly. Synchronized time also enables distributed applications on any DCE host to accurately determine whether security information has expired.

❶ When the application server starts on Host 2, it automatically stores information about its network address (and other information) in the DCE Directory Service.

❷ A user on Host 1 logs in to the distributed environment, and the user's process gets authentication information from the DCE Security Service, storing it for later use.

❸ When the user starts the application client on Host 1, the application uses the DCE client software to search the Directory Service for information about the location of the application server. The Directory Service returns the application server information to the application client.

❹ The application client uses the information from the Directory Service to communicate with the application server. The application client uses the user's authentication information to prove its identity to the application server.

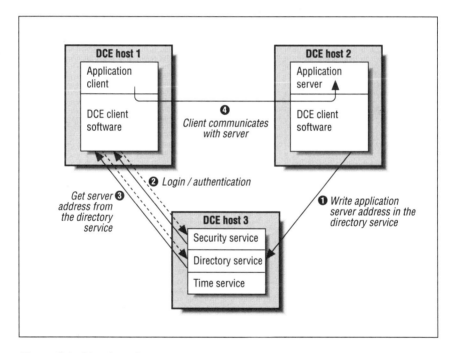

*Figure 2-1: Distributed operation in a DCE cell*

## 2.2.2 DCE Software Configurations for Clients and Servers

Now that we have an idea of how these hosts interact, we'll take a closer look at the DCE software that runs on each one. If a DCE host system runs an application client or an application server but does not run a DCE server, we'll call it a DCE client host. This host has the necessary DCE client software to interact with DCE servers and other DCE clients in the cell. We'll call a DCE host system that runs one or more DCE servers a DCE server host.

Figure 2-2 shows the necessary DCE software that runs on a DCE client host and a DCE server host. The DCE runtime library must be on every DCE host regardless of whether the host is a client or server host. This library includes the RPC and DCE threads routines as well as other DCE routines needed for DCE operations. Notice that server hosts also contain DCE client software because they need to interact with DCE servers located on other hosts in the network and with other DCE client hosts. Server hosts can also be client hosts that run distributed application client or server software.

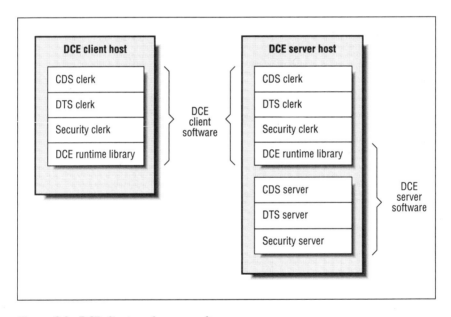

*Figure 2-2: DCE client and server software*

## 2.2.3 Some DCE Cell Examples

Figure 2-3 shows a simple DCE cell with three hosts. Hosts 1 and 2 contain DCE client software (CDS clerk, DTS clerk, security client daemon, and the DCE runtime library). Host 3 includes server software for CDS, DTS, and Security, as well as the DCE runtime library. Host 3 also contains client software. Thus any of these hosts can run a distributed application client or server.

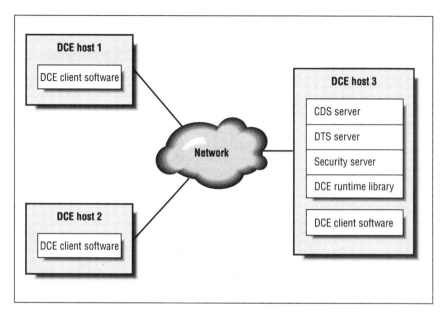

*Figure 2-3: A simple DCE cell*

Many cells will contain numerous hosts and will include other DCE services such as the DCE Distributed File Service (DCE DFS). Figure 2-4 shows such a cell. DCE Host 4 has a DCE DFS file server. Because all hosts in this cell have DCE client software that includes DFS client software, they can use files stored in the DFS file server. The security server is located on DCE Host 6. If security reasons warrant, you can place this host in a locked room to prevent tampering.

Large cells can span wide geographic areas. To reduce the time needed to move server information over long distances, you should establish copies (replicas) of servers close to the hosts that use them. For example, you can have a cell with hosts in Washington, D.C. and other hosts in Los Angeles, California. You should locate one set of servers near the Washington, D.C., hosts and replicas of these servers near the Los Angeles hosts. Part II of this book provides more information about configuring large cells.

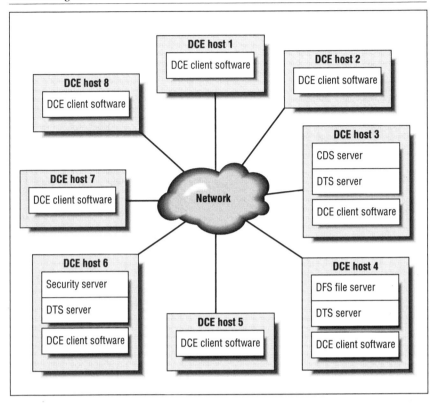

*Figure 2-4: Cell with DCE DFS and multiple DCE client hosts*

# 2.3  Cells and Naming

Once you've set up cells, you'll require access within them and probably between them. DCE provides a naming system that is flexible enough to represent any kind of resource shared between host systems and broad enough to make resources addressable from any cell in the world.

Each resource in a DCE cell, such as a person, file, device, and so on, has a unique name that distinguishes it from any other resource in any other interconnected cell. This is similar to the way a postal service uses names to deliver mail. The addressee's name on an envelope distinguishes each person from any other person in the world. Thus, John Hunter, 30 Newfield Street, Centerville is not confused with John Hunter, 30 Newfield Street, Midvale. Although these persons have the same personal name, and even the same street address, the city name distinguishes them from each other.

The DCE Directory Service stores the names of resources in the DCE. Resources include things like print servers, application servers, or other DCE services. When given a name, the DCE Directory Service returns the unique network address of the named resource. The Directory Service component that controls names inside cells is called the Cell Directory Service (CDS). Because a DCE environment can consist of multiple cells, users must be able to locate resources in other cells or outside of DCE. The Directory Service component that controls names outside cells or between cells is called the Global Directory Service (GDS). When CDS determines that the name is outside the cell, it passes the name to a global name server outside the cell using an intermediary called a Global Directory Agent.

Figure 2-5 represents a hypothetical configuration of two cells that each use GDS to access names in the other cell. Names stored directly in GDS also are accessible from each cell.

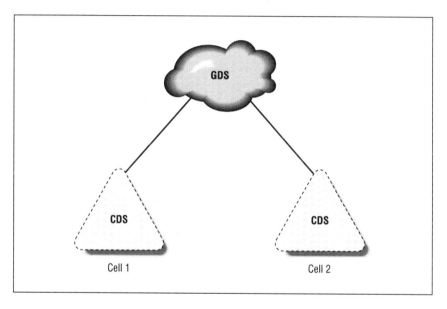

*Figure 2-5: Cell and global naming environments*

GDS is an implementation of a directory service standard known as X.500 Directory Services (XDS). This standard is specified by the CCITT X.500 series and the ISO 9594. Because it is based on a worldwide standard, GDS offers the opportunity for access to resources among users and organizations worldwide.

The Domain Name Service (**DNS**) is a widely used existing global name service. Many networks currently use DNS primarily as a name service for Internet hostnames. Although DNS is not a part of the DCE technology offering, the DCE Directory Service contains support for cells to address each other through DNS. The DCE naming environment supports the version of DNS based on Internet Request for Comments (RFC) 1034 and 1035.

Another DCE component, the Global Directory Agent (**GDA**), makes cell interaction possible. The GDA enables CDS to access a name in another cell using either of the global naming environments (GDS or DNS). The GDA is an independent process that can exist on a system separate from a CDS server. CDS must be able to contact at least one GDA to participate in the global naming environment.

Figure 2-6 shows how the GDA helps CDS access names outside of a cell. When CDS determines that a name is not in its own cell, it passes the name to a GDA, which searches the appropriate global naming environment for more information about the name. The GDA can help CDS find names in a cell that is registered in GDS (path 1) or a cell that is registered in DNS (path 2). The GDA decides which global service to use based on whether the name syntax is X.500 or DNS.

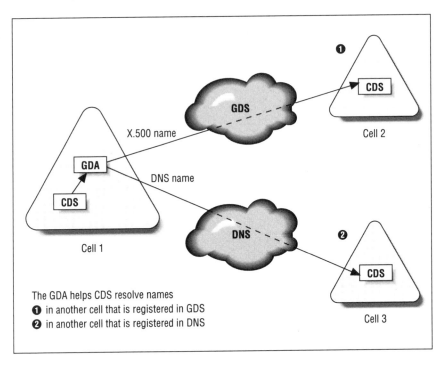

*Figure 2-6: Interaction of CDS and a GDA*

## 2.3.1 How Cells Determine Naming Environments

In addition to delineating security and administrative boundaries for users and resources, cells determine the boundaries for sets of names. Because different naming components operate within and outside of a cell, naming conventions in the cell and global environments differ as well. The DCE naming environment supports two kinds of names: **global** names and

**cell-relative**, or **local**, names. This section introduces the concept of global and local names. Later sections discuss CDS, GDS, and DNS names in detail.

## Global Names

All entries in the DCE Directory Service have a global name that is universally meaningful and usable from anywhere in the DCE naming environment. The prefix **/...** indicates that a name is global. A global name can refer to an object within a cell (named in CDS) or an object outside of a cell (named in GDS or DNS).

The following example shows the global name for an entry created in GDS. The name represents user William Ward, who works in the administrative organization unit of the Widget organization, a British corporation. The name syntax is X.500 style; each element, except the global prefix **/...**, consists of two parts separated by an equal sign (=). The abbreviations stand for country (C), organization (O), organization unit (OU), and common name (CN).

    /.../C=GB/O=Widget/OU=Admin/CN=William Ward

The following example shows a global name for a price database server named in CDS. The server is used by the Portland sales branch of XYZ Company, an organization in the United States.

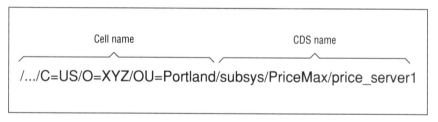

As the example illustrates, global names for entries created in CDS look slightly different from pure GDS-style names. The first portion of the name, **/.../C=US/O=XYZ/OU=Portland**, is a global **cell name** that exists in GDS. The remaining portion of the name, **/subsys/PriceMax/price_server1**, is a CDS name.

The cell name exists because cells must have names to be accessible from the global naming environment. The GDA looks up the cell name in the process of helping CDS in one cell find a name in another cell. Cell names are established during initial configuration of the DCE components. The DCE administrator must obtain a unique cell name from one of the global naming environments, depending on whether the cell needs to be accessed through GDS or DNS. Naming the cell is a critical step since all subsequent resources in that cell "inherit" the cell name as part of their own unique names. Once a cell is named, it is for now extremely difficult to change.

The next example shows the global name of a host at ABC Corporation. The global name of the company's cell, **/ . . . /abc.com**, exists in DNS.

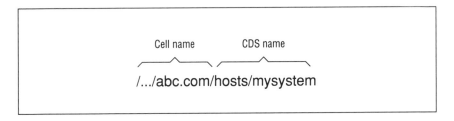

## *Local Names*

In addition to their global names, all CDS entries have a cell-relative, or local, name that is meaningful and usable only from within that entry's cell. The local name is a shortened form of a global name, and thus is a more convenient way to refer to resources within a user's own cell. Local names have the following characteristics:

- They do not include a global cell name.

- They begin with the **/.:** prefix.

Local names do not include a global cell name because the **/.:** prefix indicates that the name being referred to is within the local cell. When CDS encounters a **/.:** prefix on a name, it automatically replaces the prefix with the local cell's name, forming the global name. CDS can handle both global and local names, but it is more convenient to use the local name when referring to a name in the local cell. For example, the following two names are equally valid when used within the cell named **/ . . . /C=US/O=XYZ/OU=Portland**:

```
/.../C=US/O=XYZ/OU=Portland/subsys/PriceMax/price_server1
/.:/subsys/PriceMax/price_server1
```

The naming conventions required for the interaction of local and global directory services may seem confusing at first. In an environment in which references to names outside of the local cell are necessary, a few simple guidelines can help make the conventions easy to remember and use.

- Know your cell name.

- Know whether a name you are referring to is in your cell.

- When using a name that is within your cell, you can omit the cell name and include the **/.:** prefix.

- When using a name outside of your cell, enter its global syntax, including the **/ . . .** prefix and the cell name.

- When someone asks for the name of a resource in your cell, give its global name, including the **/...** prefix.

- When in doubt, use the global name.

- When storing a name in persistent storage (for example, in a shell script, program, or database), use its global name, including the **/...** prefix. Local names (names with a **/.:** prefix) are intended only for interactive use and generally should not be stored. (If a local name is referenced from within a foreign cell, the **/.:** prefix is resolved to the name of the foreign cell and the resulting name lookup either fails or produces the wrong name.)

- You might use local names in persistent storage like a script file to set up or use similar directory structures in multiple cells. This would allow users or programs to move to a new cell and still find services in familiar places.

## 2.3.2 *Names Outside of the DCE Directory Service*

Not all DCE names are stored directly in the DCE Directory Service. Some services connect into the cell by means of specialized CDS entries called **junctions**. A junction entry contains binding information that enables a client to connect to a server outside of the Directory Service.

For example, the DCE Security Service keeps a database of principals (users and servers) and information about them, such as their passwords. The default name of the Security Service junction is **/.:/sec**. The following example illustrates the parts of a global DCE principal name:

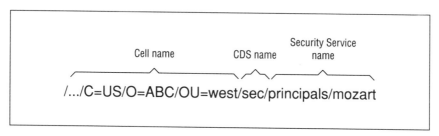

The cell name, **/.../C=US/O=ABC/OU=west**, is a GDS name. The **sec** portion is the junction entry in CDS, and **principals/mozart** is a principal name stored in the Security Service database.

Another service that uses junctions is DFS. The DFS Fileset Location Server keeps a database that maps DFS filesets to the servers where they reside. The junction to this database has a default name of **/.:/fs** that you can change if necessary. The following example illustrates the parts of a global DCE filename:

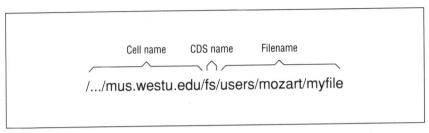

The global name contains a DNS cell name, **/.../mus.westu.edu**. The **fs** portion is the file system junction entry in CDS, and **/users/mozart/myfile** is the name of a file.

When referring to pathnames of files in the local cell, you can shorten a local filename even further by using the DFS-relative prefix (**/:**). This prefix translates to the root of the cell file system. The default name of the file system root is **/.:/fs**, one level down from the root of the cell namespace. So, for example, the following are all valid ways to refer to the same file from within the **/.../mus.westu.edu** cell:

```
/.../mus.westu.edu/fs/users/mozart/myfile

/.:/fs/users/mozart/myfile

/:/users/mozart/myfile
```

The DCE namespace is thus a connected tree of many kinds of names from many different sources. The GDA component of the Directory Service provides connections out of the cell and to other cells through a global namespace, such as GDS or DNS. In a similar manner, junctions enable connections downward from the cell namespace to other services.

## 2.3.3  Summary of Names

The following summary shows examples of the kinds of names you might encounter in a DCE environment.

| | |
|---|---|
| Global root name | /... |
| X.500 global name | /.../C=GB/O=ABC/OU=west/CN=william ward |
| X.500 global cell name | /.../C=GB/O=ABC/OU=west |
| DNS global cell name | /.../abc.com |

| Global name with a DNS cell name | `/.../abc.com/subsys/PriceMax/price_server1` |
|---|---|
| Cell root name | `/.:` |
| CDS name | `/.:/hosts/myhost` |
| Cell-relative name | `/.:/subsys/PriceMax/price_server1` |
| Security Service junction name | `/.:/sec` |
| DCE principal name | `/.:/sec/principals/john_hunter` |
| File Service junction name | `/.:/fs` |
| DCE filename | `/.:/fs/users/alfred_momonio/myfile` |
| Filesystem root name | `/:` |
| DCE filesystem filename | `/:/users/alfred_momonio/myfile` |

# 2.4  Cell and LAN Profiles Point to DCE Services

When you initially install and configure a DCE environment, the configuration procedure creates a default file and directory structure for the top level of the cell. We've already discussed several parts of this default structure: **/.:/fs** is the junction to the file system and **/.:/sec** is the junction to the security service (Section 2.3.2). There are two special files in the cell root that contain pointers to services in the cell:

```
/.:/cell-profile
/.:/lan-profile
```

DCE Security servers (and most other cellwide application servers) register their locations in the cell profile so that clients and servers can find them. Thus servers (except for CDS servers) can be found by clerks or other servers, including those outside the cell, by searching the cell profile. For cells with a single LAN, the cell profile also contains the name of the LAN profile. Multi-LAN cells have a uniquely named LAN profile for each LAN. Other profiles in the profile hierarchy also associate all hosts with the LAN to which they are connected.

Some services rely on geographic proximity for accuracy. For instance, time information from DCE time servers on the local LAN is likely to be more accurate than time information from servers on a remote LAN, which is delayed because it passes through a slow WAN link. The LAN profile contains information about time servers available on the local LAN. DCE time service clerks search the LAN profile for information about servers on the local LAN.

# 3

# *Remote Procedure Call: The Foundation of Distributed Computing*

Although DCE consists of many closely integrated components, each of which provides important functions, it is the DCE Remote Procedure Call (RPC) software that makes distributed operation possible. First, RPC offers a method for developing distributed applications that is both powerful and simple. RPC development tools promote a robust process of design and maintainance, while automating much of the code generation. Then, at run-time, RPC software manages the communication between application clients and servers.

Programmers who write distributed applications for traditional (non-DCE) environments need to understand network communication details and build communication into the application. While specific communications tasks can vary, every distributed application must:

- Open a connection and transmit data. This poses several problems for programmers. The communications tasks form a completely new programming model which usually has nothing to do with the application at hand. Communication is always transport-specific to some extent and introduces new system errors that the program has to check for and recover from, making it hard to port to other environments.

- Organize data into a stream of messages suitable for transmission. This stream is quite different from a function's argument list, which simply states the order and data types of arguments. Furthermore, programmers might need to convert the data into another machine's data format, an extremely complicated task that must be redone each time an application is ported to a different machine.

In other words, networking is a particularly complicated form of I/O that requires programmers to treat a distributed application in an entirely different way from a local (nondistributed) application.

DCE RPC automates the development and implementation of almost all communication needs associated with distributing applications, letting programmers concentrate on writing the applications themselves. RPC doesn't hide everything about the transport protocols—programmers still need to manage error checking and recovery because a program would not be acceptably robust if it terminated at every network transmission error—but RPC hides a lot and simplifies much of the rest.

This chapter describes the fundamental aspects of remote procedure call software, looking at the mechanics of application development and of distributed operation. The last section in this chapter summarizes RPC functions of interest to users, administrators, and programmers.

# 3.1 Distribution Builds on the Concept of a Local Application

In Chapter 1, we introduced the client/server model of distributing an application. The purpose of a server is to perform some activity on behalf of a client. We'll build on that model to see how distributed applications extend the familiar model of a local application. Let's look a little closer at what constitutes a client and a server.

In many ways, a server is like a library, providing a related group of general functions. For instance, a math server may provide a lot of statistical functions. A server can also be extended to include new functions or new features in existing functions, so long as the programmer maintains backward compatibility. RPC allows use of version numbers to support extension.

Unlike a library, which is inactive and simply resides on disk where the linker can extract functions from it, a server is live and continuous. It requires support from the operating system and must handle multiple calls simultaneously.

Just as we can view a server as a library, we can view a client as a calling program. Client/server relationships can be extremely varied. Some clients are tied closely to a particular server, but others call many servers, invoking just one or two functions from each.

To summarize, the client/server model builds on the model used by local applications, preserving familiar semantics of calling and returning from procedures. With DCE RPC, you can often keep the existing call statement in your application, and reuse existing procedures by writing some additional code. But remote procedure calls also invoke software that establishes and manages communication between the calling code on the client side and the remote procedures on the server side.

Keep these concepts in mind as we compare procedure call behavior in a local and distributed application.

### 3.1.1 Local Procedure Call Behavior

A local application executes on a single host and consists of a main program and a set of procedures that execute in a single address space in host memory. Figure 3-1 is a conceptual model of a nondistributed application that shows the relationship of the main program to the procedures. In this example, the main program responds to some input from a user by calling an averaging procedure from a preexisting math library.

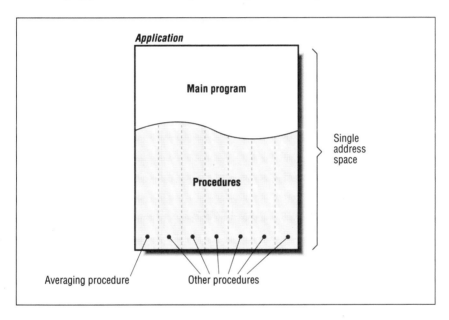

*Figure 3-1: A nondistributed application conceptual model*

The program accepts the input values from the user and calls a procedure that averages numbers, passing the numbers as arguments in the call to the procedure. The procedure executes, returning the average of the numbers to the calling program.

## *3.1.2 Remote Procedure Call Behavior*

Now, let's see how the same averaging function could execute in a distributed application. Figure 3-2 shows the main program on Host 1 (the client) and the remote procedures on Host 2 (the server). Systems may have different data requirements, so we must be able to convert data into various forms while preserving the data integrity. We'll also have to transmit the procedure call over the network.

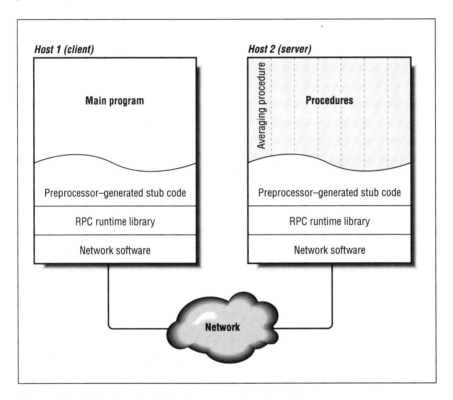

*Figure 3-2: A distributed application conceptual model*

Fortunately, the RPC application development tools automatically generate special code called **stub code** that manages communication between the main program and the remote procedures (Section 3.2). At run time, RPC software—the stub code and RPC runtime libraries that exist on client and server hosts—converts data to the appropriate formats and performs all communication between client and server.

On the client side, the stub code takes the place of the local procedures. The program makes what appears to the program to be a local procedure call, invoking instead a procedure in the client stub code. On the server side, the stub code acts like a program. It calls communication and data conversion procedures from the RPC runtime library as well as procedures originally invoked by the client application.

## The Stub Code and Run-time Libraries Transfer the Remote Procedure Call to the Server

The client stub code accepts the input arguments from the program. Then the client stub code calls routines from the RPC runtime library to find and communicate with the server. RPC runtime routines do the following:

- Determine which network transport (for example, TCP/IP or UDP/IP) to use for communication

- Search the directory service for the server's host address

- Connect to and transmit the remote procedure call to the server

In Chapter 1, we said that DCE is a layer of software that masks differences between different hardware platforms. The client and server stub code provide this vital masking function by **marshalling** the data between client and server hosts. Let's say the server machine uses data whose byte order is the reverse of that used by the client machine. The marshalling procedure on the client gets the call arguments and prepares them for transmission to the server. A similar unmarshalling procedure on the server receives the data and converts to a form needed by the server machine.

In short, the application programmer never has to worry about data formats; conversion is handled by the client and server stubs.

## The Server Invokes the Remote Procedure

A server must be prepared for incoming remote procedure calls. Thus, servers usually start as part of the host's boot procedure and run continuously, so they can detect and handle incoming calls.

When the call arrives, activity starts in the RPC server. The runtime library dispatches the call to the proper procedure in the server stub. The stub prepares the data for the server procedure by unmarshalling it and turning it back into a normal argument list.

The procedure executes, averaging the numbers, and passes the output argument back to the calling code in the server stub.

## The Server Returns the Data and Status to the Client

The server stub code gets the output argument, calling RPC runtime library routines that marshall the data and transmit it back to the client.

The client RPC runtime routines receive the data from the server and pass the data to the client stub code.

### *The RPC Software Returns Control to the Calling Program*

The client stub code unmarshalls the data, converting it to the local data representation, and returns the output argument (the average of the numbers) to the calling client application program.

# 3.2 The Development Process Enables Distribution

We mentioned that in some ways, DCE distributed applications behave like nondistributed applications. The client application program behaves as though it is calling a local procedure when, in fact, it is calling a procedure in the client stub code. Similarly, the remote procedure behaves as though the server stub is the calling program. Because the client and server can use existing interfaces between programs and procedures, writing a DCE distributed application is fairly straightforward—you can concentrate on developing the client application and the server procedures without handling communication details or worrying whether clients and servers are compatible.

RPC development tools include a compiler that automatically generates most of the code that manages communication between client and server. Communications functions include selection and use of network transports, data marshalling and preparation for transfer, and server dispatching. Optionally, you can control some aspects of network communications.

For compatibility, the client and server need to share information so that they can interpret calls in the same way. Thus, clients and servers must know the name for the interface, the name of each call, and the data types for each argument and return value. Programmers write this information in special files called interface definition files, which are used to produce the client and server stub code. These files also contain other information that helps RPC reduce data storage and the amount of data transferred over the network. This information indicates whether each argument is input, output, or both. Finally, the interface definition is a useful place to store type definitions, enumerated types, and defined constants that each side uses to manipulate data from RPC calls.

# 3.3 Interface Definitions Enable Client and Server Interaction

Now that we're aware of what clients and servers need to know about each other, let's see how the development process imparts all of the necessary information to both sides of the distributed application.

### Interface Definitions: The Root of the Client/Server Relationship

The interface definition ties the client and server application code together. It is a formal mechanism that describes the set of procedures the interface offers. The interface definition declares the name of the procedure, the data type of the value it returns, and the order and data types of its parameters. Thus, writing the interface definition is the first step in developing a distributed application.

A programmer writes the interface definition file using the Interface Definition Language (IDL). IDL closely mimics the declaration syntax and semantics of the C programming language, with the addition of attributes that help distributed applications execute efficiently in a network. An IDL compiler produces application header files that support the data types in the interface definition. Thus, if you write your code using information from the interface definition and include the IDL-generated header file in your source file, the client and server will be compatible. The IDL compiler also generates the stub files.

Figure 3-3 shows the development tools used and the files produced when developing an interface. A universal unique identifier (UUID) in the interface distinguishes this interface from any other interface on the network. You can produce a UUID as well as a template for the interface definition using the UUID generator utility **uuidgen**. Then use a text editor to write or modify the interface definition file. When the interface definition is complete, run the IDL compiler to generate client and server stub files and a C header file that are used to develop the client and server portions of the application. The IDL compiler also generates the code in the client and server stub files that marshalls data and communicates between the distributed parts.

Although using IDL to create interface definitions is a new step for many programmers, the interface definitions can actually save a lot of work in the long run. You can ensure compatibility between clients and servers by basing programs on the interfaces.

## Headers and Stubs Relate Client and Server Application Code

When each interface definition is compiled, the resulting header file, client stub, and server stub contain all the information needed to call a procedure correctly: the name of the procedure, the data type of the value it returns, and the order and data types of its parameters.

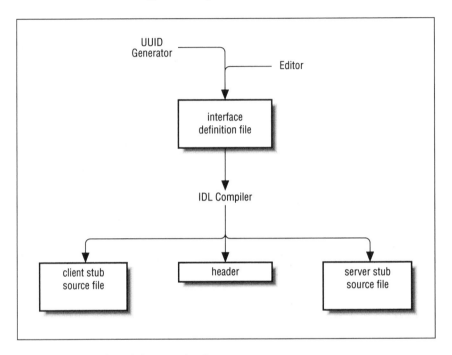

*Figure 3-3: Interface definition development steps*

For instance, this information, which clients and servers use to understand each other, is made available to the application client and server for use in their development stage.

1. **Client Development.** Developing a client is much like developing a local program except that you need to understand and adhere to the interface definition. Also, you might need to use some special coding to handle certain aspects of distribution such as network errors. Otherwise, a client application and a local application are very similar.

   The client development part of Figure 3-4 shows the files and development tools used to produce a client. Programmers write the client application code (the program) in the C language. The C #include directive reads in the header file produced by the IDL compiler, so type and constant declarations are available.

After the client application and client stub files are compiled with the C compiler, the programmer produces the executable client application by linking the client stub object files with the client application object file and the RPC libraries.

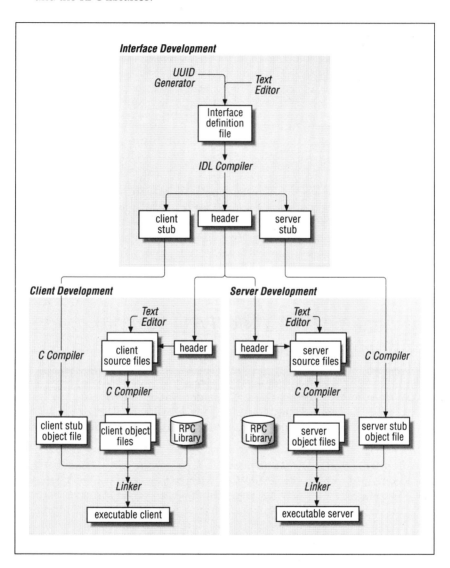

*Figure 3-4: Distributed application development tasks*

2. **Server Development.** The server development section of Figure 3-4 shows the files and development tools used to produce a server.

There are two distinct portions of code that you write for a server:

- The remote procedures themselves
- DCE calls that initialize the server

The code that implements the remote procedures is the same as code for local procedures. Consequently, you can often reuse code from existing local procedures, sometimes even binaries (object files), without change.

Code that initializes the server calls RPC runtime routines that start the server and prepare it to handle incoming remote procedure calls.

Programmers write the server application code (the implementation of the procedures and the initialization code) in the C language. The C #include directive reads in the header file produced by the IDL compiler, so type and constant declarations are available. After the server application and the server stub files are compiled with the C compiler, the programmer produces the executable server application by linking the server stub object files with the server application object files and the RPC libraries.

# *3.4 Binding: How a Client and Server Find Each Other*

We've seen how the application development process enables clients and servers to correctly interpret each other's definitions and arguments. Now, we'll see how server initialization uses the Cell Directory Service and host endpoint map to store pointers (called **binding information**) that lead clients to servers.

A client usually finds a server using a two-step process. First, the client gets the server's host address from the Cell Directory Service (CDS). Then, the client communicates with the host, finding the server process address (called an **endpoint**) by searching the host's endpoint map. An endpoint is a process address (such as a TCP/IP port number) of that specific server on the server host. Clients then use the endpoint to communicate directly with the server.

## 3.4.1   The Directory Service Identifies Server Hosts

When an application server initializes, it can place its host address in the CDS (CDS is part of the DCE Directory Service). When an application client makes a remote procedure call, the client stub code gets the server host address from CDS. The client stub uses the address to communicate with the server host.

## 3.4.2   The Endpoint Map Identifies Servers

When an application server initializes, it writes each interface name and associated endpoint into a database called the **endpoint map**. Thus, the endpoint map lists every server interface available on the local host, along with the endpoint where a client can find the server.

On each DCE server host, a daemon process called **rpcd** (RPC daemon) manages the endpoint map. Client stub code communicates directly with **rpcd** on the server host to obtain an interface's server address.

Endpoints are either **dynamic** or **well-known**. Dynamic endpoints are selected by the runtime library and vary from one invocation of the server to the next. Well-known endpoints are specific endpoints used every time a server runs. Well-known endpoints are typically used for widely-used applications such as daemons and are usually assigned by the authority responsible for a given transport protocol. The number available may be limited, so most applications use dynamic endpoints.

The RPC daemon resides at a well-known endpoint so that clients can find it. Thus, when clients know a server's host name they can communicate directly with the RPC daemon to acquire the application server's actual endpoint.

After a server stops running, the RPC daemon routinely removes the expired endpoints and associated server information from the endpoint map. Application administrators, and applications themselves, can make a running server unavailable to some clients by removing some or all of a server's endpoints. Administrators use the RPC control program **rpccp** to accomplish this.

## 3.4.3   Server Initialization Lays a Path for Clients

To find a server, a client needs to find the right host and then communicate with the right process on that host. Each time a server initializes, it can place its binding information in CDS and in the host endpoint map. Clients find and use the binding information to communicate with the server.

The basic server initialization steps include:

1. **Register each interface with the server runtime library.** Interface registration instructs the server runtime library to expect remote procedure calls to the interfaces being registered. When the runtime library receives an incoming call, it can dispatch the call to the correct interface. This step does not place the binding information in the endpoint map or in CDS.

2. **Register protocol sequences that the server will use for remote procedure calls.** A protocol sequence identifies a single type of communications protocol such as UDP/IP. You can instruct the server to use specific protocol sequences or use all available protocol sequences.

   Protocol registration also causes the server to create its endpoint. Clients must get and use the endpoint to communicate with the server.

3. **Advertise the server location to clients.** Advertising the server means making server binding information available to clients that need to find this server. The way you do this depends on the application. An application can advertise the server host binding information by:

   - Putting binding information in a directory service database

   - Storing binding information in an application-specific database

   - Printing or displaying binding information for clients.

   The most common way of advertising is by using a directory service database and an endpoint map.

   Applications can register the server address endpoint in the local endpoint map. Client stub code can search the endpoint map to get the server address on the host and then communicate directly with the server process.

4. **Listen for remote procedure calls.** Finally, the initialization procedure instructs the server to listen (wait) for incoming remote procedure calls. The initialization routine that starts the server listening does not return unless the server is requested to stop listening with a specific routine from a client or one of the remote procedures of the server.

Figure 3-5 summarizes possible initialization steps, showing the common advertising method of storing binding information in a directory service database and endpoint map.

❶ The initializing server writes the name of each interface and the host address of its server into CDS. In this example, the statistic interface (**Statistic_if**) is one of several interfaces offered by the math server.

❷ The server writes the name of each interface and its server endpoint into the host endpoint map.

❸ The server begins listening to the port named by the endpoint.

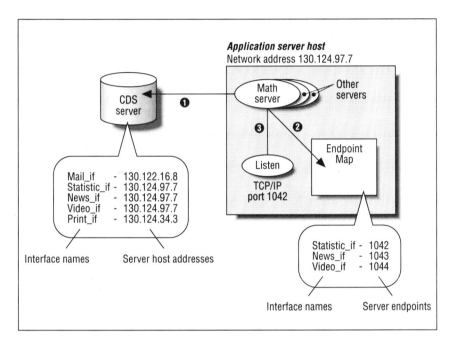

*Figure 3-5: Simplified server initialization*

## 3.4.4 Clients Follow the Path to Servers

Now the path is in place for a remote procedure call. The server has initialized and placed the interface name and its server host address into CDS. The initialization procedure has also placed the interface name and server endpoint into the host endpoint map. Finally, interfaces have been registered with the server so the server can dispatch incoming calls to the correct interface.

Figure 3-6 shows the major steps a client uses to find a server.

❶ When a client application calls a remote procedure, RPC software interacts with the CDS software on the client to acquire (import) server binding information from the DCE Directory Service. The CDS server returns the results of the search (the host address of the server offering the Statistic_if interface) to the CDS software on the client. The CDS software caches the results to speed up later requests and returns the application server's host address to the application client.

❷ Now the client knows the address of the host where the server resides. The client finds the server process endpoint by using the RPC daemon (**rpcd**) to look up the binding information in the endpoint map of the server system. **rpcd** resides at a well-known endpoint so the client can find it.

❸ Using the server endpoint information, the client communicates (binds) directly with the server.

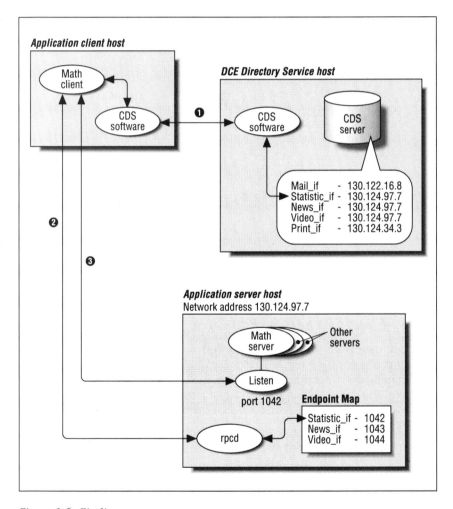

*Figure 3-6: Finding a server*

# 3.5 Executing the Remote Procedure Call

Once the client has located the server, the client can invoke the remote procedure call. Figure 3-7 shows the major steps involved in completing a remote procedure call. The routines that perform these steps are generated automatically by the IDL compiler.

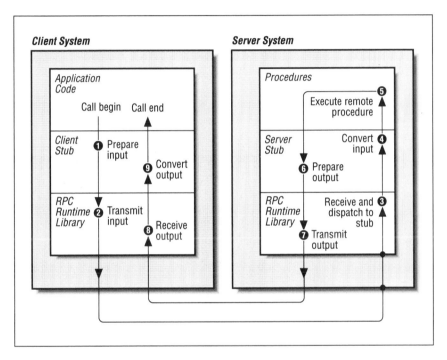

*Figure 3-7: Completing a remote procedure call*

# 3.6 Using, Administering, and Programming RPC

RPC is virtually transparent to application users who invoke and use applications in customary ways. Other than perhaps experiencing an occasional delay when performing some remote functions, users typically are not aware of the distributed nature of their application.

Except in unusual circumstances, RPC requires little or no administration. In most cases, activity such as interface registration in an endpoint map or exporting interface information to a directory service can be handled automatically by the application. If necessary, however, you can control naming and endpoints for an RPC application and its users. An RPC control program (**rpccp**) allows you to control access to servers and interfaces by viewing, adding, removing, and, in effect, modifying information in a name service database. Similarly, you can use **rpccp** to register and unregister endpoints in both local and remote endpoint maps.

As software that supports development of distributed applications, RPC provides a set of programming tools.

- The **uuidgen** utility generates templates for interface definition files that include a UUID and other code elements necessary for producing stub files.

- The Interface Definition Language compiler reads interface definition files and produces files used by programmers for creating clients and servers. The resulting files include C header files and C object-code stub files. The compiler has options that automatically generate calls to the name service (directory service) interface routines if you are using this service.

- The runtime library routines perform all operations needed to set up, control, and execute remote procedure calls.

- A nidl-to-idl converter helps you convert applications written to use Hewlett Packard's Network Computing System (NCS) Version 1.5 or Digital Equipment Corporation's DECrpc Version 1.0. The converter might not be provided by all DCE vendors.

- Error handling routines support detection of and recovery from network problems in a robust manner.

# 4

# *Threads:*
# *Improving Program Performance*

Threads are an increasingly popular way to improve application performance through parallelism. Threads have been used in various versions of UNIX and other operating systems for some years, sometimes under the term "lightweight processes." POSIX has standardized threads in a specification known as the POSIX 1003.4a standard, currently in Draft 4.

Starting multiple threads is similar to forking multiple processes from one parent process. Unlike multiple processes, however, multiple threads of a process use the same address space, so they share all static and external data, as well as open files and anything else that is available to the whole process. Thus, they make a lot of parallel-programming algorithms easier to implement. They also require less memory than multiple processes, and may require a little less time for start-up and context switching.

This chapter discusses the threads implementation provided by OSF. Vendors may substitute some other threads implementation. Although the extensions included with other implementations might differ from the OSF offering, the application programming interface for the basic set of threads routines will be compatible with the implementation we're describing here.

## 4.1  What Is DCE Threads?

DCE Threads is an implementation of threads based on the POSIX 1003.4a (Draft 4) standard, which also includes real-time priority scheduling.

To improve program performance, RPC server stub routines use threads internally, enabling RPC-based servers to handle multiple client requests simultaneously. Threads can also be useful when writing advanced client applications.

DCE Threads improve program performance on single processor systems by permitting the overlap of input and output or other slow operations with faster computational operations. Figures 4-1 and 4-2 show how concurrency affects the execution time of a threaded application. Nonthreaded applications consist of procedures that execute serially. The processor completes executing one procedure before executing another. Threaded applications consist of multiple threads that execute concurrently, with CPU time shared among the threads.

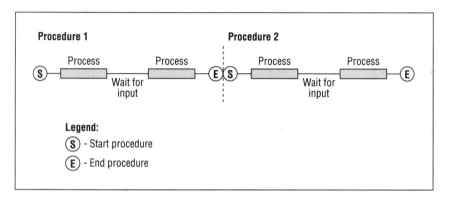

*Figure 4-1: Nonthreaded applications execute serially*

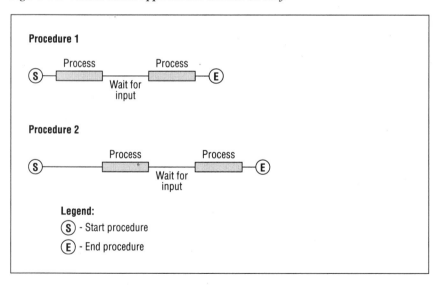

*Figure 4-2: Threaded applications execute concurrently*

# *4.2 Using Threads*

As you might expect, the increased flexibility of having multiple threads share process resources leads to increased work and responsibilities for programmers. The new items programmers have to consider fall into the categories of protecting shared resources, scheduling and synchronization activities, and handling signals, status, and exceptions.

## *Protecting Shared Resources*

Anything shared by threads—static data, external data, open files, and anything else that is a processwide resource—must be protected by locks in some manner so that no two threads try to change it at the same time. POSIX provides some primitive synchronization routines based on mutex or mutual-exclusion locks.

Figure 4-3 shows how one thread (Thread 1) can lock a value in memory to prevent premature access by another thread (Thread 2).

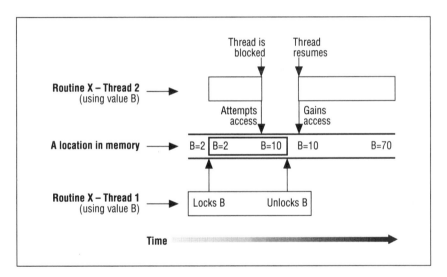

*Figure 4-3: Locking shared data*

Although DCE library routines can handle multiple concurrent calls and manage most of their own locking needs internally, if you are writing server functions, you must take explicit action to protect any resources they use. Many libraries have built-in locks so that they can be called safely by multiple threads, but others cannot handle multiple concurrent calls. Such "non-reentrant" routines must complete execution before they can be called again.

It's not always obvious when you might be using non-reentrant code. For example, say that you use the **printf()** function to assemble a string from a set of arguments passed to the function. The **printf()** function in turn, may rely on a dynamic memory allocation routine to reserve sufficient memory to store the string. The dynamic memory function may be nonreentrant because it uses a global, processwide linked list to locate free memory. Processwide variables may not be able to tolerate simultaneous access such as is likely in a threaded environment. As a rule, when in doubt, you should assume code is non-reentrant.

DCE Threads provide jacket routines for a number of nonreentrant UNIX system calls. Threads call the jacket routine instead of the UNIX system calls; this allows DCE Threads to take action on behalf of the thread before or after invoking the system call. For example, the jacket routines ensure that only one thread calls any particular service at a time to avoid problems with system calls that are not thread reentrant.

Jacket routines are provided for UNIX input and output system calls, and the **fork()** and **sigaction()** system calls. Jackets are not provided for any other UNIX system calls or for any of the C runtime library services. To protect these routines from being called concurrently, DCE Threads has a global lock. A global lock is similar to a mutex and must be unlocked before another call can be accepted. Jacket routines provided with DCE Threads use this global lock to protect non-reentrant code from multiple concurrent use. You must use the same global lock when calling code suspected of being non-reentrant.

## Synchronizing Threads

Threads interact and communicate using shared memory. When dividing work up among threads, you have to start them explicitly, and synchronize or wait for them in order to tabulate their results. Just as a parent process uses **wait()** calls or signals to check on the status of its children, one thread often waits for another to end or to reach a particular point in the program (a barrier).

You can block a thread from executing until some shared data reaches a particular state by using **condition variables**. Cooperating threads check the shared data and wait on the condition variable. For example, one thread produces work-to-do packets and another thread consumes these packets (does the work). If the work queue is empty when the consumer thread checks it, that thread waits on a work-to-do condition variable. When the producer thread puts a packet on the queue, it signals the work-to-do condition variable.

## Scheduling Activities

Normally, the operating system provides the application process with a chunk of CPU time and DCE Threads gives pieces of the available time to individual threads. Often, some threads that carry out important tasks, such as responding to real time events, can't wait for CPU time. DCE Threads lets you specify policies and priorities so that important threads can take priority over other threads, getting the necessary CPU time whenever they need it.

Real-time policies and priorities are of interest mainly for threads that perform CPU-intensive calculations and have to respond quickly to events or deliver data at frequent intervals. Programs with such threads can assign priorities to threads to ensure that important ones can run whenever they have work to do. A higher-priority thread always preempts a lower-priority one—that is, the lower-priority thread is suspended so that the higher-priority thread has the CPU. A thread can run whenever all the higher-priority threads block (for instance, while waiting for a read or write to finish) or exit.

Furthermore, programs can determine the relationships among threads of the same priority. A first in/first out policy ensures that a thread runs without interruption; it can be preempted only by a higher-priority thread. In contrast, a round robin policy assigns an equal timeslice to each thread of a given priority, so that they take turns running.

If the operating system supports threads, a DCE program with the right privileges can use real-time policies to preempt other users. If the operating system does not support threads, the policies control only the relative priorities of threads within your process.

## Handling Signals

UNIX signals are more complicated in multithreaded programs than in traditional ones, so you should generally avoid using them in your program. When a particular thread generates a signal because of an error, such as a segmentation violation or a floating-point exception, the operating system can deliver a signal to the particular thread. But many signals—including all those generated by outside processes—are delivered to the process as a whole and cannot be handled on a per-thread basis.

Instead of catching signal handlers the traditional way, you should use the implementations of the POSIX **sigwait()** and **sigaction()** services included with DCE. These services operate at a different level than signal handlers but can achieve the same results. The **sigwait()** service allows a thread to block until one of a specified set of asynchronous signals is delivered. The **sigaction()** service allows for per-thread handlers to be installed for catching synchronous signals.

## Handling Status and Exceptions

The standard P1003.4a pthreads calls report errors by setting the global *errno* variable and returning -1. Although this is perfectly suitable for many situations, some conditions can produce errors that are not handled by the client code. Such errors are simply ignored and may cause subsequent errors.

To ensure that errors are reported so they can be handled at the level in the program where proper recovery actions are known, you can use the pthread exception interface included with DCE. Before writing a multithreaded program, you must determine which interface each program module will use for receiving error notification. The status interface and the exception interface cannot be used together in the same modules of a program.

# 4.3 *Why Use Threads in an Application?*

RPC application servers are multithreaded, which allows them to handle multiple concurrent requests. Thus, you may need to control some threads operations in a server. For instance, you may have to protect shared data at the server using mutexes. Some server procedures may call other procedures that are nonreentrant, so you would have to protect these routines from concurrent calls with a global lock. There might be other considerations too, but the specifics are outside the scope of this book.

Although it's not necessary to write multithreaded client programs, there are some situations where client programs can benefit from the concurrency made possible by DCE Threads. One kind of program that can benefit uses a divide-and-conquer algorithm, in which a client divides data into blocks that can be processed separately, sends each block to a server to be processed, and then collects and combines the results. Some client application user interfaces can benefit by using threads to give the interface back to a user while a long operation takes place. Any program that does lots of distributed operations might also benefit from threads.

In short, using threads can give very real advantages to certain kinds of applications, but you must weigh these advantages against the added program complexity they bring.

# 5

# *DCE Security Service: Protecting Resources*

Many kinds of computers use a variety of measures to protect resources such as files and applications from unauthorized access. Typically, each user must first prove his or her identity by using a secret password to log on to the host. The host uses the password, which is known only to the user and the host, as proof that the user is who he or she claims to be. Once the user logs on to the host, the host resources are usually protected further by means of permissions or privileges associated with each file. The permissions regulate whether a user can read, write, or execute that file. The number of users on single hosts is typically small enough so that the host alone can manage all of the passwords and permission functions.

A distributed computing environment, on the other hand, might support thousands of users accessing files on any of hundreds or thousands of hosts in the environment. Because it is impractical to maintain every DCE user's security information on every host in the environment, DCE serves security information from a centralized database. This database, along with a distributed set of daemons and libraries, compose the DCE Security Service.

When servers enforce security, each client must provide proof of its user's identity and access rights. These are provided on the first RPC call, and sometimes, in highly secure environments, on every RPC call. Because access to every DCE resource—directories, files, printers, and so on—is controlled by a server, the servers' demands for authentication and authorization provide comprehensive network security. This applies to DCE servers, such as those of the Cell Directory Service, as well as user application servers. The server verifies the client's authenticity and authorization before allowing access to the resource.

Security Service functions must be built in to applications. In other words, clients call local security routines to acquire authentication information from a security server and pass it to other servers. Servers also call security routines to verify authentication information and enforce authorization. Authentication is the ability to prove one's identity to someone else. Authorization is the ability to regulate access based on one's identity.

# 5.1 Authentication and Authorization

The DCE Security Service provides authentication and authorization services that help protect DCE resources against illegitimate access. These services protect resources in ways that are similar to password and permission protection used on various computer systems.

## 5.1.1 Passwords Ensure Authenticity

One service provided by DCE Security is the authentication service, which enables a **principal** (user, computer, or server) to prove its identity to another principal. Every principal in a DCE cell has a secret key that is known exclusively to the user and the authentication server. Human users remember their secret key as a password. When a user enters a password, the DCE Security Service software converts it to a secret key.

During login, the authentication server (part of the security server) checks the user's password and provides the user's process with specially encrypted data structures called **tickets**. Clients within that process present the tickets to other principals as proof that they are authentic (they are who they say they are). Tickets have characteristics that make them extremely difficult to forge or reuse illegitimately.

Each application server also has a secret key (kept in a special file on the server host) and can be authenticated just like a user, acquiring tickets from the authentication server. Server authentication occurs when, say, an application server exports its network address information to a CDS server (Section 3.4.3).

Because both clients and servers can be authenticated, applications can perform mutual authentication. Note, though, that authentication is time consuming so applications shouldn't use more authentication than is necessary.

## 5.1.2 Privilege Attributes Convey Verifiable Identities

The authorization service enables a principal to determine the rights of other principals in the DCE cell based on their principal names and group memberships. When principals are registered in the Registry database, they are assigned membership in one or more groups and organizations.

**Groups** generally correspond to work groups or departments; **organizations** typically denote larger and higher-level collective entities that can include multiple groups. A principal is a member of his or her own work group and may be a member of other groups. Typically, a principal is a member of one organization. Together, a principal's name, group, and organization membership are known as the principal's **privilege attributes**.

As part of the login process, the privilege server (another part of the security server) provides a principal with his or her privilege attributes by including them in the ticket constructed by the authentication server.

## 5.1.3  Access Control Lists Protect Resources

Resources such as servers, directories, files, or even records in databases can have an associated **access control list** (ACL) that specifies which operations can be performed by which user. Let's say user Alfred Momonio tries to read a file from a DCE DFS file server. A program called an **ACL manager** on the file server looks up user Alfred Momonio on the ACL. The ACL entry for Alfred Momonio contains read and execute permission for that file, so the ACL manager allows Alfred Momonio to read the file.

DCE components and applications can use different kinds of ACLs to protect their resources. The types of ACLs and their exact effects depend on how they are defined by the ACL manager for the specific component or application. If you want to use ACLs to protect your application's resources, you must write your own ACL manager.

## 5.1.4  Special Accounts Enable Intercell Authentication

As we said in Chapter 2, a cell is the basic unit of operation and administration in DCE. A security server maintains security information about all principals in the entire cell. Because cells are independent units, security servers don't usually maintain information about principals in foreign cells. Thus, when a client tries to get a ticket to a server in a foreign cell, the security server does not have information about that foreign server and cannot issue a ticket.

In a secure DCE network, intercell communication requires some cooperation in advance between security administrators from both cells. Each cell's Registry database must contain a special account for the other cell's security server. These accounts contain a secret key that is shared between the security servers of both cells.

Figure 5-1 shows the basic steps a client uses to access an application server in a foreign cell.

❶ When a client requests a ticket to the application server in the foreign cell (Cell 2), the local security server uses the shared key to create a ticket that the client can present to the foreign security server.

❷ The foreign security server authenticates the principal (because the ticket conveys evidence of the shared key) and gives the client a ticket to the application server.

❸ The application server in Cell 2 authenticates the client.

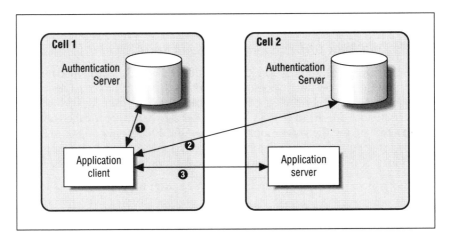

*Figure 5-1: Authentication in a foreign cell*

# 5.2 The Security Services Resist Tampering

Information used by the DCE Security Service has characteristics that resist forgery and reuse by illegitimate principals. Furthermore, administrators can protect DCE security servers from tampering by placing them on physically secure hosts.

## 5.2.1 Life Spans Protect Security Information from Illegitimate Use

A user's secret key is never passed over the network (except when changing it), and keys are never passed in an unencrypted form over the network. Generally, keys are used only on the local host to encrypt information that is passed over the network. It is extremely difficult and time-consuming to calculate a secret key by examining intercepted information that has been encrypted with the key. However, given enough time and computing power, an attacker could eventually succeed in deciphering a key from information encrypted with it. For this reason, secret keys have a life span (a time limit) after which they must be changed.

When the DCE Security Service authenticates a user, the user's process receives a ticket. The user's process caches the ticket and uses it repeatedly to access DCE resources. To prevent attackers from reusing tickets that are passed over the network, each ticket has a life span after which the user must reauthenticate and get a new ticket.

## 5.2.2  Frequent Key Substitution Protects Secret Keys

Secret keys are used only briefly during the login process and are quickly deleted from the host to avoid their discovery by attackers. Authenticated users receive substitute keys called conversation keys that encrypt data exchanged with application servers. Conversation keys have a shorter lifespan than secret keys and are much more restricted in scope; the user has a distinct conversation key for communicating with each application server being used.

## 5.2.3  Encryption Ensures Data Authenticity, Privacy, and Integrity

The user's conversation key, used for communication with a particular server, can encrypt parts of remote procedure calls sent to that server. The server acquires the conversation key from the ticket that was originally prepared by the security server and passed to the server by the client. The application server uses the conversation key to decrypt the remote procedure call, thus guaranteeing the authenticity of remote procedure calls from that user. This method of authentication is also known as authenticated RPC. Authentication can be limited to the connection, to the first remote procedure call between a client and server pair, or to every remote procedure call between these systems.

An application that requires complete data privacy can further use the conversation key to encrypt parts of remote procedure calls, including the data passed between client and server. Furthermore, applications can ensure data integrity by including encrypted checksums of the data passed between clients and servers. The data integrity feature enables recipients to check whether data has been modified in transit. The integrity checksum must be encrypted (calculated) and decrypted (verified) using the conversation key. The data portion of the RPC may or may not be encrypted, depending on whether the privacy protection level is chosen.

DCE Security Service encryption uses the Data Encryption Standard (DES) which the U.S. State Department prohibits from being exported outside the United States. Therefore, DCE source code exported outside the United

States does not include encryption. Vendors can implement local encryption methods, but should be aware that hosts using incompatible encryption methods cannot operate together.

### 5.2.4 Secure Hosts Protect Security Servers

DCE Security servers can be protected from tampering by placing them on secure hosts. Such hosts can be in a locked room and allow login using only the computer's console. Because an interactive user's host could be more vulnerable to attack than a host in a locked room, no security information is stored there, even in encrypted form.

Noninteractive principals, such as application servers, keep their secret keys in a special encrypted file that is protected by local host permissions and is not accessible on the network.

# 5.3 Groups and Organizations Simplify Security Management

As we mentioned previously, you can protect files, applications, and other DCE objects from unauthorized access by associating them with an Access Control List (ACL). An ACL includes the names of principals or groups that are allowed access to the object and specifies which permissions are granted to each.

In DCE cells with many users, it is impractical to independently manage each user's access to files or applications using his or her principal name. Each time a person joins or leaves the company, the name has to be added or deleted from many ACLs. Instead, by making each principal a member of one or more groups, you can control access on a much wider scale. Each time a person joins the company, the name needs to be added only to the desired group.

Now the security administrator can use groups in ACLs. For instance, when a group is listed in an object's ACL, all principals in that group have the same kinds of access to the object. Perhaps one group is granted read, write, and delete access while all other groups have read access only. Note though, that groups are effective only within cells. So ACLs in foreign cells can grant access based solely on principal names, not on group membership.

Administrators use organization membership to apply global security policies—the life span of tickets and passwords, for instance—to principals. For example, an organization that does not handle highly sensitive information may have a policy of long life spans on tickets and passwords. Another organization that does handle highly sensitive information may have a policy of short life spans on tickets and passwords. Stringent security policies (those with relatively short life spans on tickets and passwords) require more overhead than less restrictive policies.

# 5.4 How People Interact with the DCE Security Service

People who interact with the DCE Security Service consist of distributed application users, Security Service administrators, and application administrators.

## 5.4.1 Using the DCE Security Service

As a user who wants to run DCE distributed applications, you must log in to the DCE cell using the login facility provided with the DCE Security Service. Some DCE implementations may integrate DCE login with the standard host login. Once logged in, you can run distributed DCE applications in authenticated mode.

You can always view your tickets and attributes to check on expiration times. If tickets expire before you are finished using an application, you'll need to reauthenticate with the security server and get new tickets to continue working.

## 5.4.2 Administering DCE Security

As a DCE Security Service administrator, you can manage aspects of DCE Security using a special program called **rgy_edit**. This program enables you to view, add, delete, and modify information in the registry database. You can enter and modify the following kinds of information:

- Principal, group and organization information. Each principal, group and organization in the cell must be registered.

- Account information for each principal. In addition to traditional login information like the home directory and shell, this information includes the principal's group and organization names, password, ticket expiration times, whether a principal can operate as a client, or server, or both, whether principals can get a new ticket with a network address different from the address on the current ticket, and so on.

- Policy information for each organization, including account and password life span, password length and format, and password expiration date.

The **rgy_edit** program includes import and export functions to maintain consistency between the Registry database and individual hosts. On UNIX, import functions copy user information from UNIX **/etc/passwd** files into the Registry database. Export functions perform the reverse operation, copying relevant principal information from the Registry database into UNIX **/etc/passwd** files on individual UNIX hosts. At this writing, import and export functions are not yet available.

### 5.4.3 Administering Access Rights for Applications

As an application administrator, you can control access to DCE objects, such as files, entries in databases, directories, and printers, by using a program called **acl_edit**. You can view, add, delete, and modify entries in ACLs for applications or ACLs for objects controlled by them.

## 5.5 DCE Security in Action

Figure 5-2 shows the role security plays in the activities of the user, the client program, and the server.

❶ A DCE security administrator uses **rgy_edit** to register each principal in the Registry database. The registered information includes each principal's secret key and privilege attributes.

❷ An application administrator uses **acl_edit** to create entries in an access control list for the application or its objects (files, directories, or servers controlled by the application). Each entry names a principal, group, or organization, and specifies what a principal bearing that principal, group, or organization name can do to the object.

❸ When a user logs in to DCE, the login process inherits the identity of the user, interacting with the authentication server and privilege server to acquire the tickets needed to access other servers.

❹ The authentication server and privilege server get a principal's secret key and privilege attributes from the Registry database. The authentication server and privilege server use this information to authenticate a principal, constructing credentials the principal needs to access other servers.

❺ When a user starts an application client, the client inherits the user's identity and privilege attributes. The first remote procedure call to the application server includes user identity and privilege attribute information that the server can authenticate.

❻ Before executing the remote procedure call, the application server calls an **ACL manager**, which determines what permissions (if any) to give to the principal. The ACL manager searches the specified object's ACL for the principal or group name and, if it is found, grants any associated permissions.

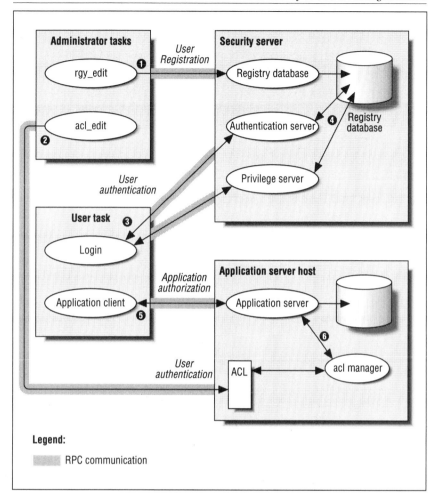

*Figure 5-2: General tasks in a secure environment*

# 5.6 *Programming the DCE Security Service*

As a programmer, you can access and control DCE Security using routines from different libraries. Some of the tasks applications have to perform include:

- Control the level and the kind of authentication within remote procedure calls, using the **Authenticated RPC API**.

- Establish and control a principal's login context using the **Login API**. This API communicates with the security server to acquire authentication and authorization information. On UNIX systems, a principal's login context is inherited by any child processes. You can export the login context so that it can be imported by other processes that are running on the same host. You are most likely to use this API when writing an application server.

- Retrieve and manage keys for noninteractive principals using the **Key Management API**. An application server must manage its own secret key, concealing it when not in use and retrieving it from local key storage when needed.

- Implement and use DCE ACL-based authorization functions using the **ACL API**.

  — **sec_acl** routines let you write clients that can browse, edit, and test ACLs.

  — **sec_acl_mgr** routines let you write ACL managers for application servers. An application server uses an ACL manager to search for a principal's privilege attributes in an ACL. The server then uses the search results to make authorization decisions.

- Resolve principal names to universal unique identifiers (UUIDs) using the **ID Map API**. These calls let programs refer to objects in different cells using identifiers that are globally unique.

- Perform security-related functions using **Registry API** calls, which are interfaces to the Registry database.

# 6

# DCE Directory Service: Locating Resources

Distributed processing involves the interaction of multiple systems to do work that is done on one system in a traditional computing environment. One challenge resulting from this network-wide working environment is the need for a universally consistent way to identify and locate people and resources anywhere in the network.

The Directory Service makes it possible to contact people and use resources such as disks, print queues, and servers anywhere in the network without knowing their physical location. The Directory Service is much like a telephone directory assistance service that provides a phone number when given a person's name. Given a unique name of a person, server, or other resource, the Directory Service can return the network address of that resource along with other information associated with the name.

The Directory Service provides DCE distributed applications with a place to store and find information about resources available in the distributed computing environment. Currently, a major use of the Directory Service is to provide DCE distributed application clients with a remote server's network address.

## 6.1 The Directory Service Controls the Naming Environment

The naming environment provides a universally consistent way for people and programs to refer to resources anywhere in the distributed environment, either inside or outside a cell.

The Directory Service, which controls the naming environment, includes the Cell Directory Service (CDS) and the Global Directory Service (GDS). CDS controls the naming environment used inside a cell (Section 2.3). CDS servers implement the naming scheme chosen for a cell, and they let you add, modify, and delete name information in CDS.

GDS controls the global naming environment outside (between) cells. GDS servers let you add, modify, and delete name information in the Global Directory Service. GDS includes an implementation of XDS so you can use X.500-style names for the global environment.

The Directory Service also allows use of another widely used global name service, the Domain Name Service (DNS). Although DNS is not included with DCE, the Directory Service has software that allows you to communicate with other cells through DNS (Section 2.3.1).

Activities that occur completely within a cell—including most of the interaction between clients and servers—use CDS exclusively. For this reason, our discussion of the Directory Service focuses primarily on CDS. Later in this chapter, we'll talk about using GDS to communicate with a foreign cell.

# 6.2   The Naming Environment Maps Names to Resources

A user or application can ask for a resource by specifying its global name or local name (Section 2.3). CDS components —the clerk and servers—navigate through the name environment, ultimately providing the user's application with the network address of the resource.

## 6.2.1   CDS Names Correspond to CDS Directories and Object Entries

Every resource in a cell has a unique name. Uniqueness is conveyed through the hierarchical nature of the names. Here are two examples of hierarchical names:

```
/.:/service/qserver_1
/.:/service/qserver_2
```

You can think of CDS names in the same way you think of files in a hierarchical filesystem: the CDS directories correspond to filesystem directories, and the entries for individual objects correspond to files. In a CDS name like **/.:/service/qserver_2**, the names **/.:** and **/service** are directory names, and **/qserver_2** is the object entry name.

It is important to realize that CDS objects are just information about resources, not the resources themselves. A program cannot gain access to a file simply by opening the corresponding CDS object. But the program can use the address obtained from the CDS object to find the file. Similarly, an object entry for a printer might store information like "color graphics printer, floor 2, network address 130.124.97.7." After getting this descriptive information (called **object attributes**) from CDS, a program can create a print request and spool it to the printer. Note that RPC takes care of getting the address information from CDS so the application doesn't have to.

The Cell Directory Service enables cell administrators to impose a directory hierarchy within a cell. The exact kind of hierarchy chosen for a cell depends on the needs of the organization. Some companies might choose an organizational hierarchy in which directories correspond to organizations within the company. Others may choose a geographical organization in which directories correspond to sites located in different geographic areas. It is also possible to mix organizational and geographic hierarchies or other kinds of hierarchies.

So far in this chapter we've discussed CDS from an abstract point of view— its logical organization. But its physical distribution, and the various shortcuts it offers, help make it usable.

## 6.2.2  Distribution Ensures Access to Directories

To make name information accessible, administrators copy it into multiple servers located near the users most likely to need it. Because multiple copies of name information are available on different servers, name data can be available even if a server fails.

CDS uses a process called **replication** to maintain replicas (copies) of directories and the information they contain. CDS administrators create replicas and place them in **clearinghouses**. A clearinghouse is the name database managed by a CDS server. Then CDS ensures that all replicas contain up-to-date information. Some cells may contain more than one clearinghouse, especially if the cell covers a wide geographic area. It is not necessary—and indeed, it could be cumbersome—to replicate the entire name environment for the entire cell in every clearinghouse. So clearinghouses contain only those replicas needed by nearby users.

Now let's look at some special contents of directories to see how they unify separate parts of this distributed name environment.

## 6.2.3  Child Pointers Link the Name Environment Together

Because a cell's name environment can be distributed across many clearinghouses, it is essential to maintain a path of connectivity between them.

This path of connectivity enables CDS servers to find every directory (and thus every entry) in the name environment.

Every CDS directory knows how to get to its child directories (directories immediately beneath it). Each time someone creates a child directory, CDS automatically creates a **child pointer** in the parent directory (the directory immediately above the new child). The child pointer tracks the location of the child directory, even if someone moves it to another clearinghouse.

Every clearinghouse also contains a copy of the **cell root directory**. The root directory contains child pointers to all of its child directories. Those directories, in turn, contain child pointers to all of their child directories.

A CDS server can determine whether it contains a target name by looking at the names of directories in its clearinghouse. For instance, a server gets a name of a target entry called **/.:/service/qserver_1**. Because it has a directory named **/.:/service**, it searches that directory, returning information contained in the object entry called **qserver_1**.

When a CDS server gets a name that is not in its clearinghouse, the server looks in its replica of the root directory for the most relevant child pointer (the pointer whose name is closest to the entry being sought). CDS moves the search to a clearinghouse more likely to contain the entry. CDS continues searching in this manner, though rarely in more than two or three clearinghouses, until it finds the entry. Once CDS finds an entry, it caches the information for subsequent use.

## 6.2.4  *Soft Links Customize a Name Environment*

A soft link is a pointer that provides an alternate name for an object entry, directory, or other soft link in the Directory Service. You can do minor restructuring of the directory hierarchy by creating soft links that point from an existing name to a new name. Soft links also can be a way to give something multiple names, so that different kinds of users can refer to a name in a way that makes the most sense to them.

## 6.2.5  *Object Attributes Define Resources*

Applications use the attributes in an object entry to determine how to use the resource they describe. When client applications create names for resources, they also store attributes about those resources in CDS on behalf of their users. Through a client application, a user can store additional attributes in an object entry. When a user refers to the resource by its CDS name, CDS retrieves data from the attributes for use by the client application.

Client applications cannot request information from CDS based on attributes. However, you can use attributes to filter the output of CDS control program (**cdscp**) commands that show or list directory contents. Also, client applications can conduct attribute-based searching in the global directory service (GDS).

## 6.2.6  Putting the Parts Together

Figure 6-1 shows the parts of a CDS server. Every server manages at least one clearinghouse containing directory replicas. A replica can contain object entries, soft links, and child pointers. The figure shows only one replica and one of each type of entry possible in a replica. Normally, a clearinghouse contains many replicas, and a replica contains many entries.

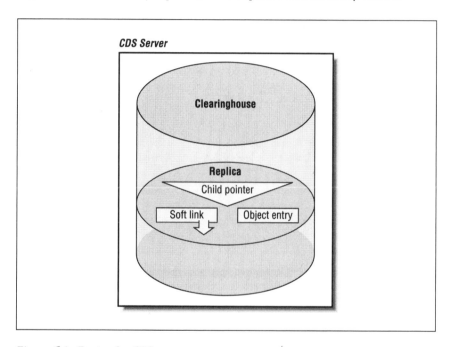

*Figure 6-1: Parts of a CDS server*

Imagine an organization that has a marketing group in Building 1 and a group that does technical work in Building 2. The marketing group maintains a CDS clearinghouse called **Bldg1_CH**, while the technical group has a clearinghouse called **Bldg2_CH**. The _CH suffix is a recommended convention for naming clearinghouses.

One CDS subdirectory, called **subsys**, has child directories for two sets of printers, **Print_staff** and **Print_trade**. The technical group routinely sends documents used for staff training or other internal purposes to printers in **Print_staff**. The marketing group also sends some documents to printers in **Print_staff**, but the group also has a regular need to print color proofs for trade journals on the high-quality color printers in **Print_trade**; the technical group rarely has to use the high-quality printers.

Figure 6-2 shows how these directories and their contents are physically implemented in two clearinghouses. The clearinghouses themselves have CDS names: **/.:/Bldg1_CH** on Host 1 and **/.:/Bldg2_CH** on Host 2.

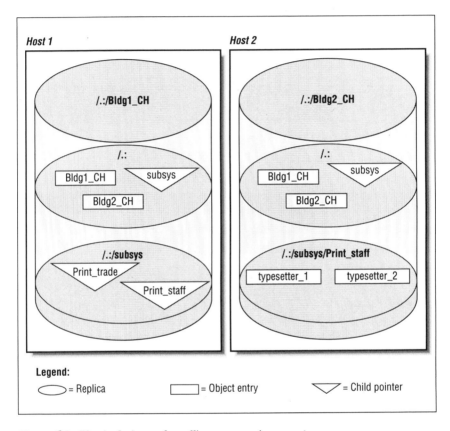

*Figure 6-2: Physical views of a cell's name environment*

The Building 1 clearinghouse contains replicas of the root directory and of **/.:/subsys**. The contents for **Print_staff** or **Print_trade** are not listed in the clearinghouse, but the **/.:/subsys** directory has enough information about those directories to refer CDS clerks to other clearinghouses. Thus, the marketing group in Building 1 can find any printer with a small amount of searching.

The Building 2 clearinghouse contains replicas of the root directory and the **/.:/subsys/Print_staff** directory. On the rare occasions that the technical group needs any printer directory besides **Print_staff**, CDS can find it by searching from the cell root until it finds the **/.:/subsys/Print_trade** directory in some other clearinghouse; the process simply takes longer.

Organizations should create at least two replicas of every CDS directory. Therefore, both the **/.:/subsys** and the **/.:/subsys/Print_staff** directories should be replicated in at least one other clearinghouse somewhere in the cell.

## *6.2.7 Update Operations Keep Name Information Current*

Once names are entered into CDS, users who have the appropriate access can make changes to the data associated with the names. Any addition, modification, or deletion of CDS data happens initially in only one replica: the master replica. The two main methods CDS uses to keep name information in other replicas current are **update propagation** and the **skulk** operation.

An update propagation is an immediate attempt to apply one change to all replicas of the directory in which the change was made. Its main benefit is that it delivers each change in an efficient and timely way. Unlike a skulk operation, however, update propagation does not guarantee that the change gets made in all replicas. If a particular replica is not available, the update propagation does not fail; the change is simply not made in that replica. The skulk operation ensures that when the replica is available again, it becomes consistent with the other replicas in its set. The skulk operation is a periodic distribution of a collection of updates. Its main functions are to ensure that replicas receive changes that might not have reached them during an update propagation and to remove outdated information. These maintenance functions include:

- Removing soft links that have expired. (You can specify an expiration time when you create a soft link.)

- Maintaining child pointers, which includes removing pointers to directories that were deleted.

- Removing information about deleted replicas.

## *6.2.8 DCE Security Protects Directory Service Information*

The information stored in the Directory Service is critical to the correct operation of a DCE cell, and it must be protected from unauthorized or casual tampering. The Directory Service uses the DCE Security Service to protect its information (Chapter 5).

In a secure DCE cell, a server does not complete a user's request unless the user's identity has been verified through the DCE Authentication Service.

So, for example, a CDS server allows a user to create a new directory only if that user's identity has been verified.

Once the identity of a principal has been verified, the software must next determine whether that principal has the permissions required to perform a requested action. This is called authorization. Therefore, to create a new directory, the user in the previous example must not only be authenticated, but must also have the appropriate permissions.

The CDS permissions are **read**, **write**, **delete**, **test**, **control**, and **administer**. Although the exact meaning of each permission can vary somewhat depending on the kind of name it's associated with, their general meanings are as follows:

- **Read** permission lets users view data.

- **Write** permission lets users create entries.

- **Delete** permission lets users delete entries.

- **Test** permission lets users test whether an attribute of a name has a specific value without being able to see any values (that is, without having read permission to the name). The main advantage of this permission is that it gives application programmers a more efficient way to check for a value: rather than reading a whole set of values, the application can test for a particular one.

- **Control** permission lets users manage the access control list (ACL) of an entry.

- **Administer** permission lets users manage directory replication.

Servers need to be authenticated to each other because they share and modify replicated data. For example, suppose server A and server B both store a replica of the same directory. Associated with each directory is a list of all the servers authorized to maintain that directory. When a user modifies an entry in the replica at server B, server B must notify server A of the change. Server A does not accept the update unless server B is an authenticated principal and is one of the principals authorized to modify that directory.

# 6.3 The DCE Directory Service Uses the Client/Server Model

The Directory Service uses an extended form of the client/server model. An application that stores and retrieves information from CDS is a **client** of CDS. Client applications create names for resources and store attributes about those resources in CDS on behalf of their users. Through a client application, a user can store additional attributes in CDS. When the user refs to the resource by its CDS name, CDS retrieves data from the attributes for use by the client application.

A system running CDS server software is a **CDS server**. A CDS server stores and maintains CDS names and handles requests to create, modify, or look up data.

CDS operations are complex, especially when they involve searching multiple clearinghouses for information. Requiring applications to manage such operations would impose too much overhead, so CDS uses an intermediary called a **clerk**, which runs on every host that uses CDS.

The clerk receives a request from a client application, sends the request to a server, and returns the resulting information to the client. This process is called a **lookup**. The clerk is also the interface through which client applications create and modify names and attributes.

## 6.3.1 Caching Improves Performance

The clerk caches, or saves, the results of lookups so that it does not have to go to a server for the same information repeatedly. The cache is written to disk periodically so that the information can survive a system reboot or the restart of an application. Caching improves performance and reduces network traffic.

## 6.3.2 Clerks Find CDS Servers in Several Ways

Before CDS begins looking up information about a name, the CDS clerk must know how to find the name. If a name does not yet exist in the clerk's cache, the clerk must know of at least one CDS server to contact in search of the name.

The clerk can learn about CDS servers and their locations in any of three ways:

- **Through the solicitation and advertisement protocol**. Clerks and servers on the same LAN communicate using the solicitation and advertisement protocol. A server broadcasts messages at regular intervals to advertise its existence to clerks on its LAN. The advertisement message contains data about the cell that the server belongs to, the server's network address, and the clearinghouse it manages. Clerks learn about servers by listening for these advertisements on the LAN. A clerk also sends out solicitation messages, which request advertisements, at startup.

- **During a lookup**. During a lookup, if a clearinghouse does not contain a name that the clerk is searching for, the server managing that clearinghouse gives the clerk as much data as it can about other places to search for the name. If a clearinghouse contains replicas that are part of the full name being looked up, but not the replica containing the actual object name, it returns data from a relevant child pointer in the replica it does have. The data helps the clerk find the next child directory in the path toward the object name.

- **By management command.** A DCE administrator can use the CDS control program to create knowledge in the clerk's cache about a server. This command is useful when the server and clerk are separated by a WAN, and the clerk, therefore, cannot learn about the server from advertisements on a LAN.

# *6.4  CDS in Action*

Now that we have an idea of who the players are in CDS, we'll see some examples of how a client application gets information about a host from a CDS server. We'll also take a closer look at CDS to see the interaction among some of the CDS processes.

## *6.4.1  A Simple Lookup Example*

Figure 6-3 shows the interaction between a CDS client, clerk, server, and clearinghouse during a simple lookup.

❶ The client application on Host 1 sends a lookup request to the local clerk.

❷ The clerk checks its cache and, not finding the name there, contacts the server on Host 2.

❸ The server checks to see whether the name is in its clearinghouse.

❹ The name exists in the clearinghouse, so the server gets the requested information.

❺ The server returns the information to the clerk on Host 1.

❻ The clerk passes the requested data to the client application. The clerk also caches the information so that it does not have to contact a server the next time a client requests a lookup of that same name.

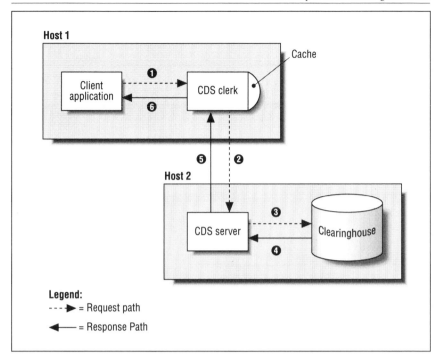

*Figure 6-3: A simple CDS lookup*

## 6.4.2 A Complex Lookup Example

A CDS cell can have more than one clearinghouse storing replicas of CDS directories. This example shows a possible sequence of events that occurs when a server cannot find a requested name in its clearinghouse.

In Figure 6-4, the clerk works downward from the root of the cell hierarchy to locate an object entry. The object entry, **/.:/Sales/Spell**, describes a spell-checking server at a company's London sales headquarters.

❶ On Host 1, a spell-checking application requests the network address of the **/.:/Sales/Spell** server. The clerk does not have that name in its cache, and so far it only knows about the **/.:/Bristol_CH** clearinghouse on Host 2.

❷ The clerk contacts the server on Host 2 with the lookup request.

❸ The **/.:/Bristol_CH** clearinghouse does not contain the target object entry, but it does contain a replica of the root directory. From the **/.:/Sales** child pointer in the root, the clerk can learn how to contact clearinghouses that have a replica of the **/.:/Sales** directory. The server on Host 2 returns this data to the clerk, informing it that a replica of **/.:/Sales** is in the **/.:/London_CH** clearinghouse on Host 3.

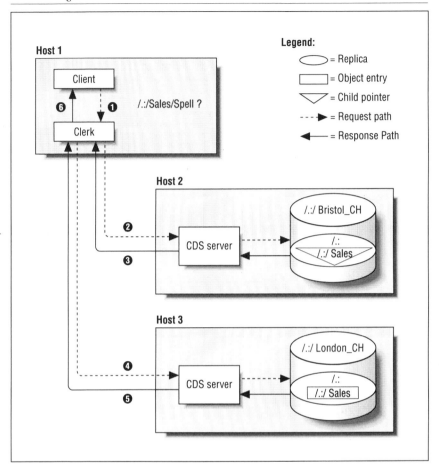

*Figure 6-4: A complex CDS lookup*

❹ The clerk contacts the server on Host 3 with the lookup request.

❺ The **/.:/Sales** replica in the clearinghouse on Host 3 contains the **/.:/Sales/Spell** object entry, so the server passes the address of the spell-checking server to the clerk.

❻ The clerk returns the information to the client application, which can now make a remote call to the spell-checking server.

Long lookups like the one illustrated in the Figure 6-4 do not happen often after a clerk establishes its cache and becomes more knowledgeable about clearinghouses and their contents. However, the figure illustrates the resources and connections that could be involved in an initial lookup. The figure also illustrates the importance of maintaining connectivity between parent and child directories. If somewhere the directory path is broken or a clearinghouse is unreachable, a clerk may not be able to find a name. This danger is greatly reduced by having two or more replicas in each cell.

## 6.4.3  A Deeper Look at CDS

A CDS lookup operation involves numerous processes and relies on several interprocess communication methods. Figure 6-5 identifies the major processes and the interprocess communication methods involved in a CDS lookup for a UNIX client.

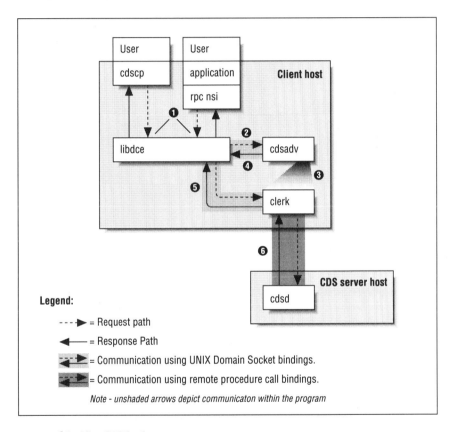

*Figure 6-5:  The CDS lookup process*

❶ Applications call the CDS application programming interface (API) in the **libdce** library. An application like the CDS control program (**cdscp**) makes direct calls to **libdce**. Other applications call by using the RPC name service interface (**rpc nsi**).

❷  **libdce** queries the advertiser (**cdsadv**) for information about the clerk.

❸  The advertiser creates a clerk process (if a clerk does not already exist).

❹  The advertiser returns the clerk's UNIX domain socket address to **libdce**. (On systems that do not support UNIX domain sockets, the clerk and **libdce** use whatever forms of local interprocess communication are available.)

❺  **libdce** binds to the clerk using its UNIX domain socket.

❻  The clerk binds to the server (**cdsd**) using remote procedure call bindings.

# 6.5  *Communicating with a Foreign Cell*

To find names outside the local cell, CDS clerks must have a way to locate directory servers in other cells. The Global Directory Agent (GDA) enables intercell communication, serving as a connection to other cells through the global naming environment.

The GDA is an intermediary between CDS clerks in the local cell and CDS servers in other cells. A CDS clerk treats the GDA like any other CDS server, passing it name lookup requests. However, the GDA provides the clerk with only one specific service: it looks up a cell name in the Global Directory Service or the Domain Name Service (Section 2.3) and returns the results to the clerk. The clerk then uses those results to contact a CDS server in the foreign cell.

A GDA must exist inside any cell that needs to communicate with other cells. It can be on the same system as a CDS server, or it can exist independently on another system. You can configure more than one GDA in a cell for increased availability and reliability. Like a CDS server, a GDA is a principal and must authenticate itself to clerks.

CDS finds a GDA by reading address information stored in a CDS server. Whenever a GDA process starts, it creates new information or updates existing information in the server. The information contains the address of the host on which the GDA is currently running. If multiple GDAs exist in a cell, they each create and maintain their own address information in the CDS server.

Even though the DCE Directory Service automates the process of finding host addresses, it's helpful to know the steps involved in intercell communication.

1.  When a CDS server receives a request for a name that is not in the local cell, the server searches the directory to find the location of one or more GDAs, returning the GDA host address information to the CDS clerk.

2.  The clerk passes the lookup request to the GDA.

3.  The GDA detects whether the name is X.500 style or DNS style. Depending on the style, the GDA passes the name to a GDS server or a DNS server (Section 2.3).

4.  The GDS or DNS server looks up and returns to the GDA information associated with the name. The information includes the addresses of CDS servers in the foreign cell.

5.  The GDA passes the information about the foreign CDS servers to the clerk.

6.  The clerk contacts the CDS server in the foreign cell, passing it a lookup request. The foreign CDS server authenticates the user before proceeding (refer to Figure 5-1).

7.  The server looks up the name and passes the requested information back to the clerk. In this example, the clerk contacts only one server in the foreign cell. While resolving a full name, a clerk might actually receive referrals to and contact several servers in the foreign cell.

8.  The clerk passes the information to the client application that requested it.

# 6.6  How People Interact with the DCE Directory Service

People who interact with the DCE Directory Service include distributed application users, Directory Service administrators, and programmers who write distributed applications.

## 6.6.1  Using the DCE Directory Service

Users can indirectly access the directory service by using applications that create, modify, or delete directory service entries.

Users' direct access to directory service entries is limited to the use of a browsing utility. The Browser is a tool for viewing the content and structure of cell directories. It runs on workstations with windowing software based on the OSF/Motif® graphical user interface. The Browser can display an overall directory structure as well as show the contents of directories. You also can customize the Browser so that it displays specific kinds of entries. You can see only the entries in the directory service to which you have read permission. Entries to which you do not have read permission are not displayed.

## *6.6.2 Administering the DCE Directory Service*

The amount of administration needed to maintain the DCE Directory Service depends largely on the number of users and objects (files and devices) that belong to the distributed environment. Generally, the more users and objects you want to track, the more effort you have to spend on administration. Initial configuration choices can also affect administration. Part II mentions some of these configuration choices.

Administrators control the Cell Directory Service by distributing various directories to servers where they're likely to be used and specifying replication and update details.

Administrators can also control the structure of Global Directory Service entries and their attributes and can create **schemas** (sets of rules) that specify the kind and form of information stored in these entries.

To prevent unauthorized users from deleting or modifying important information, administrators of parts of the Directory Service can use the DCE Security Service **acl_edit** program (Section 5-4) to control access to Directory Service entries. For an application that creates Directory Service entries, the programmer or another application administrator can be responsible for controlling access to those entries.

Administrators can also help users find resources using soft links. Soft links are aliases that provide alternate names for resources, allowing different groups to refer to the same resources by names that are meaningful to them.

## *6.6.3 Programming with the DCE Directory Service*

Usually, programmers use the Directory Service only to export and import server location information. Note that even this use of the Directory Service is indirect. A distributed application's server initialization code uses the RPC Name Service Interface (NSI) routines to export server location information to the Directory Service. Code that searches CDS for server information can be automatically included in the client stub by the Interface Definition Language (IDL) compiler (Section 3-2).

To write an application that makes direct calls to the Directory Service, use the XDS application programming interface. This API is consistent with the 1988 CCITT X.500 Series of Recommendations and the ISO 9594 Standard and provides access to directory service functions in both the Global Directory Service and the Cell Directory Service. Using this API, you can create, modify, and delete entries.

# 7

# *DCE Time Service: Synchronizing Network Time*

Many applications use time to control operations. Astronomers use applications that can focus telescopes on specific regions of space at particular times. Automated teller machines wait prescribed amounts of time for customers to respond to menu choices, signalling those who wait too long to enter information. As long as the clocks controlling events are properly synchronized either with real time or with related events, applications can execute quite smoothly.

Problems can occur, however, when clocks are not synchronized. This is a special problem in networks because they consist of multiple hosts. Each host has its own clock and its own time reference, with slower clocks drifting ever farther behind faster clocks.

Time skew between two networked hosts can cause problems for a tool such as **make**, which selects files for compilation based on their creation time. Modified source files on a tardy host can appear older than corresponding object files on the host with the faster clock. In this case, **make** does not recompile files that should be recompiled.

On a larger scale, a stock trading wire service might have big problems when brokers in London learn of deal-making events five minutes after brokers in New York and Hong Kong have already acted on the news.

The DCE Distributed Time Service (DTS) helps you avoid such situations by synchronizing host clocks in LANs and WANs. Clock synchronization enables distributed applications to determine the sequencing, duration, and scheduling of events, independently of where they occur.

# 7.1  How Does DTS Work?

DTS is a client/server application that is distributed using RPC. In general, each DCE cell has one or more DTS servers that provide time information to client hosts and applications through intermediaries called clerks.\* DTS clerks interact with DTS servers, relieving client applications from this overhead. Each host that is not a DTS server has a DTS clerk. (At installation time, you choose whether to configure the DTS software as a server or clerk. You can reconfigure software later, if necessary.) DTS servers export their names to a LAN profile (Section 2.4) so other DTS servers and clerks can find them.

Because no device can measure the exact time at a particular instant, DTS servers express the time as an **interval** containing the correct time. In the DTS model, clerks obtain time intervals from several servers and compute the intersection at which the intervals overlap. Clerks then adjust the system clocks of their client systems to the midpoint of the computed intersection. When clerks receive a time interval that does not intersect with the majority, the clerks declare the nonintersecting value to be faulty. Clerks ignore faulty values when computing new times, thereby ensuring that defective server clocks do not affect clients.

Figure 7-1 shows how DTS clerks compute time from the intersection of time intervals received from several DTS servers. In this figure, the clerk ignores time interval 2 because it does not intersect with the other intervals.

DTS servers synchronize themselves by obtaining time information from all other DTS servers on the LAN. Like clerks, servers compute the intersection at which the intervals overlap and adjust their host clocks to the midpoint of the computed intersection. Alone, DTS ensures that DCE hosts share a consistent notion of time. However, this time is not necessarily the correct time. Servers can synchronize with external time standards by setting the time manually or by connecting an external time provider (Section 7.3) to one or more servers in the LAN.

---

\*DTS servers improve confidence in the accuracy of time and help detect faulty servers by sampling time from at least two other DTS servers. Thus vendors generally recommend that three servers be available on each LAN to provide time information.

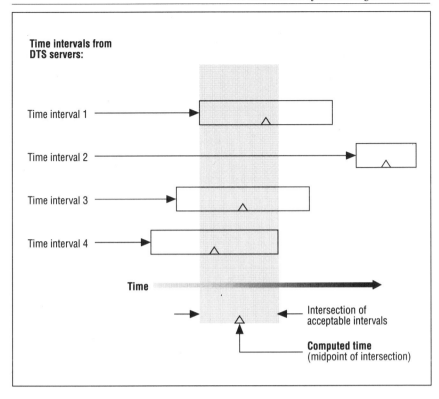

**Time intervals from
DTS servers:**

Time interval 1

Time interval 2

Time interval 3

Time interval 4

**Time**

Intersection of
acceptable intervals

**Computed time**
(midpoint of intersection)

*Figure 7-1: Computing Time from Intersecting Time Intervals*

# 7.2 DTS Time Is Cellwide

DCE cells can include multiple LANs and extended LANs. Because local
DTS servers communicate only with DTS servers on the same LAN, DTS
uses two special servers, global servers and couriers, to synchronize time
among interconnected LANs or extended LANs.

**Global servers** are available throughout a cell. The number of global
servers is usually small (one on each LAN), but global servers enable DTS
to synchronize every host in the network. We recommend connecting an
external time provider (Section 7.3) to a global server.

Local servers called **couriers** maintain synchronization with other LANs by
using time information from their global servers. Couriers use the
responses of all local servers and one global server when synchronizing
their own clocks. In a multi-LAN cell in which more than one global server
is present, couriers eventually get time information from all LANs by choosing global servers at random for each synchronization.

Figure 7-2 shows global servers on three LANs in a cell. In this case, the global servers also act as local servers and as couriers. Each courier helps maintain cellwide synchronization by obtaining time information from global servers on other LANs as well as from local servers on its own LAN.

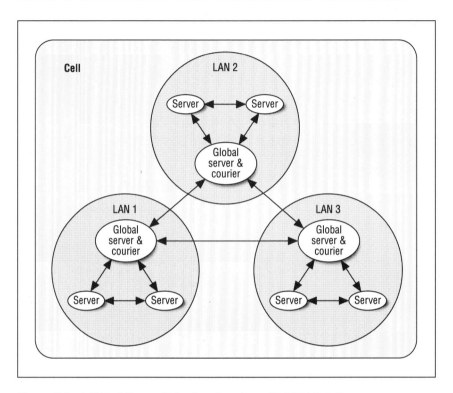

*Figure 7-2: A Global Server Helps Synchronize a Multi-LAN Cell*

# 7.3 Synchronizing Cell Time with External Time Sources

You can connect an external time source to the DCE Time Service. This allows the use of time signals such as those of the U.S. National Institute for Standards and Technology (NIST). DTS uses the Coordinated Universal Time (UTC) standard that has largely replaced Greenwich mean time (GMT) as a reference. Many standards bodies disseminate UTC by radio, telephone, and satellite; commercial devices (time providers) are available to receive and interpret these signals. DTS has a **Time Provider Interface** (TPI), which describes how a time provider process can pass UTC time values to a DTS server and propagate them through the network. The TPI also permits other distributed time services such as the Network Time Protocol (NTP) to work with DTS.

# 7.4 Using DTS

DTS is transparent to DCE users. Users cannot access DTS directly; however, applications can use time functions available from the DTS application programming interface (API). For example, a conference call scheduling application can get time zone information from the DTS API to determine the best times to schedule conference calls that span multiple time zones.

# 7.5 Administering DTS

A DTS administrator's primary goal is to maintain synchronization among all clocks in the distributed environment. To control DTS servers and clerks, use the DTS control program **dtscp**. Typical administrative tasks are few and fairly straightforward, and can include the following kinds of duties:

- Once DTS has been running on your network for some time, you may want to optimize DTS operation using **dtscp** to set various DTS parameters such as the maximum inaccuracy, number of servers required, and error tolerance. The default parameters are adequate for many network configurations.

- If your network does not use time providers and the network systems have been running for some time, you may occasionally set the time on DTS servers to match UTC or another external reference.

- As your network grows or its topology changes, you may need to relocate servers. Rather than moving software physically, you can change clerks into servers or servers into clerks. You can also change local servers into global servers or couriers.

- You should monitor time-related distributed activities for signs of DTS server problems. Occasionally, you may need to restart or resynchronize a server. When you need to remove a DTS server for any reason, you can disable the server and replace it by changing a clerk into a server.

# 7.6 Programming with DTS

DTS synchronizes host clocks with other host clocks in the distributed environment. Because applications normally get time from the host clock, you need not modify applications to benefit from DTS time synchronization.

You can, however, include many time-related functions in applications, using DTS API routines to:

- Retrieve time information

- Convert binary time information from one time structure to another

- Convert between binary and ASCII representations of time

- Convert to local time

- Manipulate binary time information

- Compare two binary time values

- Calculate binary time values

- Obtain time zone information

These time operations give you many ways to design time functions into applications and to use time to control your application's execution.

# 8

# *DCE Distributed File Service: Providing Cellwide Access to Files*

Wherever organizations use computers, people and programs frequently need to share files. Although it can be difficult to share files between computers that have incompatible file systems, software like Sun's Network File System (NFS) facilitates this task. NFS allows users to mount common file systems from other computers. Once mounted, users can use their favorite tools or editors to process the mounted files. Alternatively, users can share files by logging in to the foreign system, but now they're in an unfamiliar environment without their favorite tools.

A DCE cell offers a single integrated file system, the DCE Distributed File Service (DFS), that is shared among all DCE users and host computers in a DCE cell. Everyone in the environment has his or her own directory in the file system and uses the same interface to move around in it. Consequently, sharing files and the information in those files is easy. And as an integrated part of DCE, files can be protected by DCE security's authentication and authorization functions. Thus, files are accessible on a controlled basis to anyone needing access, while access is limited to other users.

## *8.1 Some Good Reasons to Use DFS*

The DCE Distributed File System is a distributed DCE application. As such, it offers benefits derived from its integration with and use of DCE services. Let's look at some advantages of using DFS:

- DFS makes sharing information easy because everyone in a cell has access to one seamless file system. Furthermore, DFS keeps track of where a file is being used, thus preventing different users from simultaneously modifying the same information.

- DFS files are manageable. You can divide large numbers of files into smaller groups called **filesets** (filesets are groups of related files that should stay together). DFS allows multiple filesets per disk partition, a management advantage over NFS, which allows a single fileset per partition.

- DFS facilitates load balancing because you can easily move filesets to underutilized machines. DFS automatically tracks files that move.

- DFS scales well, accommodating a virtually unlimited number of filesets in a cell. The number of files in a fileset is controlled by a diskspace quota associated with the fileset. DFS servers can exist across multiple heterogeneous hosts; when you need more space for files, just install DFS file server software on hosts of your choice and move filesets to the new hosts. DFS automatically tracks host addresses on which filesets reside.

- In place of the three UNIX file permissions, DFS offers six permissions, allowing more precise definition of access to files and directories. Li DFS server data is highly available through replication. DFS replicates (copies) files to other machines so that if one copy becomes unavailable, data is still available on other machines.

- DFS has the advantage of being integrated with DCE. All communication between clients and servers uses RPC, taking advantage of RPC authentication provided by the DCE Security Service. DFS files can then be further protected by DCE ACLs. Moreover, DFS servers use a native protection scheme of administrative lists to control access to DFS server processes. DFS servers use threads to perform more efficiently. DFS clients use the DCE Directory Service to find fileset location servers, allowing you to move these DFS servers freely. Client and server hosts can use the Distributed Time Service (DTS) to synchronize file activities across multiple systems.

# 8.2 DFS Is a Comprehensive File System

Aside from the benefits of being integrated with DCE, DFS is a comprehensive file system, providing all of the supporting backup and maintenance services.

## 8.2.1  The DCE Local File System can Coexist with a Host's Native File System

When you install and configure a DFS file server on a host, the DCE Local File System (DCE LFS) can exist alongside the native file system, such as the UNIX file system. Like the native file system, LFS is bounded by the host on which it is installed. LFS, however provides many of DFS's most valuable benefits by allowing replication (copying part of a file system to another host), precise authorization using DCE authorization, and fast recovery from crashes through the use of logging.

DFS allows you to use a UNIX file system (UFS) as an alternative to LFS. DFS exports UFS, but does not provide the replication and backup services available with LFS. Furthermore, UFS is not protected by the DCE Security Service ACLs.

## 8.2.2  DFS Acts on Groups of Files Called Filesets

Files reside on machines called **file servers**. Each file server stores one or more filesets. A fileset is a group of files that are administered as a set. It is easier to back up or move files as a group rather than on a file-by-file basis. A fileset can contain the files of a single user or a group of users.

## 8.2.3  DFS Tracks Files as They Move

If a fileset moves to another machine, a server called a **fileset location server** records the move, storing the address of the new location with addresses of all other filesets in the cell. The server keeps the information about fileset locations in the server's fileset location database. When given the name of a file by a DFS client, the fileset location server returns the address of the machine serving the fileset that contains the file.

## 8.2.4  DFS Locates and Backs Up Filesets

DFS can be quite large, with filesets residing on many machines in a cell. Furthermore, administrators can move filesets from one machine to another, which can make backing up such a system a real nightmare. Fortunately, DFS **backup servers** ease this critical task by maintaining fileset backup schedules for all filesets in a cell. When it's time to dump one or more filesets to tape, the backup server gets the fileset's location from the fileset location server and then initiates the dump. The backup database (only one per cell, please) stores all backup information for all filesets in the cell. The backup server uses the backup information to restore backed up files to a file server if files have been lost or corrupted.

## 8.2.5   DFS Protects Files Using DCE Access Control Lists

DFS precisely controls access to files and directories using DCE ACLs. DFS defines six permissions for access to files and directories. These include the standard UNIX permissions **read**, **write**, and **execute**, and three additional permissions: **control**, **insert**, and **delete**.

## 8.2.6   DFS Protects Its Servers by Using DFS Distributed Security

DFS controls access to its servers and processes by using **administrative lists**. An administrative list contains the names of principals (users and server machines) or groups that can execute commands affecting a DFS server or process on a particular machine. As DFS administrators change roles or new people are assigned to DFS administration, maintaining separate lists for multiple servers and processes on multiple machines could be quite difficult. To simplify the task of updating administrative lists and other common configuration information, this information is maintained and served from a central update server on a **system control machine**.

## 8.2.7   DFS Ensures Server Software Consistency

To perform correctly, all DFS server machines in a cell with identical CPUs and operating systems must run the same versions of DFS processes. DFS relies on **binary distribution machines** to distribute consistent versions of DFS processes and command suites to machines with identical CPUs and operating systems. Each set of machines with a particular CPU and operating system requires a binary distribution machine with the same CPU and operating system.

## 8.2.8   DFS Simplifies Management Using Administrative Domains

Large cells with many users and files can require many DFS server machines. To simplify DFS management and to provide more precise control over DFS, you can group sets of DFS server machines into administrative units called **administrative domains**. A DCE cell that includes DFS consists of one or more DFS administrative domains. Each administrative domain includes a set of server machines necessary for running DFS. Some DFS server machines must belong to a single administrative domain. Other machines provide cellwide services and can belong to multiple administrative domains.

## *8.2.9  DFS Clients Use Caching to Speed Operations*

DFS clients are typically workstations that provide access to DFS files for their users. Each DFS client machine runs a process called the **cache manager**, which handles lookups and stores versions of data retrieved from file server machines. The cache manager stores versions of retrieved data in a portion of the local disk referred to as the DFS cache. To speed file operations, an application acts on the data stored in the client cache, which is then written back to the file server. Acting on data stored locally is much quicker than acting on data stored across a network. Furthermore, if the file server becomes unavailable for some reason, the local data remains available for use and is written back when the server next becomes available.

## *8.2.10  DFS Clients Can Include Diskless Workstations*

DFS clients without local disks for storing cached DFS data can store data in local memory. DCE software called DCE Diskless Support Service software helps diskless computers act as DFS client machines by helping these machines connect to DFS file servers. Diskless machines need a place to store idle blocks of memory used by one process so that the memory can be used for other processes, a function called swapping. The DCE Diskless Support Service software helps diskless computers perform swapping by using disk space on remote machines to store idle data.

# *8.3  How DFS Works*

This quick walkthrough of a DFS file lookup will give you an idea of how clients use the DCE Directory Service to locate the file system and subsequently find the correct file. Figure 8-1 shows servers that might participate in the first lookup of a file.

❶ When given a filename, a DFS client cache manager queries the CDS for the address of a fileset location server. The cache manager stores the address for subsequent use.

❷ The cache manager makes a remote procedure call to the fileset location server to get the address of the file server serving the target file.

❸ The cache manager makes a remote procedure call (request to open the file) to the file server. The file server verifies the client's authenticity and, if the client is authorized, serves the file to the client.

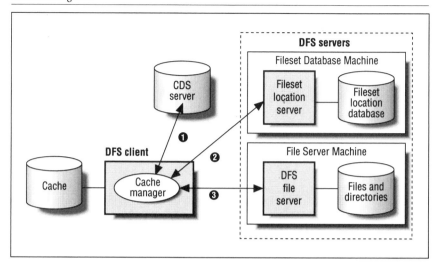

*Figure 8-1: Simple DFS file operation*

# 8.4 DFS Files Connect to the Larger World

The DFS file system does not simply float in a cell; it is directly connected to the cell root. If a cell is connected to the global directory service, file names are globally unique. Files are accessible from any other DCE cell that is also connected to the global directory service, provided that principals have the proper authorization. You can refer to a file in any of several ways: by its global name (an Internet or X.500-style name), by a cell-relative name, and by a DFS-relative name. Figure 8-2 shows examples of these kinds of file names.

---

**Global file name (Internet format):**
> /.../goodcompany.com/fs/usr/w_rosenberry/proj/plan.doc

**Global file name (X.500 format):**
> /.../C=US/O=goodcompany/fs/usr/w_rosenberry/proj/plan.doc

**Cell-relative file name:**
> /.:/fs/usr/w_rosenberry/proj/plan.doc

**DFS-relative file name:**
> /:/usr/w_rosenberry/proj/plan.doc

---

*Figure 8-2: DFS file names are globally unique*

# 8.5 How People Interact with the DCE Distributed File Service

People who interact with DCE DFS include distributed application users, administrators, and programmers who write distributed applications.

## 8.5.1 Using the DCE Distributed File Service

DCE application users will store their files in the Distributed File Service. As the premier DCE application, users will notice DFS more than any other DCE component. DFS uses native operating system commands to control directory and file operations so users won't have to spend time learning new commands. Thus users on UNIX systems will use **cd** to change directories, **ls** to list directory contents, **mkdir** to create new directories, and so on. DFS also includes several of its own commands to show things like quotas and locations of files.

## 8.5.2 Administering the DCE Distributed File Service

The amount of administration needed to maintain the DCE Distributed File Service depends largely on the number of files stored in DFS. Initial configuration choices can also affect administration.

If you locate file servers physically close to their users, it can make DFS administration easier. You can delegate tasks to the people most familiar with local user needs, and most able to handle administrative tasks more efficiently. Administrators will specify details about replication, backing up and restoring filesets, and installing or removing DFS file servers as needs change. They will also move filesets to other machines to balance the load across all file server machines in a cell. Administrators will be responsible for monitoring and adjusting DFS performance.

Administrators will also use DCE access control lists to control access to files and directories. To prevent unauthorized principals from tinkering with DFS servers, administrators will use administrative lists to control DFS server access.

## 8.5.3 Writing Programs that Use DFS Programming Interfaces

Most application programmers will probably layer their applications on DFS, letting DFS manage the underlying tasks, such as communication and server functions. By simply using standard file system calls like **fopen()** and **fclose()** programmers can avoid having to duplicate functions already available in DFS.

Fearless programmers who thrive by plunging deep into system internals will be happy to learn that all routines used by DFS are available to those who want to write their own file system or customize the stock DFS applications provided to DCE vendors from OSF.

# *9*

# *A Look at Writing DCE Applications*

A theme running through the previous chapters has been "DCE is based on the client/server model." Section 3.4 cited the Remote Procedure Call (RPC) as the foundation for the client/server computing model, Section 4.2 described the role of DCE Threads within that model, Section 3.4.3 described how the Cell Directory Service (CDS) helps clients to find servers, and Section 5.5 showed how servers can check a client's privileges.

This chapter addresses experienced application designers or programmers who are new to networking, to distributed programming, or just to DCE. We'll discuss an approach toward application design, provide an overview of the program-development process, and address briefly some programming-language considerations. The chapter focuses on RPC, Threads, and Security, and mentions CDS briefly.

We realize that the topic of distributed programming—from design to coding to maintaining—is worthy of several books, never mind a single chapter. But we'd like to raise questions, flag potential pitfalls, and provide a very basic "first step" for people just getting their feet wet with distributed-application coding. Remember that we don't intend to deliver The One And Only Best Way. Our goal is to provide A Good Way To Start.

So let's get started!

## *9.1 Designing Your Client/Server Application*

If we had to sum up the most important design guideline in one sentence, we'd say this: Understand your users like never before, understand how to write thread-safe code, and be flexible.

But you'd probably like a little more detail, so here's our more thorough recommendation of the steps required for designing your client/server application:

1. Develop a comprehensive user model (Section 9.1.1).

2. Refer to the user model and design code modules for your application (Sections 9.1.2 through 9.1.6).

3. Determine the level of security required for each client/server pair (Section 9.1.7).

4. Design an interface for each server (Section 9.1.8).

5. Design the routines of your application and use threads for routines whose tasks are slow (Section 9.1.9).

6. Code, debug, and test your servers; identify performance bottlenecks and tune your use of threads.

7. Code, debug, and test your clients; identify performance bottlenecks and tune your use of threads.

During each step, it's important to remain flexible. We'll give you hints in this chapter about which decisions you can expect to revisit and how to develop a practical application while leaving some decisions open.

## Let's compare traditional and client/server designs

Some of the design steps in the preceding list are the same as those for traditional, nondistributed programming. For instance, you are probably already designing applications with an eye toward the user, and rapid prototyping tends to blur the distinction between coding and designing. Figure 9-1 provides one way of looking at the traditional design process, where a single computer system runs the entire application.

The application is usually given one task to accomplish; for instance, an application can implement an expense-voucher system. If using a rapid prototyping, concurrent engineering process, you may go through the cycle once for the user interface, show it to users, and then go through it again for internal, coding issues.

After testing and initial implementation, you may need to add a routine here or there, or you may need to modify a routine, but the design issues are minimal. And, if maintenance becomes burdensome, there's always the option of rewriting the application.

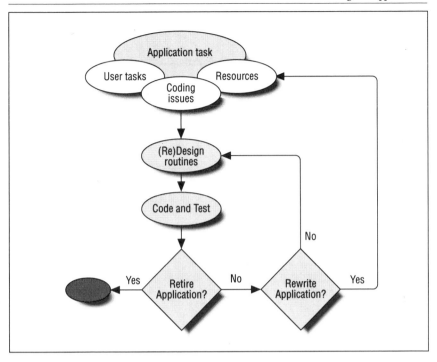

*Figure 9-1: Traditional designs: the application task and geography
remain constant*

Now let's take a look at the design process for a DCE client/server application, shown in Figure 9-2.

With a client/server application, the design process still operates within a single hierarchy, but the top is very different. Also, Security and Threads alter the bottom of the hierarchy. At the top, you'll see the label "Module task." We define a **module** as being the collection of routines that constitute a client or a server; we'll discuss the formation of modules later in this chapter.

Notice that we didn't mention rewriting the application; redesigning and rewriting are constant. Why? Because the group of somewhat interdependent clients and servers across the network probably won't be thrown away at the same time, and the use of threads reveals—over time—ways in which your application can be redesigned. Here's the implication: you must deal with backward compatibility forever. The good news is that DCE makes it easier to maintain compatibility, mainly by separating code from its declaration and by automating the ways an application can locate its distributed pieces after one piece changes location.

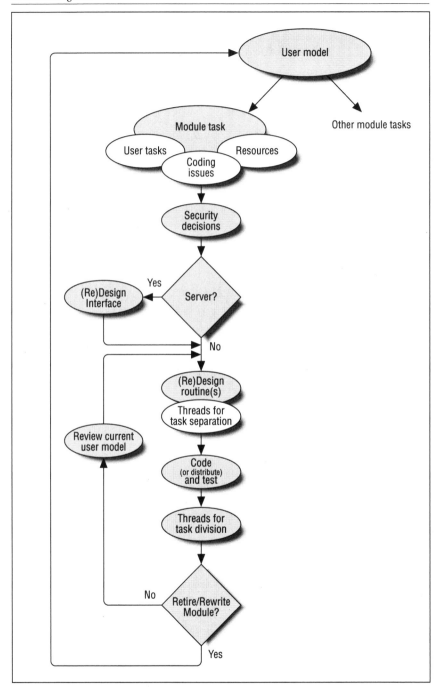

*Figure 9-2: Client/server designs: the user model and threads play a large role*

## *A good client/server design won't redesign people*

Client/server applications are powerful in part because they map better to the ways in which people and groups of people use computers to do their work. They operate in harmony with different people doing different things in various locations that have different resources. Yet even the most powerful software can't compensate for certain facts of life: that people are not predictable, that job descriptions are altered, that departmental groups change course (sometimes without quickly notifying other groups), and that programming environments—especially across a network—do not remain constant.

Clearly, DCE can't force the various departments, users, system administrators, and application programmers to check assumptions about foreign environments, to design for change, or to communicate changes in a timely manner. ("Whoops! I forgot to tell you that I deactivated that print queue!") So when you implement distributed applications, people must talk to one another more frequently (programmer to programmer, department to department, programmer to user, programmer to system administrator). DCE can distribute the code, but you have to distribute the level of communication and cooperation that goes along with this new technology. One recommendation that we'd always make is to buy more copies of this book to give to your coworkers!

With that sage advice in mind, let's look at the design process in detail.

## *9.1.1  Developing a Comprehensive User Model Is Critical*

To get off on the right foot, you need to develop an excellent user model. A **user model** is a deep understanding of the work flow of groups of people using your application and what they need to get their jobs done. The term **work flow** means the day-to-day methods and resources that people use to do a job. The user model involves a constellation of psychological and organizational issues; this chapter focuses only on the user's work flow as it affects the distributed application.

To begin, let's review the simple distributed application from Chapter 1, as shown in Figure 9-3.

Although the traditional design process is a hierarchy, the distributed process is a matrix of hierarchies. To create the matrix, compare your application's user groups with the distributed resources they need to complete their work. Figure 9-4 shows a very basic matrix that applies to the distributed application in Figure 9-3.

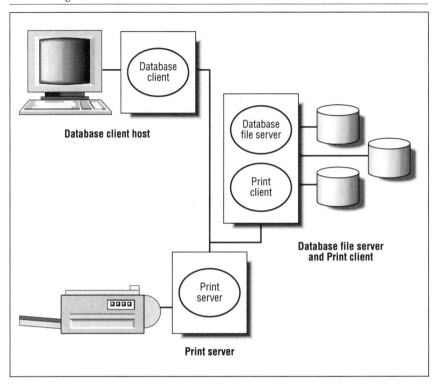

*Figure 9-3: A simple client/server configuration*

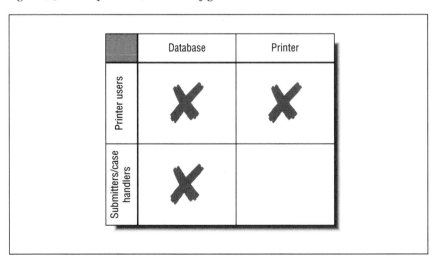

*Figure 9-4: Determine which user groups need which resources*

Each X in a matrix represents the modules of code distributed across the network; the users reside on one host system and use one user interface. When you design more complex applications, the X's in each box will indicate a type of code module, but the needs of your application may require multiple instances of that module. For example, you may need a printer client on multiple host systems. Notice also that, unlike this simple application, yours may have distributed users and multiple user interfaces.

You may be saying, "I see the matrix, but where are the hierarchies?" Well, every X in the matrix requires the design process outlined in Figure 9-2, and you need to balance code-module interdependencies constantly. Figure 9-5 shows what we were getting at when we mentioned the hierarchy of matrixes.

How do you make decisions about user tasks and threads and coding issues and interrelated modules and everything else? We recommend taking the time to thoroughly answer the questions that follow; the answers will form a rough cut at a user model for your application.

## 9.1.2 *What is the job and how will your application facilitate work flow?*

Let's start with the users of your application. As a first step, you may want to define the work flow according to a producer/consumer model. Does the application require a single producer and multiple consumers (as in a read-only electronic bulletin board)? Multiple producer and multiple consumers (as in an electronic mail server)? Multiple producers and a single consumer (as in employee expense vouchers)?

An expense-voucher application, for instance, has two groups of users: many people supplying vouchers and one user group approving or rejecting the vouchers. Someone may be required to maintain the expense-voucher database, which would be a third user group. Notice that the user group may not automatically map one-to-one onto a single client and server. You may need a combination of clients and servers to meet the needs of your user groups.

Once the user groups are clearly defined, develop descriptions of the tasks a user group can invoke, possibly from different host systems, that can be used together to accomplish a large job. These are examples of task descriptions: submitting an expense voucher, approving a voucher, maintaining the database of vouchers, checking to make sure that the requester has permission to receive money, and printing the vouchers. Don't impose an order on the tasks if an order is not required by the work flow.

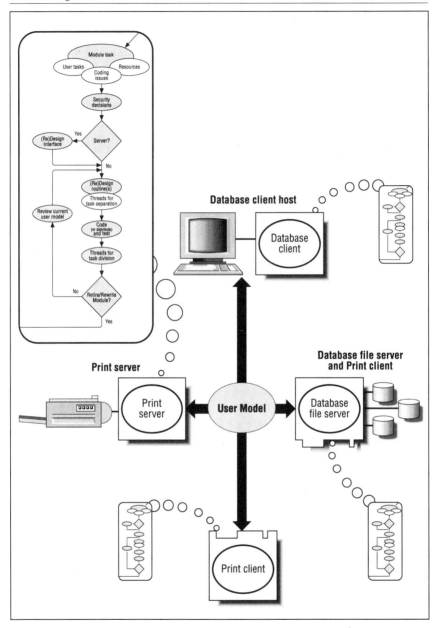

*Figure 9-5: A user model is the definition of all client/server relationships*

This method of design is similar to object-oriented programming design (Section 9.3). It strongly associates an element (a particular set of users at a particular location with a particular set of resources) with a set of tasks (tuning a database or submitting expense vouchers), then treats that grouping as a single object to be "invoked" by a larger application.

You can produce task descriptions by answering the following questions: who are the people using this application, what are their job categories, and what tasks do they perform on the job? Is your "user group" an application or a group of people? Do application and human-user tasks overlap at all? What types of resources will users need to access? For instance, will they need to use code, queues, or a database? Will the users be centrally located or distributed? If they are distributed, are certain tasks performed only in certain locations or do all users perform the same tasks? How do users use a resource provided by the application?

Later we'll address the implications of different answers to these questions. The main point is that having some answers during the design process makes it a lot easier to modify and maintain your application later.

## 9.1.3 What resources do you require and where are the resources located?

For the sake of convenience, resources can be viewed as hardware, software, or information. Hardware resources may be multiprocessors, array processors, vector processors, or color printers; a software resource may be a remote runtime library; an information resource may be a database, a file, or an electronic bulletin board.

Sometimes, the need for a resource comes from a user group; for instance, a group may need to enter an expense voucher into a database before it's approved. Sometimes, the application may require a resource or the creation of a resource; for instance, you may need to write a routine, which will "talk" in the database query language to enter new vouchers.

You might ask the following questions to gain a deeper understanding of how resources fit into the user model: What resources do users require? Does this requirement clarify where the application belongs in the producer/consumer model? Do different types of users require this resource? (Referring to the expense-voucher example, employees, managers, and Personnel may need access to the database of vouchers; a system manager may need to access the database, too.)

Would other resources on the network help either the user or application, for instance, a machine with multiple processors or a machine hooked up to an external service like a time provider? Can you move a resource from its current location? Can you split a resource into several resources at several locations? From whom would you need approval or help to redeploy resources across the network? Do you need new resources (a new color printer)? If your resource is code, is there existing code or do you have to write it? If you have to write it, how many different types of users need to use it? (We'll discuss the decision to distribute code a little bit later.)

In developing the user model, it helps to brainstorm about the possibilities of current resources, their creation, and their possible division and redistribution. For example, consider an application that purchases and sells stocks for customers. You can read one database for customer portfolios and one for current stock prices. The two functions can be divided so that the databases can be closer to their users. For instance, the price database requires constant access to the stock exchange, and that might require special hardware and software already located on a certain host system. The client databases can be split up, one for each office. Or, if there is a central location that can serve all offices efficiently, then one client database might be sufficient.

In summary, DCE gives you new and sometimes unexpected opportunities for distribution. Besides the well-known access it gives to remote resources, it provides you with the power to split and redistribute other types of resources.

## 9.1.4 How can you connect groups of people effectively with the resources they need to do their jobs?

One module of your distributed application will allow one or more groups of users to access a subset of the resources. For example, one group of distributed users will want to submit expense vouchers that will, in turn, need to be stored in a central database. You will need to design a user interface for those users and create the code modules that accomplish that set of tasks. Some of those tasks can be performed by the local client code, such as collecting data from the person submitting the report, while other tasks may require a remote call to server code; for instance, you may need code to place a voucher request into the distributed database.

Continue this mapping process for each group of users, then design the clients and servers necessary to implement the system. In other words, for each mapping of a major user group to a required resource, you'll need to design a code module—collection of routines—to perform required tasks; the task will determine whether the code module is a client or a server.

Remember that large distributed applications may require configuration and maintenance from someone such as a network administrator. For instance, you may need to create a user interface and task modules for someone to maintain the database of expense vouchers, and a database maintainer may need to add and delete permissions, perform database tuning, and so forth. Database administration is not directly related to the submission and approval of vouchers, but it is essential for the efficient and proper running of your application. Plan maintenance for applications that will require it.

## 9.1.5   A Client/Server Application Is a Series of Related Mini-Applications

At this point, you probably have a good feel for the code modules that you need to write. Now you need to decide whether to distribute code or implement it locally, possibly duplicating the code on several host systems.

In general, the decision to distribute a task or to do it locally requires a trade-off between the cost of execution (how large is the program's **granularity**), and the cost of communication and data transfer (remote procedure calls). You need to judge at which point an application's granularity becomes large enough to justify the overhead of a remote call. For instance, is it worth it to you to make a remote call to add two numbers? (No.) To compute a vector? (Usually not.) To convolve a graphical image in order to scan it for a particular object? (Probably yes.) You may also want to distribute a routine that uses a fairly complex algorithm required by different modules in your application; although the routine may not be incredibly compute intensive, you may want to prevent client programmers from duplicating their efforts.

In essence, the routines in a server can be viewed as a catalogue of services—similar to a runtime library—for various groups of users. Think through the details that a developer of a runtime library might need to consider, especially around communicating about the existence and capabilities of the routines. How do you let people know that the routines are available for use? How will you explain how the routines work? Are there groups of users that you don't want to use the routines? Is there a way to divide the catalogue to make it easier for users to access the services? We'll revisit these questions soon (Section 9.1.8).

## 9.1.6   Take Cell Configuration and Network Topology into Consideration

The network topology is another factor that you need to consider when designing your application. Figure 9-6 illustrates two possible Local Area Network (LAN) configurations within a single cell. Accessing resources across a cell or Wide Area Network (WAN) can take extra time, and the total access time will be less consistent. For instance, naming communication from CDS to the Global Directory Service (GDS) can slow intercell communication, and network traffic may be low or high on any given day, making WAN use inconsistent. Once again it's time to ask a series of questions whose collective answers will tell you where to locate clients, servers, and resources. Can the user afford the time it might take to cross a cell boundary or communicate among different LANs to access a resource? Will your intercell or WAN requests be frequent or infrequent? Do your intercell or WAN requests involve the transmission of large or small amounts of data? Which tasks require intensive computing power? Now for a few questions specific to choosing a host for a server. Does the server access a physical resource that doesn't move, like print queues? Does the host system have enough compute cycles to be the service nexus for a series of clients? Is the host system well-administered, so that down time and inefficiencies are minimized? Is there a server in the same cell or on the same LAN as a user group? Are there security and trust issues that would cause you to limit server access only to users within a single cell?

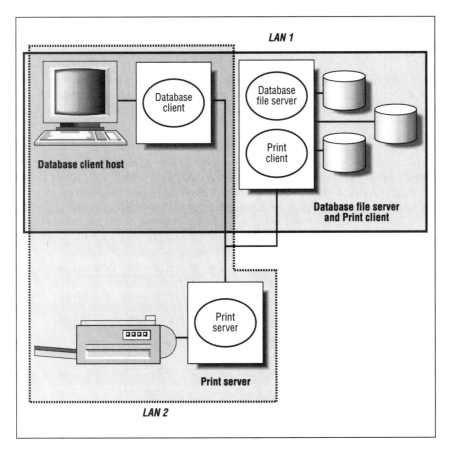

*Figure 9-6: Consider network topology when distributing code*

If your application provides a catalogue of routines for other applications and if the user needs quick access to these routines, you can locate a server in every LAN. If the routines are fairly generic and non-time-critical to the user, you can send a remote call across the WAN to a server in another LAN or perhaps across a cell boundary. (In these cases, you may want to design a thread in your client to do other work while waiting for the remote call across the WAN to complete.)

If your application provides access to a large database, chances are that you can't replicate the database in every LAN. Can you make the call across the WAN and create threads to execute other routines while the client waits? Or, can you locate servers in every LAN, locate the database in one LAN, and code the servers so that they cache information fetched from the distributed database? Or do you cache the information in the client? Or can the information be divided and distributed to better meet the needs of your user groups? The answers to these questions depend on the user's needs, the amount of the information to be fetched, and the frequency of the fetching. However, look for ways—like caching—in which clients can "remember" information, requiring fewer remote calls and placing less importance on the location of a server on the network.

## 9.1.7 *The Level of Security Is Up to You*

While designing your clients and servers, think about how much security their interactions will require. The security level may be the same for all clients, may be the same for one group of clients and different for others, or may vary for every client/server pair. The breakdown on security levels depends on the uniqueness of your application's client/server pairings.

The relationship between a client and a server is very much like a relationship between people. For example, most people share a limited amount of information with a stranger or a casual acquaintance, more information with a friend, even more information with family members, and the most amount of information with a spouse. Sometimes, there may be one friend with whom you share more information than most other friends; you make an exception in this one case.

Carrying the analogy a bit further, the way that you exchange information with another person may differ depending on how you're communicating. The directness of your communication may vary depending on whether the two of you are talking alone in a room, in a room with others, over the telephone, or are writing letters. Sometimes you'll use code words, winks, and nods to communicate, so that others won't catch on to what you're saying. Sometimes you'll make the communication formal to ensure that the message is received, like an invitation requiring an R.S.V.P, a court order, or registered mail.

To determine security levels for your application, you need to gain a deep understanding of the various client/server relationships, the types of transactions taking place between them, and the sensitivity of the data being sent across the network. We'll pose a series of questions to help you understand your application's security needs. Later, we'll discuss how to set security levels.

Is it important for the server to reject clients or make other decisions based on the identity or privileges of the client? Is it important for the client to choose a server or to check the server's privileges? (For instance, a database client may want to verify that it's talking to the right server.) Are there legal implications that would require levels of security? (Many financial and medical organizations must prove they have reasonable protection for their customers' data.)

Also, how vulnerable is your application to outsiders who may want to intercept data on the network and substitute false data? Will you be sending sensitive information outside the more trustworthy users in a cell or LAN? Is it important for your servers to record who they send data to (auditing)? Does your application run across national boundaries, or will it someday soon? (At the time of this writing, you can't use encryption with international applications, as we'll explain later.) Should your application's users be able to set the protection for a given operation? (For instance, with a Mail application, users might be able to set and modify the protection on stored messages.)

## *The Application Controls Its Own Security Levels*

If your server must implement a level of security for all clients, then call the **rpc_binding_set_auth_info** routine in the server-initialization file (Section 9.2.1); each client must make a nearly identical call in their code to communicate with that server. A **level of security** is a combination of three Security elements placed on a given RPC interaction: authentication, authorization, and data protection. By default, DCE applies no security. If a client and server attempt to communicate using different security levels, DCE generates an error instead of choosing between the server's or client's security level.

(Although by default DCE applies no security, your application does have some protection from network errors. DCE relies on the underlying network software—such as TCP/IP—to transport data reliably and to fix network-error situations that may inject bad data into the data stream. On the other hand, DCE Security was designed to protect clients and servers from a malicious third party who tries to substitute data.)

The level of security applies to the binding between the client and server, and stays in effect either until the client and server process choose another level or until one process terminates. It's possible for either the client or the server to **negotiate** a mutual security level. However, negotiating security levels is like deciding on how many threads to use (Section 9.1.9): you need to choose between overhead and application need. We recommend that you find one appropriate security level for a client/server pairing and stick with it, unless there's an application need that offsets the negotiation overhead (like the Mail application mentioned previously).

Let's take a look at setting a security level and at the options available for each of the three Security elements. You can set two of the three elements—authentication and data protection—with one argument to the **rpc_binding_set_auth_info** routine, and you can indicate that authorization will take place by passing a constant as a separate parameter.

Here are the seven options for authentication and data protection:

- **rpc_c_protect_level_none**

  There will be no authentication or data protection placed on the client/server RPC communication.

- **rpc_c_protect_level_default**

  The client or server will use a cellwide default for authorization or data protection, which can be any of the other constants in this list.

- **rpc_c_protect_level_connect**

  Upon initial connection, the client, server, and a DCE Security server work together to prove that the client and server are who they say they are. This process is called **mutual authentication** (Section A.3).

- **rpc_c_protect_level_call**

  Upon every remote call, RPC will perform an operation on the transmitted data that mutually authenticates the client and server.

  The data transmission for a remote call is broken into chunks called "packets" (PKT). For **rpc_c_protect_level_call** authentication and data protection, RPC performs an MD5 checksum on the RPC-internal part of the first transmitted packet only. To calculate the checksum and access the data, the client and server need to use their secret key, which proves their identity.

- **rpc_c_protect_level_pkt**

  Upon every packet in a remote call, RPC will perform an operation that mutually authenticates the client and server. This process involves performing a checksum on the RPC-internal portions of all packets in the transmission.

- **rpc_c_protect_level_pkt_integrity**

  RPC will perform a checksum on every packet, including the application-specific data. In addition to mutual authentication, this ensures that the data sent is the data received.

- **rpc_c_protect_level_privacy**

  RPC will encrypt the contents of every packet, including application-specific data. This protects clients and servers from a malicious third party on the network who wants to intercept their transmitted data. The encrypted data requires the secret key of both the client and server for decryption.

Each subsequent authorization and data protection level includes the protection offered in the previous level. And, along with the added protection of each subsequent level, higher levels involve more application overhead.

You may be asking why you'd want to authenticate at all. In general, authentication allows the application to audit remote calls or to enable authorization. (You can't check privileges effectively unless you can be sure of the principal's identity.) When you authenticate on every remote call, it's also called **authenticated RPC**. Authenticated RPC is useful for servers that receive random requests spread out over potentially long periods of time. Some database services may find this authentication useful.

When choosing a security level, select the elements needed by your application. Just mix and match. For instance, a relatively high level of security would include data privacy (which implicitly involves PKT authentication) and privileges checked. A relatively low level of security would involve connection authorization (which implicitly involves no data protection) and no privileges checked.

## *Authorization: Server Routines Decide Whether to Execute*

Authorization involves one body of code (usually a server) checking whether a principal (usually a client) has enough privileges to access a particular **object** (a database, routines, or files, for instance). To check for privileges, the code places a call to the DCE Security API, passing another principal's name and the name of the object that the principal wants to use.

Let's use the expense-voucher application to shed light on this process. A server might check whether a client has privileges to access the expense-voucher database. Perhaps clients for employees will have only **read** and **write** privileges, while clients for Personnel or management will be granted a fuller set of privileges . For this application's server to perform authorization, the client and server must first establish the same security level. Let's say that the client then makes a remote call to the **modify_voucher** routine. On the server's side, the RPC runtime library creates a thread and executes **modify_voucher**. Finally, the server routine itself must decide whether the client has enough privileges to continue executing the routine.

It wouldn't be difficult for a server routine to check the access control list (ACL) to see whether the client has enough privileges (Section 5.1). The Security API provides routines to access the client's principal name. The server routine can then pass the client's and database's principal names to another Security routine, which determines whether the client has the right to modify the database. However, we recommend that you write a separate body of code, called an Access Control Manager (ACM), that each server routine calls to check a client's privileges. The ACM can be a black box, calling security routines and simply returning Yes (continue to execute) or No (abort due to lack of privileges) to the server routine that called it.

## A Few Pointers About Using DCE Security

Here are some information and advice to keep in mind while designing and implementing levels of security for your application.

- Data protection involves high overhead.

  Data protection requires a significant amount of work by the RPC runtime library and DCE Security, due to checksum computation and encryption. Both integrity and privacy are time-consuming operations, so be sure to use data protection judiciously.

  Since authentication and authorization take place before the remote call, they tend to have minimal impact on performance compared to the impact of data protection. However, remember that your application's use of authorization can create noticeable overhead. If the application makes many decisions based on different clients, different resources, different privileges, time, and the context of application conditions, then overhead can be significant.

- Use multiple interface definitions instead of security-level negotiation.

  DCE Security, like all aspects of a distributed application, requires less time and effort if you plan ahead with interface definitions that suit your application's user model. Making different types of client calls from a single, large interface often entails unnecessary overhead or inappropriately easy access, depending on the security level you chose. Consider Figure 9-7. If you create one interface for each set of routines that perform the same type of task, then the security level will be appropriate for all the remote calls in a given interface. Figure 9-8 shows how three interfaces would serve the task groupings better and improve the efficiency of the application.

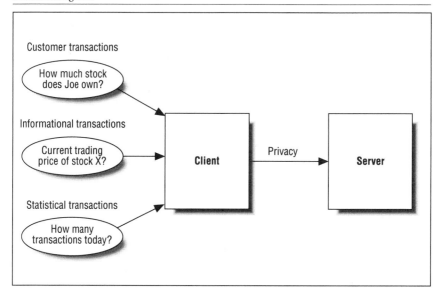

*Figure 9-7: A poorly designed interface hampers security performance*

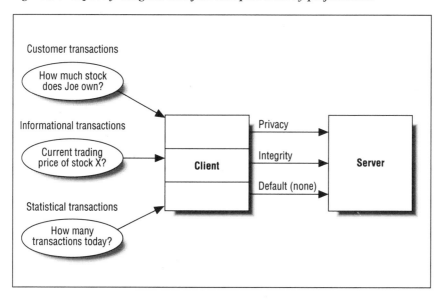

*Figure 9-8: Well-designed interfaces improve security performance*

- Determine the appropriate security level for an interface and stick with it.

  It is possible to negotiate levels of security during execution, but, given various issues involving performance and complexity, we recommend that you avoid this as much as possible.

- Use integrity for international applications.

  Privacy automatically ensures data integrity, and both data-protection methods involve almost the same overhead. Why not always use privacy over integrity? Because privacy limits the scalability and portability of your application.

  Companies are not allowed to ship certain software—such as DCE—out of the United States, because it performs encryption to application data according to the Data Encryption Standard (DES). (Briefly, product-internal DES encryption is exportable; DES encryption of user's data is not exportable.)

  This means that the DCE encryption implementation in France will probably be different than the encryption capabilities of an implementation in the United States. If there is a remote chance that your distributed application will become international, then use integrity protection.

## 9.1.8  A Well-Designed Interface Aids Scalability and Maintainability

Before you rush off to code modules, let's look at the process of developing a client/server interface and how the contents of that file can improve scalability and ease of use.

The design model that DCE uses is the **interface** and **implementation** model. The interface file contains the declarations, and the implementation files contain function code.

Creating a client/server application is similar to creating separately compilable modules, where you need one general file to define or declare routines, symbols, data structures, and global data for all other files. In the C language (used by almost all DCE programmers at the time of this writing), the interface is a **.h** header file to declare global data and functions. Figure 9-9 illustrates the use of the **.idl** and **.h** files as an interface to DCE source-code modules.

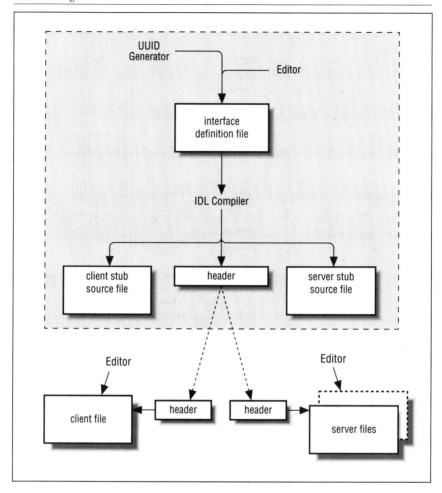

*Figure 9-9: Client/server implementations and their interface*

Your **.idl** file declares the client/server global types and function declarations of the server routines. The IDL language, which is very much like C, includes attributes that facilitate data flow and the portability of remote calls (Section 9.3). To mark the interface uniquely so that an application's clients and servers can be identified by the RPC runtime library and by CDS, IDL requires that the interface file contain an identifier generated by the **uuidgen** command.

The IDL compiler accepts a **.idl** file, then creates a **.h** file to be included in your client and server source code. The IDL compiler also creates stub code, which uses the RPC runtime library to execute the remote procedure, and to transfer data to and from the client and server.

All this leads to design issues. Creating multiple interfaces to a single server often facilitates ease of use. For instance, the expense-voucher system probably includes modules of code that assist employees in creating and submitting forms, that help maintain the database, that allow someone with the proper privileges to approve or reject submissions, and perhaps that allow financial analysts to run reports against the database. If there are 100 server routines to a single interface, the four clients described previously might have executable files containing stub code for all 100 routines, when they may use only 7 or 8 of them.

It's a good idea to split up the interface file according to your user model. Using the example from the preceding paragraph, there are at least five interfaces: one with routines commonly used by all clients, one for the Approval clients, one for the Employee clients, one for the Database Maintainer clients, and one for the Financial Analyst clients.

The **.idl** file is often the only documentation that the server implementer provides to her or his client coders. Like any documentation, books included, if it's hard to read and understand, people won't read it and won't write clients for your server. Consider documenting this information in your **.idl** file: how to call the remote procedures, in what order to call them, and the meaning and acceptable values of the routine parameters.

Finally, it's easier to expand your application if you create interfaces that map closely to the user model and to the resource availability. For instance, you can move pieces of your server code to servers in other LANs or cells more easily, if that becomes necessary. In general, the interfaces will be more reusable. If you have only one interface and you need to make a change, all clients and servers need to recompile their code. Remember also that most production-ready applications contain code that directly reads and manipulates data structures affecting the client/server binding (Section 9.2.2); if you break up an interface later, you will have to recode pieces of your server-initialization file or server routines that manipulate bindings.

## 9.1.9 Threads Present New Challenges to Application Designers

We recommend that you learn the threads paradigm right away and that you implement threads in your earliest client/server applications. There are two reasons for our recommendation. First, you'll find it easier to use threads in the first place, rather than retrofitting them into an application. Second, threads can have profound implications for the design of your application, in particular how you structure and access global variables and how you design your subroutines.

## Threads Improve Performance for Both the Server and Client

Let's take a look at how clients and servers use threads. For decades, servers in the UNIX socket-programming world have forked processes to handle client requests, which come in the form of TCP/IP connections. DCE uses this same principle, adding some flexibility and efficiency. For DCE applications, the RPC run time on the server's host creates one or more threads to handle incoming client requests. Figure 9-10 shows a server's use of DCE Threads.

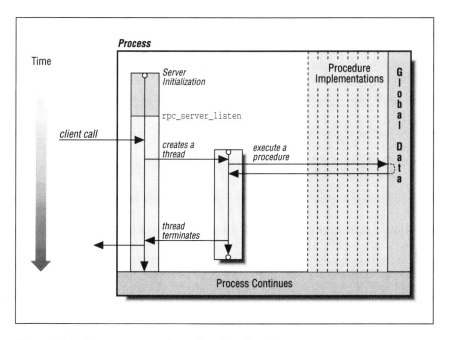

*Figure 9-10: A server creates threads to handle client requests*

In the server-initialization file, the call to **rpc_server_listen** establishes the maximum number of server threads. If you want DCE to choose the maximum number, then specify 0 as the argument to this routine. The operating system may impose a limit on the number of threads concurrently executing.

A server initialized to serve more than one client request at a time is called a **multithreaded server**. If the server receives more requests than the maximum threads allowed, it places the requests in a queue until one of the currently executing threads terminates.

Remember that all multithreaded server routines need to be reentrant (thread safe). These routines need to be designed to run concurrently in the same process, sharing the same global data. It's good programming

practice to write reentrant code for your entire DCE client/server application. Later, we'll give you some tips on writing reentrant code.

On the client side, threads fit neatly into the structure by providing a place
for time-consuming routines to execute concurrently with the main program. They can also speed up execution, allowing you to divide a task into
subtasks that can execute at the same time. Figure 9-11 shows a client's use
of threads.

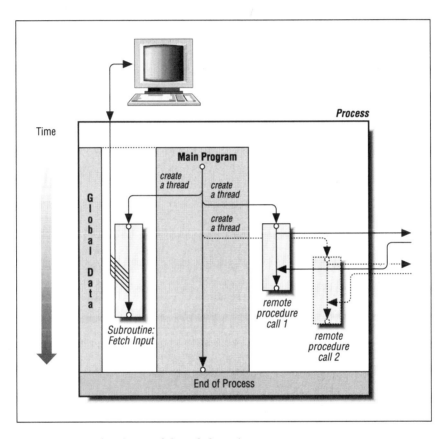

*Figure 9-11: A client's use of threaded routines*

## Threads Help Task Separation and Task Division

Threads affect the bottom part of the client/server design hierarchy (Figure
9-2). One helpful way to view the role of threads is to divide their use
into two categories: task separation and task division. In the first case, you
simply designate which application routines should run in separate threads.
Some examples of threaded task separation include routines that drive slow
devices, respond to user input, or make remote procedure calls. A good

example of an application that can increase its speed using task separation is this: a chess program that takes advantage of a thread to allow the program to "think" on its opponent's time, computing possibilities for its next move while it waits for the opponent to choose a move. This threading technique structures execution much like structured languages organize the flow of your source code.

In the second case, task division, you can sometimes speed up your application by breaking a slow task into smaller chunks and executing them in separate threads. Some examples of threaded task division include concurrently executing subtasks, deferred work (for instance, modifying a balanced tree, returning to the user, and then rebalancing in a separate thread), or utilizing special hardware processors.

Opportunities for task separation are usually easier to spot than those for task division. Until you gain more experience with threaded programming, it's important to use the Coding and Testing steps of the design process to monitor the efficiency of your program. During a compute-intensive portion of your application, you should be thinking to yourself: is there work that my application can be doing while this task is chugging away in a separate thread? Or, is there a way that I can break this task down and execute the pieces in separate threads?

This point in the design process is why we recommend being flexible from the beginning. It can be frustrating to get past the debugging and testing steps and find that you need to seriously rethink the design of your module's routines. For instance, if you decide to break up a slow task into six pieces and execute them in separate threads, then that entails creating six routines that the original algorithm didn't call for. In other cases, the use of threads may cause the extreme alteration of a previously written routine, perhaps involving the protection of global data to make the routine reentrant. The good news is that, with experience, you will begin to spot task separation and division opportunities much earlier in the design process.

## Some Tips for Designing and Using Threads

The use of threads, like that of RPC, is a balancing act. Always weigh program simplicity—so that subsequent programmers can understand and maintain it—against the need for reentrant protection. Which is more important: execution efficiency or code maintainability?

Let's put it this way: make your use of mutexes, condition variables, and scheduling as simple as possible, but no simpler. If you use a global lock on all global data, then you increase the risk of blocked threads, because other threads will surely need to use small pieces of that global data. But if you use locks on every small piece of global data that you can, the source code will be difficult to read and the runtime behavior of threads will be more difficult to predict.

One thing you can do to make threaded programming easier is to design your global data well. Try to be more conservative in your use of globally defined variables, defining them to facilitate the use of mutexes. For example, if you need to protect a small piece of a larger variable, consider declaring the large variable locally, copying a piece of it to a small global variable, and then locking the small global variable. You can also pass sensitive data as parameters, causing them to be stored on the routine's local stack, thereby making them unavailable to other threads as global data.

We also find that a certain mind set is helpful when working with threads and writing reentrant code. While writing your code, constantly imagine that another invocation of this same routine is executing concurrently. Imagine your current thread blocking on any statement—perhaps in the middle of storing a multibyte variable—allowing another thread the opportunity to change the value of your global data out from under you. Then, use condition variables and mutexes to secure the lines of code in which you need to be sure of the value of the variable.

Be mindful of what it might be like for another thread to access a global variable in between the time you define it (did you initialize it?) and the time you lock it. How can you ensure that the value is what it is supposed to be when you use the variable? One method is to reset the variable to its original value before you unlock it, allowing other threads to use it. This type of variable resetting is called **invariant data**, because it's always the same value when another thread unlocks it for use.

Here's a warning about mutexes: they lock a mutex variable, *not* the data that you are trying to protect. Therefore, a routine that doesn't use mutexes can access data that is supposedly "locked" by a routine in another thread. If every programmer working on your application is very disciplined about unlocking the mutex variable before accessing the protected data, then everything is peachy. However, one rogue routine can cause reentrancy problems in your application.

When programming with threads, you should also beware of the idiosyncrasies of your hardware and software systems. The number of processors, whether your machine code accesses data in an uninterrupted process (**atomicity**), the threads implementation, the program's algorithm, and your language compiler all have an effect on the predictable functioning of designed threads in an application.

Porting and debugging can be difficult with threaded programs. For example, imagine that your compiler packs fields of records so tightly that they cannot be accessed using atomic operations. If you protect two packed fields using two mutexes, you might end up with the wrong answer. Both threads will be accessing the same memory at the same time, properly using two valid locks. This kind of bug is difficult to catch, because a change in compiler can hide or reveal it, or because it might require an improbable set of threads executing certain routines at precisely the wrong moment.

Finally, you need to be concerned with overloading your system. Too few threads can create a bottleneck. For instance, remote calls executed without separate threads can really slow things down. However, too many threads can slow your program down, too. Each thread must be managed by the Thread Scheduler, which creates overhead and taxes your system. Later, we'll talk about debugging threaded programs (Section 9.3).

# 9.2 Implementing Your Client/Server Application

Once you've designed your application, it's time to take a look at what it takes to code, test, and debug your application. Here are the topics covered in this section:

- Coding a test application from scratch (Section 9.2.1).

- Implementing a production-ready application (Section 9.2.2).

- Working with previously written code (Section 9.2.3).

## 9.2.1 Coding Your First DCE Client/Server Application

Frequently, programmers develop a practice application that tests whether underlying software is functional and in place (a "ping" application). After coding, debugging, testing, and implementing this simple code, a programmer then can more confidently move on to a production-ready application.

In the C world of programming, the most common get-your-feet-wet application is the Hello World program, which simply writes "hello world" to the terminal screen. Appendix A provides a distributed version of the Hello World program in increasing complexity, and talks briefly about specific coding details. The rest of this section describes the design and structure of this application.

Before writing the code to Hello World, we need to create a user model. To do that, we'll answer the following questions:

- What is the goal of Hello World?

  The goal of this application is to test for the presence of DCE RPC, Threads, and Security, and to authenticate the client and server. In essence, this is a database application. The application provides one remote procedure that accesses the data, and the server's "database" contains one piece of data ("hello world"). The client handles all I/O with the user.

- Which producer/consumer model applies to this application?

  Hello World is a single-producer/single-consumer application. However, it would take very little effort to allow multiple, concurrent client calls. All you need to do to make it a multiple-consumer application is change the argument to the **rpc_server_listen** routine in the server-initialization code (see Appendix A). If you design remote procedures to be reentrant, then it is easier to scale the application later.

  Modifying this application by creating multiple producers is also very straightforward. As long as the servers are registered with CDS, the RPC run-time library can hook up its client with a server that's close by. Since the overhead of marshalling one character string is very low and all servers do the same thing, it doesn't matter which server a particular client uses.

- Who are the users of this application?

  In the single-producer/single-consumer model, there's only one user group. The user group wants to see the data in the database to ensure that DCE is up and running.

- What and where are the resources? Will they move in the future?

  The resources are one database containing a character string and one remote procedure. Since the "database" is embedded into the remote procedure and uses very little memory, it isn't tied to a specific host system; we could easily duplicate this "database" across the network. If the resource moves, CDS can provide updated information to the clients; the move requires no special notice to application users or system managers.

  Even in a small application like this, you should be very cautious about memory use on both the client and server. In the client, we sidestep the problem of arbitrary-length strings by deciding on a maximum length and declaring a static character array. In a more sophisticated application, the client stub can allocate memory as part of a remote call.

- Will there be a need to distribute code?

  This application distributes one remote procedure that defines the data and sends it to the client. We don't foresee a need to distribute any other code in the near future.

- Do the cell/LAN configurations affect the application design?

  No. Servers and clients use CDS to communicate, and marshalling presents no efficiency issues that would require special processing by the client. So clients can use a server inside or outside their cell or LAN.

- Can threads aid task division or speed up the application?

  The application uses an extra thread in the client to communicate with the users while waiting for completion of the remote call and uses another one to make the remote call. Any attempts to use threads for more speed in this simple application will create more overhead than savings in execution time.

The two main concerns when using threads are synchronization and data sharing. This application synchronizes its three threads using a flag that indicates the status of the remote call. Once the remote call is complete, the main thread joins all three threads into one.

As for data protection, the client requires none and the server routine is nonreentrant. (Section A.4 provides an example of a reentrant version of the server routine.)

- Does the application require security?

  We'd like to make sure that the client and server are who they say they are, so we'll use authentication at the time of connection.

- Are there any additional interface design issues?

  Since the interface includes only one procedure declaration and some simple type definitions, there is no need to divide the interface for efficiency.

Let's take a brief look at what the sample application in Appendix A does. Figure 9-12 shows the flow of events and how data passes between programs.

❶ The client code creates two threads, one that communicates with the user and one that makes a remote call.

❷ This application's global data includes a flag that indicates the status of the remote call and includes a buffer for the returned string. (The reentrant version of this application includes a counter and a mutex in the global data.)

❸ At this point, the stub code and RPC runtime library take over (Section 3.5). The RPC runtime library marshalls the data across the network.

❹ The RPC runtime library creates a thread in which to execute the procedure specified by the client.

❺ The procedure writes "hello world" to one output parameter and writes a "terminated" flag value to the second output parameter.

❻ The thread terminates, and the RPC runtime library marshalls the output parameters back to the client.

❼ The client reads the new value of the flag and joins all three threads.

❽ The client writes the returned string to the terminal and terminates.

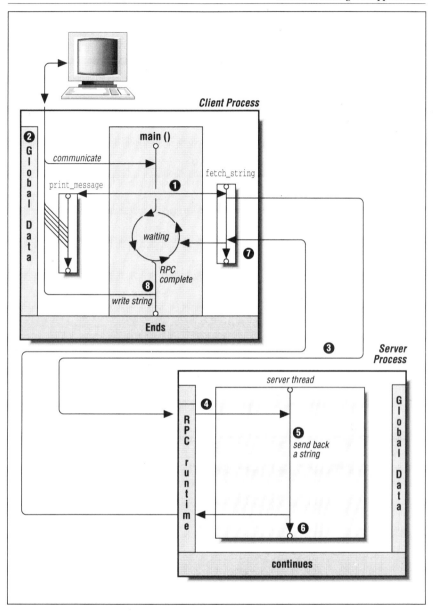

*Figure 9-12: What the sample application does*

With the exception of programming-language and debugging issues (Section 9.3), writing and developing application code differs very little from writing a nondistributed application, whose routines are divided into separately compilable files. However, there are some differences. You need to do the following—among other things that production-ready applications require—to develop your DCE client/server application:

1. Generate an interface for each client/server task grouping.

   You use the **uuidgen** command to create an IDL file template, then add appropriate type definitions and remote procedure declarations.

2. Compile the IDL file to create the **.h** file, and the client and server stub code (Section 3.3).

3. Write a server-initialization file for each server.

   The server-initialization file establishes client/server communication protocols, determines how many client requests the server can execute concurrently, defines module-wide data, and performs other tasks (Section A.2).

   Depending on your user model, the server may have several interfaces, each with a different set of server routines and a different level of security. The mapping of interface files between client and server does not have to be one-to-one. The server registers as many interfaces as it takes to provide all server routines. A client can include as many of the **.h** interface files as is appropriate.

4. For both the client and server, link the application code with the RPC runtime library and with the appropriate stub code. If the code module is a server, link everything with the server-initialization file.

## 9.2.2 Creating a Production-Ready Application

This chapter and Appendix A provide a good first step toward DCE client/server programming. We hate to break this to you, but there are a few more steps that you'll need to master before you're creating production-ready applications. For those who hate surprises, we've collected these brief descriptions of other RPC features, which are useful for more complex applications:

- Binding handles and methods

  If you put together all the information that the client has to know in order to find a server and place it in a data structure, you have a binding handle. The Hello World application makes things very easy for the client by using the **automatic binding** method, which creates and uses a binding handle through a whole crew of behind-the-scenes actors provided by DCE.

  Two other binding methods are very useful: **implicit** and **explicit** binding. Use implicit binding when you want to choose a server for a client to call. For instance, your client may need to use data from a particular host. Use explicit binding when you want to make remote calls to different servers from the same client. You can use both methods together. For instance, you can use implicit binding to establish a default server and explicit binding to make exceptions.

- String binding

  If you want to read binding handles and make decisions based on their contents, then use **string binding**. This method allows you to search an ASCII version of the binding handle for information, such as the principal name of the server or client.

- Attribute Configuration Files (ACFs)

  The ACF is an auxiliary file that contains decisions that do not belong in the interface file. Such decisions include whether to exclude object code for some routines in the interface, temporary binding methods, and so forth.

- Full and reference pointers

  DCE implemented two types of pointers that allow you to use memory wisely across the network. A **full pointer** has all the capability of a pointer in C. You must use this type of pointer for remote return values, as part of a double pointer for an output parameter of unknown size, and for all NULL pointers.

  A **reference pointer** has limited capabilities, but using it reduces overhead. Use reference pointers for non-NULL input and output parameters, and use them for in-place operations like a Fast Fourier Transform (FFT).

- Conformant and varying arrays

  DCE provides extra memory flexibility with arrays. A **conformant array** allows you to use array parameters of different lengths. On input, conformant arrays allow you to call the remote routine with a single parameter, which can take different lengths for different invocations. (For those familiar with C, this use of a conformant array is similar to a distributed version of **varargs**).

  As an output parameter, a conformant array lets the client accept data of an unknown length from the server. You should apply a double pointer (two asterisks) to this type of parameter. The client's stub allocates memory for the data received.

- **ignore** IDL attribute

  The **ignore** IDL attribute enables you to specify a large variable—such as a large structure—as a parameter, but pass only a small portion or two. This attribute tells RPC which members to ignore.

- **code** and **nocode** IDL attributes

  These IDL attributes are used in the ACF, and allow you to eliminate or include a routine's object code in the client. We recommend that you use these attributes to reduce the size of the client executables; to allow an orphan, production-ready client to use only a few routines in the interface; and to test and debug individual server routines. However, if there are large numbers of clients that need to use **code** and **nocode** frequently, then you should consider dividing a larger interface into smaller ones, better serving your user model.

- **inline** and **out_of_line** IDL attributes

  These IDL attributes determine whether the object code makes a remote or local procedure call. (For you C programmers, **inline** is similar to a C macro and to inlining in C++.) The tradeoff is to make your executable larger to get faster data marshalling. The **out_of_line** attribute tells the RPC runtime library to perform marshalling in separate subroutines, which are included only once in your application code.

- **byte** IDL data type

  You can use the **byte** IDL type in two ways. First, use this type for all byte data, such as an array of bytes. Second, use this type to code untyped or opaque data when your client and server hosts have the same machine architecture. No conversion is performed on the data by the RPC runtime library, which reduces the marshalling time considerably.

- Pipes

  This IDL data type is useful for transferring very, very large amounts of data across the network. It's particularly useful when the input is continuous (such as from a data-acquisition device) or of an unknown size.

- Context and customized binding handles

  These data structures are the equivalent of static variables in a non-distributed application. You use the customized binding handle to call one or more server routines that use a data object, which in turn requires implicit location information; one common reason for requiring such location information is to maintain the state of that data object from one server call to the next. If maintaining state, you need to use a context handle.

  Here are a few guidelines: if you want to link the state and binding information, passing the same information for every call to a particular server, then use the customized binding handle. This handle makes the custom information inseparable from the binding handle, so that you send all the information together on every call. If you want to separate state information from binding information, then use the context handle and a regular binding handle.

Applications that need to do the following server tasks are good candidates for maintaining state: file operations, opening a database, working with complex data structures, and so forth.

- **comm_status** and **fault_status** attributes

  Communications and server errors are raised as exceptions. Unless you design your program to handle the exceptions, the program will exit. An exception is a software state indicating an event that could not be handled within the normal flow of control. Such an event may be produced by hardware (such as memory access violations) or software (such as specifying an array subscript that is outside the declared range).

  An ACF can save you the trouble of writing extra layers of exception handling code. The **comm_status** and **fault_status** attributes apply to procedure parameters or return values. If these attributes are present, communication and server errors are communicated to the client as values in its named parameters rather than raised as exceptions.

- **rpc_ss_allocate** and **rpc_ss_free** routines

  There are certain situations in which your application may allocate memory in the server. For example, a server procedure may allocate memory for a conformant array, whose bounds are not determined until runtime. If the application doesn't clean up memory on the server, it may severely limit the amount of memory left over to perform other application tasks.

  Since a client cannot use the C runtime library function **free** to deallocate memory on a server, DCE provides the stub-support functions **rpc_ss_allocate** and **rpc_ss_free** for use on the server side; these are used in a complementary manner, like **malloc** and **free**.

## 9.2.3   Distributing Existing Code

Most of the focus in this section has been on newly developed applications. However, nearly every site has a significant body of code that can be distributed. Here we discuss recoding existing applications and writing clients for existing servers.

### Existing Applications Can Work Within the Distributed Model

When recoding an existing application for distribution, these are the subjects to be aware of:

- Revisit your user model.

  Many traditional applications used a simpler user  model and did not consider where to locate physical or information-based resources on the network. It may be worth your time to revisit design issues by creating a user-model matrix (Section 9.1), mapping user groups against available resources, and seeing where the existing code fits into the larger picture.

- Get a clean definition of the interface.

First, the interface should allow the old code to be separately compilable. Second, it should reflect the expanded user model (remember the user group that needs only five remote procedures out of the 100 available on your server). There are also language-specific concerns about the interface files (Section 9.3).

- Make decisions about the use of threads.

As mentioned earlier (Section 9.1.9), threading previously written code in an unaltered state may be problematic. The optimal solution—redesigning the global data of your application—is also the most time consuming. Also, that redesign effort will surely ripple into recoding some of the procedure bodies. Suddenly, it's not old code anymore that you're distributing.

Beware of subtle nonreentrant coding in existing applications. In other words, the code may appear to be reentrant, but closer inspection will reveal otherwise. For example, any code that calls the C runtime library directly is nonreentrant (at the time of this writing). If you place the **pthreads.h** file in old C code, the application will call DCE Threads-supplied jacket routines, making the call reentrant.

You may want to use fewer threads than in a new application and use **pthread_lock_global_np** for all threaded procedure calls. It may cost you in execution speed, but it will be safe.

We have another recommendation: if mutex design is troublesome and if large granularity locking is unacceptable, then create a single-threaded server. Again, you must make this decision based on the needs of the application. To make this determination, ask yourself these questions: Is it acceptable to cause a preliminary delay, forcing remote calls to wait in queue? Or is it more important to begin execution requests quickly at the expense of slow execution times for each routine?

- Make sure that your use of pointers, arrays, memory allocation, and large data structures (in parameters) fits the rules of the Interface Definition Language, as mentioned previously (Section 9.2.1).

- Consider writing **jacket** (sometimes called **wrapper**) routines to distribute information.

Instead of putting an existing routine into your interface definition, you can write a new procedure—which uses RPC protocols and is reentrant—that in turn calls the existing routine. You may need to use a global lock. All in all, despite some sacrifice in efficiency, this programming technique can be an effective way to reuse old code without having to rewrite it. And the amount of new code should be minimal, because its only purpose is to use RPC and to be reentrant.

You can also write code to be executed remotely that in turn uses a local database application. In this way, the remote procedures provide information from a local application to clients across the network without a substantial code rewrite.

## Follow the Interface When Writing Clients for Existing Servers

When writing clients for existing servers, these are the subjects to be aware of:

- Obtain a copy of the **.idl** interface file and code to it.

  Depending on how well you know the implementers or the server-host system managers, just getting a copy of the interface may be the most challenging part of this task. Also, this situation reinforces the importance of a good interface design based on a sound user model. The comments in the interface code will possibly constitute the only, or at least the most accessible, documentation.

- Define your user group within the larger application's user model. Then communicate the needs of your user group to those people maintaining the server.

  No matter how well an application is designed, a user almost always finds some idiosyncratic way to use the software. If you communicate how the remote procedures met or didn't meet your needs back to the implementers, they can expand their own user model to include your needs for the next version of the application. At least that's the theory.

- Make sure that there is a server within reasonable distance from your client.

  If you don't have a server in your LAN and if your remote calls have a critical time element, you may need to work on configuration. You can try to get the network or system administrator to install a server on your LAN.

- Design and use threads from the start.

  They are more difficult to retrofit than to design in from the start. You can also make the client subroutines more reusable by making them reentrant, in case you decide to call them from multiple threads in the future.

# 9.3 DCE Programming-language Considerations

Previous sections have prepared you for application design and for making some RPC, Security, and Threads routine calls. However, you won't be making these calls in a vacuum. Before you rush off to begin your application design, let's briefly discuss the nuts and bolts of using programming languages and debuggers with a DCE client/server application.

Discussing certain issues up front will help you to plan. What compilers do you have? Do you need a new one? Are your debugging tools adequate for distributed applications? Can you write your own tools? Do you have the programmers who know the necessary languages? Can you train them? How long will training take? How long will it take people to code application modules, especially if they'll be working in an unfamiliar language? How can you estimate debugging time, if your programmers have never debugged a distributed application before?

To summarize DCE language support in a sentence, DCE requires the use of IDL, fully supports the use of the C language, and can be used with other programming languages—at your own risk. This section discusses IDL use, C use, issues involved with using other languages, and some typical distributed debugging situations.

## The Interface Definition Language is Similar to C

To write robust applications, you need to be able to code IDL and ACF files using the Interface Definition Language (IDL). IDL is very similar to the C language, but it extends C through the use of attributes, which appear within brackets ([]) in the **.idl** file. We can't cover all of the IDL attributes, but we'd like to give you an idea of what you'll be working with.

Consider the **.idl** file from the sample application in Appendix A:

```
/*  File name:    hello_world.idl                             */
/*  Purpose:      The interface for the application,          */
/*                containing global declarations and type     */
/*                declarations.                                */
[
uuid(AAB038A0-3709-11CB-BFC4-08002B0F4644),
version(1.0)
]
interface hello_world
{
/* Global data */
const long                    MAX_STRING = 11;
/*  The "+1" adds a byte for null char  */
typedef [string] char    string_type[MAX_STRING+1];
/* Function declaration */
```

```
void hello_world(
    [out] string_type return_string, /* string passed to clients  */
    [out] short int          *flag  );/* flag signals completion */
}
```

The UUID is an attribute that distinguishes this interface from any other. The **out** attribute specifies output parameters. Remember that all data used by a remote procedure must be passed as parameters and transmitted over the network. The **string** attribute tells the stub code that the array is really a string, so it can look for the terminating null byte.

When the IDL compiler creates the **.h** header file, it translates IDL data types to portable data types—defined with C **typedef** statements—that facilitate transmission and translation to various machine-storage formats. This process ensures that data storage and use requested by a programmer on one system is equivalent to the storage allocated and used on another system.

## *"Do I Really Have to Use C?"*

Here are the three biggest concerns about using programming languages with DCE:

- You must define IDL types that map to your language's data types, as demonstrated previously by adding a byte to an IDL string type, which will hold the C-required null character.

- At the time of this writing, most implementations of the IDL compiler will generate a **.h** file and stub code only in C.

- At the time of this writing, most implementations of Threads have only **.h** header files for their data types, function declarations, and most important, declarations for the C runtime library jacket routines.

Therefore, at the time of this writing, we strongly recommend that you write your application in C. However, if it's an absolute necessity to use another language—for previously or newly written code—then please realize that you are in DCE-unsupported territory. Here's the extra work that you'd have to do:

- Translate your application's **.h** files to ones that are supported in your language.

- Be knowledgeable enough about C calling conventions to use the remote procedures' stub code.

- Use large-scale mutexes or a single-threaded server.

Above all else, maintain your sense of humor, and hang in there until you can rewrite your application in C or until DCE supports more languages. (It's highly likely that DCE will support more languages, but there is no commitment on a time frame or on the additional languages targeted for support.)

We've encountered more varying and heated expert opinions on programming languages than on any other topic involving client/server programming. Reflecting on the feedback, it became apparent that opinions depended on the culture (company culture, operating-system culture, and programming-language culture) of the person with the opinion. For instance, responses from DCE experts on the task of rewriting the application's **.h** file ranged from "What's the big deal?" to "You just can't use DCE safely from a language other than C! The application-to-stub communication and reentrancy issues will kill you!"

So what you eventually do depends on how much of a hacker and gambler you are and how much your management wants to support the gamble. It's our job to make sure that you understand why not using C increases the risk and affects the efficiency of application code. You can make the rest of the decisions. However, if you choose to venture into this unsupported swamp, take this information along for some protection:

- Support for reentrancy in your language

  Here's a simple rule of thumb: if you can write a recursively called routine—one that calls itself—then your compiler supports reentrant code. For instance, most Ada and Pascal compilers support reentrant code. Most FORTRAN 77 and COBOL compilers do not. (FORTRAN 90 supports limited reentrancy.) Check the appropriate language documentation.

- Difficulty of translating types to or from the **.h** file

  The type translation difficulty may increase dramatically when using a language other than C. Some languages may not enable the creation of a type that duplicates the type in the **.h** file. For example, it may be difficult to reproduce the **handle_t** or **pipe** data types in other languages or to find an IDL type that maps well to the Pascal pointer data type.

  You can choose to change the interface file to map to your language more easily or to hardcode the data in a very generic type. For instance, you can have remote calls pass *n* number of bits back and forth, with the application figuring out how to translate it to meaningful data.

- Stubs are always C-generated

  At the time of this writing, there is no way to produce stub files using a language other than C. This simply means that you must use the C calling conventions when making a remote call from your application, regardless of the language used to implement that remote call. (The flow goes from application code, to C client-stub code, to C server-stub code, to server routine, and back.)

For example, since FORTRAN expects all arguments to be passed by reference, there is no equivalent in that language for the IDL code [in] long a (where a is an integer). If the type of FORTRAN being used has a language extension that supports passing by values, then all is well. If not, you must write a C jacket routine that accepts the argument and passes the parameter's address to the other routine. However, you can code the **.idl** file to map to FORTRAN better by using the [in] long *a IDL expression.

Also, be aware of differences in data representation. For example, the array element A(1,2) in FORTRAN is not the same element as A[1][2] in C, because of language differences in row-column ordering.

- Server initialization language choice

  You can write the server-initialization file in languages other than C, so long as you use the proper C calling conventions for the RPC routines. However, since new code is required for DCE client/server applications, we recommend that you give yourself a break and write it in C.

- Hidden dependencies regarding reentrancy

  As mentioned earlier (Section 9.1.9), it's not easy to eyeball code to determine whether it's thread-safe, and this job becomes more difficult if you use a language other than C. For example, we know of at least one FORTRAN runtime library that, unbeknownst to its users and in the bowels of the code, calls nonreentrant C routines. Routines compiled using this implementation of FORTRAN can muck up calls to the C runtime library in other concurrent threads, even if the other threads are using proper mutexes. The programmer can place a global lock on the whole routine—if she or he realizes what's going wrong. It's a debugging nightmare. (If you use C, the **pthreads.h** jackets prevent this type of hidden glitch.)

  As another example, beware of a language's use of exception handling. We know of a case in which a compiler's use of a firmware-provided exception dispatcher interferes with the Threads signaling system.

- Using C++

  In general, if you refrain from using C++ specific data types and objects when using DCE APIs, then you can write client/server applications using this language. For instance, you can create threads for routines whose arguments are classes, and you can create threads to execute a member function, as long as it's static. This means that a programmer would write jacketing code that takes the data from an object of a certain class on one end, passes it to RPC using C-supported data types, and places the data back into objects of an equivalent class on the other end. You can distribute the data from classes and objects, but you can't distribute them intact; RPC doesn't recognize them.

You can include the IDL-generated **.h** file in your C++ source code. The **.h** file specifies to the C++ compiler that generated code should use C calling conventions and linkage.

- Using Ada

  A programmer can use either the Ada tasking package or DCE Threads, but not both, because they use conflicting protocols. Beware of built-in, hidden uses of the Ada tasking package.

## *Debugging Client/Server Applications Presents New Challenges*

We recommend that you debug all servers on their local hosts, then distribute and debug the entire application. Once you have the server routines up and running, you can create local dummy clients to provide the server's library of routines with stress testing. If you follow our advice to stabilize your server code first, the step to distributed debugging involving client code is relatively easy.

If you have the appropriate tools support, the easiest way to debug a client/server application is to use one window to debug the client and one window to debug the server routines, moving through both bodies of code one line at a time. If you don't have windows, then use terminal software that allows you to work on multiple processes or use two different terminals. Another common technique is to set a break point at the beginning of each server routine, causing the caller in the client to block until you've stepped through the code on the server.

If there's reason to believe that debugging the application locally will save time, then you can use conditionalized code to create both a distributed and a local application. You can use a preprocessor line such as `#ifdef LOCAL` in C code, and `-DLOCAL` in the makefile or on the command line to compile a local version. Linking the local version of your application is identical to linking a nondistributed application.

When you've finished local debugging, be sure to delete all old object code and to recompile the application before distributing pieces of code. This will prevent linking with mismatched pieces of the application.

Let's look at some common distribution bugs and how you can prevent them:

- Mismatched parameter declarations and definitions declarations

  There is no way to do argument validation across the network. If your C compiler has prototype checking, then this error may be caught at compilation time. If your compiler doesn't have this feature (or if it's turned off), the error may show up as an access violation in the stub code, usually on the client side, but sometimes on the server side.

This error can show up in the early development process, when the server routines may change the number, the order, or the types of parameters. To prevent this error, client implementers should check the **.idl** file periodically for changes to the parameter list.

- Missing binding-handle parameter

  Sometimes you may change the binding method for a particular routine. If you change the method from automatic or implicit to explicit, then you must add a parameter to the remote routine's parameter list (either in the source code or in an Access Control File). The error shows up as an access violation on the client side.

- Mismatched type definitions

  In nondistributed programming, if a function prototype contains a parameter declared to be of the **char** data type, then you'd probably declare the parameter to be **char** in the function code, too. In distributed programming, this may not work. Various compilers may map **char** to various types, while the IDL compiler always maps it to **unsigned char**. If the client and server hosts map **char** to different underlying types, then the code generates an error.

  The solution to this problem is to use IDL data types in the IDL file and for the parameters of the server routines. You can also check the **idlbase.h** file to gain a better understanding of the portable data types created by the IDL compiler.

- Exhausted heap memory in the server

  Signs of this error are obvious: the process runs out of memory on the server side. The source of this problem is memory leakage caused by improper use of **malloc** and **free** on the server side. It's good RPC programming practice to use the RPC memory allocation and deallocation routines, which enable the RPC runtime library to free memory automatically, once the remote call completes.

  To test for this bug, you can run the server for long periods of time, having multiple, local clients flood the server with calls, and manually watch the amount of memory used by the server's process. Also, you may want to perform this type of stress testing incrementally. Test a few routines, and then a few more, and then a few more. If your server contains 100 routines and you have a memory leakage, it can be difficult to narrow it down to the problematic routine. (This problem is another good reason for breaking your server routines into smaller, logical groupings, each with its own interface file.)

- Problematic error handling in the server

  If you don't handle an exception properly on the server, RPC will raise a generic "fault on server" exception in the client. Since it's more difficult for the client to track the source of the error, especially if it called several remote procedures at a given time, it's imperative to handle exceptions well on the server side and to stress test the server before testing with clients. You may want to consider establishing some way for the server to communicate information about errors to the client, perhaps with an additional parameter to the remote routine.

Here are various issues involved with tools support . . . or the lack of it:

- Logic bugs for multiple invocations of one remote procedure

  The problem is reentrancy and its complexity (Section 9.1.9). The best way to avoid these bugs is with a good design and stress testing. To date, there are no debugging tools that test for the presence or efficiency of reentrance techniques.

- Debugger support for multiple threads

  In a perfect world, your debugger would provide a different window for each thread; would access the state of the Threads Scheduler---"tell me which threads were running when I hit this break point and which thread issued the break"; would allow you to set condition variables, causing a thread to begin executing again; and would allow you to create or stop threads.

  As you know, this isn't a perfect world, and DCE Threads is relatively new. Look for these future features in a debugger near you!

- Consider building tools to help with debugging

  One group of engineers created macros for memory allocation and deallocation. The macros write to an external file, keeping tabs on the number of times memory is allocated and deallocated for a particular piece of data. If the application blows up due to memory leakage, the table should show a bloated allocation count for one or more pieces of data.

  For those who like to see code, we'll give you a portion of the code needed for this tool, and you write the rest. The following code is a wrapper for **malloc**. In addition to calling **malloc**, it locks a global data structure and adds information to it: who allocated the memory and how much was allocated.

```
/*  Define an object (table entry) for each type to be tracked.  */
#define memory_available        0
#define data_type_1_entry       1       /* Description... */
#define data_type_2_entry       2       /* Description... */
```

.
.
.

```
/*  Define a table to hold memory-allocation information.    */
typedef struct
{
    unsigned32 inuse;          /* number currently allocated */
    unsigned32 calls;          /* total ever allocated */
    unsigned32 fails;          /* denied alloc requests */
    unsigned32 maxsize;        /* max size allocated for this type */
}   mem_stats_elt_t, *mem_stats_elt_p_t;
EXTERNAL mem_stats_elt_t g_mem_stats[];
/*  Values for the 'flags' argument to MEM_ALLOC               */
#define mem_waitok    0
#define mem_nowait    1
/*                                                             */
/*  M E M _ A L L O C _ I L    macro                           */
/*                                                             */
/* (addr) == NULL iff "no memory available"                    */
/*                                                             */
/* Sample use:                                                 */
/*      dg_ccall_p_t ccall;                                    */
/*      MEM_ALLOC_IL(ccall, data_type_1_entry_p_t,             */
/*              sizeof *data_type_1_entry_p_t,                 */
/*            data_type_1_entry, mem_nowait);                  */
/*      if (ccall == NULL)                                     */
/*          alloc failed                                       */
#define MEM_ALLOC_IL(addr, cast, size, type, flags) \
{ \
    LOG_MEM_ALLOC_NTR; \
    (addr) = (cast) malloc(size); \
    MEM_LOCK (0);                         /*  lock a mutex     */
    g_mem_stats[type].calls++; \
    if ((addr) == NULL) { \
        g_mem_stats[type].fails++; \
        DIE("(MEM_ALLOC) Memory allocation failed \n"); \
    } else \
        g_mem_stats[type].inuse++; \
    if ((size) > g_mem_stats[type].maxsize) \
        g_mem_stats[type].maxsize = (size); \
    MEM_UNLOCK (0); \                     /*  unlock mutex     */
    LOG_MEM_ALLOC_XIT; \
}
```

# 9.4  What Next?

We certainly hope that this chapter helped you to get a feel for DCE client-server programming. For those of you who prefer to learn from code, take a look at the programs in Appendix A. One of those programs presents a reentrant version of the Hello World server routine.

The chapters that follow address some of the same design issues (Section 9.1) from another angle. What impact does the cell's configuration, the LAN/WAN configuration, the placement of clients and servers, the need for security, the implications of user models for various applications, and the available hardware have on system and network managers? This information is useful to application programmers, too. Once your server and client are ready to go out into the world, you'll need to work with the system and network administrators on lots of issues, including the location of your servers and general security.

PART II

*Configuration and Management Considerations*

# 10

# *Getting Started with DCE*

Prospective DCE administrators sometimes feel a bit bewildered as they first contemplate the task of installing and configuring DCE on their networks. After all, DCE is new and, for most organizations, the idea of distributed computing itself is new. In many ways, DCE constitutes a sort of *terra incognita* for most network service providers, application developers, and users.

While the life of a typical DCE administrator may not always be a bed of roses, neither will it be a bed of nails. Despite its novelty and complexity, DCE is a lot more approachable than it might first appear. In this chapter, we'll briefly discuss several concepts of DCE implementation that may help to mitigate some of your concerns.

## 10.1 Low Impact on Physical Network Components

DCE doesn't require any modifications to the physical components of your current network environment. You don't need to rip out any of your Ethernet cable, reroute your droplines, relocate your router boxes, or otherwise physically redesign or retrofit any part of your existing network. This is because DCE doesn't really replace anything. Instead, DCE simply layers itself on top of your network as it currently exists. You might need to redeploy or purchase a few systems, but otherwise most elements of your network's topology can remain as they are.

# 10.2 Low Impact on Non-DCE Users

Eventually, you may want all systems and users on your network to participate in DCE, but there's no need to migrate everything and everybody simultaneously. DCE systems can coexist quite comfortably on the same network with non-DCE systems. When you configure a system as a DCE client (running client software for the DCE core services, the CDS, the Distributed Time Service (DTS), and the Security Service), that system becomes a participant in the cell. Users on systems that are not running DCE client software may not even be aware that a cell exists on the network and can go about their business as usual, communicating through the network services to which they are accustomed. DCE doesn't change how non-DCE users make use of the network.

# 10.3 You Can Choose Your Own Pace

The collective opinion of most DCE developers overwhelmingly suggests that, no matter what your ultimate goal is for your cell, you should *start small.* One of the alternative configurations we'll examine is to locate server software for the three core DCE services on a single system. Then, you can spend some time test driving the cell until you're accustomed to setting up and managing the core services.

After you become familiar with the basic administrative tasks, you can begin to configure additional DCE client-only systems until all systems that you want to participate in the cell are running DCE client software. You could, for instance, first configure DCE client software on all the systems that support your engineering groups, then configure the systems used by your administration or sales groups into the cell. Alternatively, you could configure your cell in stages based on the physical location of the systems involved, configuring client software on all the systems at your corporate headquarters first, followed by systems at your satellite business locations.

You should think about the development of your cell as a process, not as an event. Implementing DCE doesn't mean that you have to send everybody home, or to *Intro to DCE 101*, and shut down your network for three weeks until the cell's final configuration is "complete." DCE implementations can grow and change over time as the needs of their participants dictate.

# 10.4   DCE Implementations Permit Planning in Stages

Formal planning for configuring and managing DCE can also be handled in stages. We're not suggesting here that you don't need to do some advance planning. On the contrary, any planning you can do will work to your advantage. The point is that you don't really need to set your final implementation plan in stone before you create your first cell and get started with DCE. It's going to be difficult to know from the start how your cell will develop over time. Having a grand scheme is great, but don't be surprised if things turn out a little differently than you had originally anticipated.

Once you've got your cell up and running, most of the performance and management problems you encounter shouldn't take you by surprise. For example, suppose you decide, as an initial implementation, to configure a sort of monster server system running the master servers for each of the DCE services you've chosen to configure. Such a configuration will work fine for a while, but as your cell grows, one or more of these servers may eventually become a performance bottleneck because of competition for local computing power and disk space. When this happens, it's a fairly simple matter to relocate the server that is causing the problem to another system or to replicate a portion of the information on the overloaded server to another system, effectively off-loading some of the traffic from the master server.

In most cases, performance degradation of your DCE services won't just happen overnight. If you pay attention and routinely monitor performance, you'll see potential problems far enough in advance to put a remedy in place before things get out of hand. Potential administrative bottlenecks in DCE can often be foreseen and averted in the same way.

# 10.5   DCE Is Dynamic

DCE Version 1.0 is impressive, but follow-on versions will undoubtedly be even more convenient to use and to manage. As a product, you can expect DCE to be quite dynamic.

Various software tools and utilities are likely to emerge that will make it easier for you to perform some of the more laborious DCE management tasks, including relocating servers on other machines, moving blocks of users out of one cell and into another, and modifying or deleting access control entries on a cellwide basis. Some DCE vendors are considering the development of a graphical management interface that supports distributed management of all DCE services. (Witness the Open Software Foundation's

(OSF) specification for their Distributed Management Environment (DME) software.)

When these proposed enhancements become available, they will probably be fully compatible with DCE Version 1.0 and will simply be layered on top of the existing DCE software. As a prospective DCE administrator, you shouldn't be overly concerned that you're getting yourself and your organization into something that will never change or that will become obsolete any time soon. DCE is modular in its design and will be able to support the future needs of cell users.

# 10.6 Where We'll Go from Here

In the remaining chapters, we'll take a look at factors that influence the size and boundaries of a DCE cell. We'll discuss some of the routine administrative tasks for each of the DCE services to give you a better idea of what you're up against in terms of day-to-day management and longer range administrative planning. We'll also explore some important factors you'll need to consider while getting your cell off the ground, including choosing a cell name, deciding on an initial cell configuration, setting up cell security, and distributing and replicating DCE services.

# 11

# *Determining Your Cell's Boundaries*

Before you create a cell, you should try to establish as accurate a picture as you can of your cell's physical and conceptual boundaries. You need to determine where you want your cell to end and the greater networking world (including other cells) to begin. In this chapter, we'll explore some of the more important factors you should consider to ensure that the cell you establish not only fulfills its intended functional purpose, but also maintains the level of security you require and can be managed within the limitations of your administrative resources. You want to create a cell that you can live with.

## *11.1  Factors that Influence the Boundaries of a Cell*

A cell typically consists of a group of systems that are located in a common geographic area, for example, on the same LAN. Geography, however, need not limit your cell's boundaries. A cell can be self-contained on a single system or be distributed across as many as several thousand systems. While a small organization may have only one cell, a large, multinational corporation can have many cells.

When planning your cell's implementation, there are several factors you should keep in mind that are common to all cells and that can help you determine your cell's configuration and boundaries. Begin by asking yourself the following questions:

- For whom are you creating the cell and why?

- What are your security requirements?

- What are your projected administrative requirements?

- How will DCE affect computing and network overhead?

## 11.2    For Whom the Cell Tolls—And Why?

Because the concept of a cell centers on shared DCE services, shared resources, and a common purpose, one useful step in determining the boundaries of your cell is to identify a body of users who need access to the same set of resources and are working toward the same goal. For example, software engineers working together to develop a new product may all want to belong to the same cell. Depending on your preferences, the documentation, marketing, manufacturing, and support groups associated with the new product might also participate in the same cell. Alternatively, if your company is function-oriented rather than product-oriented, the development, marketing, manufacturing, and support groups might each maintain their own cells in communication with but exclusive of the others. Yet another approach is to create a single cell that supports your entire organization and in which all your functional groups participate.

Although the criteria for establishing the scope of a cell lie mostly in the cell's purpose or function, the geographic dispersement of cell participants can be an important factor. For example, if a new software product is being developed partially in New York and partially in California, both the New York and California engineering groups should probably participate in the same cell. Keep in mind, however, that across such long distances, additional considerations such as the reliability of connections, slower response times, and security across a WAN become important.

## 11.3    What Are Your Security Requirements?

The security requirements of cell users directly influence the boundaries of a cell. Does the nature of your business demand an ultrasecure computing environment? Or, can you permit your user population less restricted access to the information and resources your cell provides? You need to determine just how secure an environment you require and how far trust boundaries should extend to the general user population both within and beyond the limits of your LAN or extended network. A cell should encompass a group of users and applications that frequently share a common set of resources and are, therefore, more inclined to establish relationships of trust with each other than with users and applications from other cells.

In a secure cell, all users and applications (including DCE server and client systems and processes) share a common security mechanism. DCE Security offers a fully authenticated environment in which users, systems, and processes must verify their identities to each other before they are able to exchange information. Even before a server initiates a response to a user's request, both the user and server must prove, one to another, that their identities are authentic. They must prove that *they really are who they say they are*. This proof is rendered in the form of a special kind of password. When a user enters a password at DCE login, an authentication server verifies the password against the data stored for that user in the cell's Registry database.

## 11.3.1 Authentication Across Cells

Authentication across cells is really no less secure than authentication within an individual cell, but it does increase computing overhead. Response times, therefore, are likely to be a bit slower, especially on initial connections.

Setting up mutual authentication, especially with many foreign cells, also creates some additional administrative overhead. Cross-cell authentication consists of a mutual agreement of trust between the security administrators of the two cells. The administrators of each cell authenticate their local users using the required degree of security. To make intercell communication work, the security administrators in each cell must create an account in their own Registry database for the security server from the foreign cell. These accounts share a unique secret key (Section 5.1.4).

As Security administrator, you'll have to set up such an arrangement with each of the foreign cells with which you want to employ cross-cell authentication. If you've got a group of several cells, the number of separate accounts and secret keys that must be exchanged among them grows exponentially. For example, if five cells all want to enjoy cross-cell authentication with each other, then each cell must make arrangements with each of the other four cells. Collectively, that's 20 separate accounts and secret keys.

Administration of cross-cell security, however, is not as bad as it sounds. Once you've set up the accounts, your management work is essentially complete. The security credentials for the security servers involved will expire periodically, but unless you're dealing with hundreds of foreign cells, renewing this information should not be much of a task.

## 11.3.2 Repairing a Breach of Your Cell's Security

Another security factor to consider is the amount of work that would be required to restore security if the integrity of your cell's Registry database were to be compromised. For example, suppose an intruder gains access to your security server and copies the file that contains the secret keys for your cell's user accounts. With this information (and enough time and computing power to decipher the keys), the intruder could potentially impersonate any user, server, or process defined in your Registry database. To repair this damage, you'd have to renew the secret keys and passwords for every principal registered in the cell. You'd also have to renew the secret keys your cell shares with other foreign cells. The larger the cell, and the more foreign cells with which you enjoy cross-cell authentication, the more work and, perhaps more important in this scenario, the more time you'll need to make the cell secure again.

# 11.4  What Are Your Projected Administrative Requirements?

Sometime before you're actually faced with the responsibilities of cell administration, you should make a list of the various tasks required to manage your DCE services and take stock of the human resources available to perform those tasks.

If your cell supports only a small, stable number of users and is restricted to the core cell components, it may be possible for one individual to handle the cell's day-to-day management. After a cell is up and running, the amount of work involved to maintain DCE services will vary according to the rate at which your cell grows and changes. Let's look at some of the more routine DCE administrative tasks.

- **Accommodating New Users**. Whenever new users join the cell, you'll have to define them as principals in the Registry database. You may also need to add their names to one or more authorization groups or create ACL entries on their behalf to grant the permissions needed to access the resources used in their daily work. If the size of your cell's user population is relatively stable or grows at a slow rate, these tasks shouldn't require much of your time. If you're doing a lot of hiring or otherwise acquiring large groups of new users or distributed applications, you'll need to do more work.

- **Removing Users from the Cell**. When a user leaves your cell, you should remove the user's principal name from the Registry database and from any authorization groups of which the user was a member. You should probably also delete any ACL entries that refer specifically to that user. This can be a lot of work, but such entries constitute useless (and, potentially dangerous) clutter once the user for whom they were created no longer participates in the cell. Again, if your head count is relatively stable, you won't need to spend much time expunging users from the cell. If your organization has a high employee turnover, you'll have to perform these tasks more frequently.

- **Managing Access Control**. The ACL entries that you create and the permissions that you grant to principals collectively determine who can use DCE resources and what management operations they are allowed to perform. As projects and their associated work teams come and go, you may find yourself creating and populating, then deleting many authorization groups. If users switch projects frequently, you'll need to remove their names from one group and add them to another. Many users will undoubtedly need to be included in, and later removed from, multiple authorization groups. Occasionally, users and applications may find they have insufficient access to perform their requested operations. You'll have to track down and troubleshoot such problems in order to grant or restore access.

In a low- or medium-security cell with a small user population, access control management should be minimal. However, in a cell with a large user base and a restrictive access control policy, centralized access management can constitute a full-time job.

- **Managing the Cell Directory Service**. Some users or user groups will want you to create new CDS directories for them. They may also ask you to replicate certain directories on servers that are closer to their own work areas, or may want you to delete directories that they no longer need. You may prefer to delegate some of this work by granting users and application developers the permissions they need to create and manage their own CDS directories. This gives users complete control of their own portions of the CDS hierarchy, without risking the integrity of CDS directories closer to the cell root.

- **Managing the Distributed File Service**. If you're using DFS, you can count on the additional work involved in defining administrative domains and administrative lists, maintaining and replicating filesets, overseeing the automatic backup and binary distribution facilities, and a certain amount of access control maintainance as well. See Chapter 8 and Section 12.2.4 for more information on DFS management tasks.

- **Accommodating Distributed RPC Applications**. Your cell is likely to include one or more RPC-based distributed applications. You'll need to establish host identities in the Registry for application servers so that they can communicate with other services in the cell. You'll probably also need to create CDS directories in which applications can store the names they'll use. Again, you might consider delegating this work to the application administrators themselves. But if you do, you'll have to extend to them rather more access to DCE services (especially the Registry) than might be appropriate from a security point of view. Some cell administrators will not be willing to grant applications access to their Registry databases.

Granting permissions to CDS on behalf of application administrators to create CDS directories for their own use is not quite so risky an idea, but could still pose a security problem in some very secure cells. Anyway, unless you intend to leave the management of future applications entirely to the people who develop or purchase them, some DCE administrator will have to perform this work.

These tasks, in themselves, may not seem like a great administrative burden. And, for a small cell in which the size of the user base remains fairly stable, this is generally true. However, when you begin to increase the number of cell users and applications, the volume and frequency with which such tasks will need to be performed can eventually require considerable administrative resources. Note also that other common network and system maintainance tasks have been omitted from our discussion. If you've been designated as the only DCE administrator for a new cell and your job description already includes the performance of other tasks, you may eventually need to delegate some of your non-DCE work to other employees.

In any case, as a cell grows, the daily work load of the typical DCE administrator is likely to grow incrementally at a slow and predictable pace. This leaves you plenty of time to recruit, train, and organize additional DCE administrative staff members if necessary. As your cell grows, you'll probably want to delegate administrative tasks among several individuals. You can start by assigning one manager for each of the DCE services you've configured. As the cell continues to expand, you may eventually find it necessary to assign a separate team of administrators to manage and troubleshoot each of your DCE services.

The important thing to remember is that it's not necessary for all DCE services in a cell to be managed by the same person or group. You can delegate administrative tasks in whatever way is most practical and reasonable, based on the size, complexity, and geographic dispersement of the cell.

# 11.5 How Will DCE Affect Computing and Network Overhead?

The fixed overhead on your network imposed by the internal operations of DCE software components turns out to be almost negligible. Some DCE servers and clerks do transmit messages between and among themselves at fairly frequent intervals. For instance, CDS servers broadcast so-called *advertisement* messages onto the LAN every 10 minutes to inform CDS clerks that they're still out there and where on the network they can be found. When CDS clerks need this information, they can send out their own *solicit* messages rather than waiting for the next advertisement message to come down the wire. DTS servers and clerks also send out messages to keep system clocks synchronized. DTS servers dispatch a few messages to each other every five minutes. DTS clerks (there's one on every machine in the cell) send out a message to the DTS servers every 10 minutes.

This may seem like a lot of traffic, but both the CDS and DTS messages contain only a small amount of information. Even with numerous CDS and DTS clerks and servers out there, the combined messages they exchange are unlikely to account for much additional network use.

RPC, because it provides the communications management underlying all transactions between DCE servers and clients, will have a significant presence on the network, but is unlikely to impose any greater impact on network traffic than does your current networking software. Even if your cell supports distributed applications that perform checksumming on all their transactions or that transmit constant or lengthy data streams, network traffic should increase only slightly above the levels to which you are accustomed in your current network environment.

If your cell communicates with a lot of foreign cells, you can count on another slight increase in network use. This is because operations such as name resolution and authentication incur more software interaction and network traffic between cells than they do within the same cell.

In conclusion, your DCE implementation should have little influence on the total amount of traffic on your network. There will, of course, be bursts of heavier activity. If everyone in your network participates in a cell, DCE login time in the morning may be an exceptionally busy time. The computing burden that users place on certain DCE server systems and on gateway systems between LANs may also be significant periodically.

# 12

# *Initial Cell Configuration Guidelines*

In this chapter, we'll explore some of the choices you'll need to make while getting your cell off the ground. It should come as no surprise to you at this point that there is no single, definitive, *correct* way to implement DCE. How you configure your cell depends on many interrelated factors, including the ultimate scope of the cell, your computing, data storage, and administrative resources, and the level of security that you require.

The advice in this chapter and in the chapters that follow is based largely on information gathered from people who know a lot about DCE and, in many cases, participated in its creation. Some of the advice may not immediately apply to your particular situation, and sometimes you'll be faced with mutually exclusive options that require you to evaluate the trade-offs for your own cell. Our intention here is not to provide a cookbook, but rather to give you an overview of some of the decisions you'll face during your cell's initial configuration. First, we'll warn you about some of the factors you should consider when naming your cell; then we'll look at configuring the DCE services.

## *12.1 Choosing a Name for Your Cell*

Even before you initialize your cell, the first decision to make is whether or not you want the cell to be able to participate in one of the global naming environments supported by DCE. A cell can communicate with other cells that exist outside its boundaries with the assistance of one of two global name services: the Global Directory Service (otherwise known as GDS or X.500) or the Internet Domain Name System (also known as DNS or BIND).

## 12.1.1 GDS or DNS?—You've Got to Pick One

The way DCE Version 1.0 is implemented, all global cell names must be unique. Because GDS and DNS enforce naming conventions and syntax requirements that are mutually exclusive, you cannot register the same cell in both global name services. You've got to pick *one* service or the other and then name your cell based on that decision.

The main reason for this restriction is that DCE, especially the Security component, is not designed to support the use of multiple cell names or aliases for cell names. For example, when a DCE server or client system starts up, it reads a local configuration file containing the name of the cell to which the system belongs. The software currently expects to find only one cell name in this file and is not designed to handle a list of cell names. Similarly, routines in the DCE Security API that parse full principal names into cell and user simple names expect only one cell name to be returned. Future releases of DCE may allow you to name your cell in both GDS and DNS. But, for the time being, you'll have to choose one or the other.

## 12.1.2 Cell Names are Difficult to Change

Be aware that choosing a cell name is one of the few decisions you'll make while setting up your cell that is truly difficult to reverse. Your cell's name is embedded in every name in the cell and is stored and referenced in many locations locally and in foreign cells as well. For example, your cell's name appears in the principal specifications of every ACL entry in your cell.

It's not impossible for you to change your cell's name, but for a large, mature cell it might as well be. For starters, you'd have to discard and re-create much of your CDS naming information. Changing your cell name would also render useless all references to your old cell name in local ACLs as well as those in foreign cells with which your cell's principals have communicated. If you're going to change your cell name, do it while the cell is still young and before you've communicated with any foreign cells.

## 12.1.3 The Cell Name You Choose Must Be Unique Within Your Organization

The global cell name you choose will typically include your company's global name and must be unique within your own organization. (Registering a global cell name presupposes that your company itself has already registered its name with the appropriate global naming service.) The authorities that administer the X.500 and DNS global name services make sure that duplication of *company* names never happens within their respective jurisdictions. This, however, is where their responsibility for preventing or detecting lower level duplicate names ends.

It's your job, or rather the job of some authority within your organization, to make sure that no other cell within your company or organization is permitted to identify itself with the same name. If this were to happen, the identical cell names would be ambiguous to all other cells and spurious lookup results would occur.

Probably the easiest way to make sure your proposed cell name is unique is to try looking up the name in X.500 or DNS. If you find it, you'll have to choose another name.

## 12.1.4 Get In-House Approval for Your Cell Name Before You Register

Few official guidelines presently exist on how to go about selecting a cell name. And, because nobody ever needed a cell name until DCE came along, there's unlikely to be any group within your company officially charged with the task of dreaming up cell names. Exactly who you should contact about your cell name will vary from one organization to another. If your company's name or any of its site names are already registered with X.500 or DNS, you should talk to the people in your organization who assigned those names. If your company doesn't yet use a global reference, you'll have to look elsewhere for advice.

Many larger companies and institutions have some sort of official standards group in place that is responsible for assigning unique names for various things around their networks. For example, a network's administrators are frequently responsible for assigning unique names for nodes and other common resources such as printers, file servers, or storage devices. The administrators may not actually choose the names themselves, but they can tell you whether anyone else is already using a particular name and whether the name you have in mind complies with their naming conventions. Another group may be responsible for assigning unique names for such things as facilities, site codes, mail stops, and internal telephone exchanges. Such a group may be inclined to start assigning unique names for cells.

In a company of any size, there is sure to be some authority that will take an interest in how you name your cell. Whoever this authority turns out to be in your organization, be sure at the very least to make your intentions known to them. If necessary, get their permission, their blessing, or some other kind of official approval for your cell name *before* you register the name with GDS or DNS. Remember that once in use, a cell name is inconvenient to change.

## 12.1.5  Caveats for Naming Isolated Cells

If you intend to create a private cell and are *certain* that you won't later want or need to communicate with other cells or services that exist outside the boundaries of your cell, then you can choose any cell name that suits your fancy, and you won't need to worry about officially registering a cell name with either global name service. Similarly, if you are creating a cell with which you intend only to experiment and which you will soon abandon, you need not be too concerned about how you name the cell. Some DCE developers have suggested that creating a few expendable cells is a good way to gain practical DCE experience and to get an idea of how you'll want to configure and administer a permanent cell later on. Potential DCE administrators who feel more confident in their knowledge base may prefer to go directly to the real thing rather than devoting time and resources to such a get-acquainted exercise.

If you decide to create an isolated cell, be sure you abandon the cell before you or your organization grow too attached to it. It's especially difficult to transfer CDS structure and content from one cell into another. When your preliminary learning experience is over, abandon the temporary cell and choose a cell name and a global name service with which to register a permanent cell.

# 12.2  Configuring DCE Server and Client Systems

Once you've chosen a cell name, you can get to work configuring the cell itself. To begin, you'll need to decide where you want to locate and configure DCE server and client software.

## 12.2.1  Reasons to Configure DCE Core Services on One System

For your initial cell configuration, many DCE developers suggest that you select one system in your network and configure it as the primary server for the three core DCE services: the Cell Directory Service (CDS), the Security service, and the Distributed Time Service (DTS). That's a lot of servers on one system, but there are some practical advantages to locating them on one machine, at least to get started.

- **Ease of Installation and Configuration**. Installation and configuration are more convenient. There are fewer questions to answer during the configuration process, and you'll need to go through the process only once on one machine.

- **Ease of Administration**. With only one system to manage, day-to-day administration is much simpler. Although nearly all DCE services can be managed remotely, the physical systems on which they reside (at least until some distributed management application becomes available) must be managed locally.

- **Increased Performance and Reliability**. Locating all your core servers on one machine enables them to communicate with each other without going over the network. Assuming that the machine is configured with adequate CPU and memory, response times will be as fast as they can get. In addition, you won't have to worry about connectivity failures across the network between and among the services you configure.

- **Economy**. Although there is no way to predict how all vendors will package DCE, it's likely that no matter whose flavor of DCE you purchase, you'll only have to pay for one set of server licenses if you configure the core services on one machine. This also means that you need to come up with only one machine to get started with DCE.

- **Convenience in an Application Development Environment**. If you're creating a small cell, specifically to provide an environment in which an engineering group can develop and test distributed RPC-based applications, then configuring one master server system is definitely the way to go. Because such a cell is intended for use only by the application development team, you won't need to worry about supporting large numbers of users. And, since most development team members are likely to work at the same site, there's no immediate requirement to distribute the services of the cell to other user groups.

The machine you select as your cell's master server should be the most robust and reliable system in your environment. Availability and connectivity are also important factors to consider. You want a system that stays up and to which network traffic can be directed with high confidence of making fast and stable connections. If possible, you should locate your master server somewhere near the topological center of your network.

## 12.2.2 Reasons to Disperse DCE Core Services from the Start

In spite of these significant advantages, there are reasons why some DCE administrators may prefer not to initially configure their core services on one system.

- **Avoiding a Single Point of Failure**. If you locate all your servers on one machine, you run the risk of encountering a classic example of the fabled single point of failure. If your master server system crashes, needs maintenance, or goes down due to a power spike or failure, your cell is temporarily unusable until the system comes back up. If the disk gets clobbered by an irate employee with a fire axe, your cell may be out of business for quite some time to come. For a temporary, experimental cell or a small private cell, such misfortunes may not matter too much. For a production cell designed to support your entire organization and intended to have a permanent lifespan, these potential failures warrant a lot more concern. Without at least one CDS server and one Security server functioning, your cell effectively ceases to exist.

The obvious solution to these problems is to replicate and distribute the core services on several machines. CDS, Security, and DTS all permit you to replicate the information they store or distribute the services they provide across multiple servers. By configuring at least two CDS servers and two Security servers on separate machines, you increase the survivability of those particular services (and the cell itself) by 100 percent.

Although the presence of a DTS server is not absolutely vital to a cell's survival, the time synchronization DTS provides is essential for coordinating most distributed operations. You should eventually configure a minimum of three DTS servers on separate machines. Additional DTS servers are strongly recommended if your cell spans multiple LANs. See Sections 7.2 and 14.3 for more information.

So, if you're in a hurry and want to increase the survivability of your cell right from the start, you should consider distributing CDS and Security services across multiple machines. And, even if you do decide to start off by configuring all services on one machine, you should create at least one additional CDS and Security server as soon after you complete your initial configuration as possible. See Chapter 14 for more information on distributing and replicating DCE services.

- **Avoiding Predictable Performance Bottlenecks**. As you continue to add new users and applications to the cell, you will eventually begin to overburden your master server system. As the number of users accessing a particular service and the size of its databases grows, the performance and response time of that server (and of the other servers located on the system) will inevitably begin to degrade. We can't offer any predictions about what service will first manifest an unacceptable degradation or exactly when it will occur. The answer depends on the computing and storage capacity of the system, which services you locate there, how those services are being used, and how many people and applications are using them.

  Because DCE is so new, there are no reliable metrics yet available to help you determine how many DCE services you can expect to run on a particular make and model of system before you bring the system to its knees, but common sense can help you here. For instance, if you're creating a large cell that will immediately support a very large user population, your Registry database is going to require a lot of disk space. In such a case, you should probably locate your Security server on a system of its own.

- **Accommodating Special Security Requirements**. If your organization has strict security requirements, you should locate the cell's Security server on a machine of its own. In addition to being an essential component of the cell's operation, your Security server safeguards the integrity of your security database. It stores the data that defines accounts, principals, private keys, and passwords for every user, process, and application registered in the cell, and it regulates the intervals at which their passwords and tickets expire.

  It's no easy task to compromise DCE Security (unless, of course, you get access to an account that happens to have unlimited DCE permissions), but an easily accessible, unattended security server is especially vulnerable and makes a tempting target. Administrators of ultrasecure cells will probably want to locate their Security servers on machines that are kept under lock and key and made accessible to only a handful of authorized operators. If the organization for which you are creating a cell deals with sensitive information and has already surrounded its facility with a moat and stockade, you'd better verify where they want you to locate their security server *before* you configure it on a machine with other DCE services.

- **Suiting the Machine to the Service**. If you've got a lot of machines at your disposal and don't mind paying a few extra server license fees, you can afford to be more imaginative about where you initially locate your core services. Although most DCE services can reside happily on any machine equipped with reasonable computing power and storage capacity, certain DCE services perform better when they are located on systems configured to accommodate their special needs. The nature of the services and the demand you intend to place on them can influence your decision about initially locating them all on one machine. For instance, your Security server, whose Registry database may quickly become very large, will perform better on a machine configured from the start with a lot of storage capacity. DTS servers provide another example; they can reside on virtually any system, but are always more reliable when located on systems that do not experience a lot of interrupts and that are equipped with accurate clocks. See Chapter 14 for more information on the system preferences of CDS, Security, and DTS.

## 12.2.3 Configuring Client-only Systems

Once you've configured CDS, DTS, and Security servers somewhere, you've got a functional cell. To enable other systems to participate in the cell, you need to configure them as client-only systems. That is, you need to install and configure client software for the three core DCE services: CDS, Security, and DTS. If you've configured DFS in the cell, you'll also need to configure DFS client software on the systems that you want to make use of that service. The client software for GDS is included in the CDS server software, so there's nothing more you need to do to support GDS client operations.

Now that you're bringing more systems on line to DCE, you'll have performance considerations to think about on a system-by-system basis. While the operation of the DCE client software doesn't always create a lot of additional computing overhead, the limited memory and disk space on some smaller systems is a factor you should consider when selecting client machines.

The precise memory and disk space requirements for DCE client systems will vary, perhaps dramatically, from one vendor, machine architecture, and operating system to another. We're not prepared to quote the exact image sizes for each of the DCE client daemons here, but we can offer some information on the advantages of using shared libraries, and give you some ballpark figures on the default cache requirements for CDS and DFS clients.

On systems whose operating systems support their use, shared libraries can help reduce the amount of disk space needed by DCE clients. Some DCE libraries (**libdce**, for example, which contains the entry points for all RPC calls used by DCE) are very large. Using shared libraries helps keep the size of the client executables to a minimum. Without shared libraries, disk usage on a client system increases dramatically.

Both CDS and DFS clients cache pertinent information to help them operate more efficiently. For a CDS cache, allocation of disk space is linked to the available physical memory on the system. The CDS client calculates the total amount of available physical memory on the system, then allocates roughly one-half of one percent of this figure in disk space for the cache. If you've got 100MB (or less) of physical memory on your system, the CDS cache size defaults to the minimum of 512KB. If you've got more than 100MB of available memory, the cache will be fractionally larger.

A DFS client cache can potentially require a fair amount of disk space because it needs to accommodate the sections (or so-called "chunks") of working files that are copied to the client from a DFS server. A cache size smaller than 5MB can hamper Cache Manager performance. Also, don't let a disk cache take up more than 90% of a cache directory's partition, and don't let a memory cache take up more than 25% of memory.

When you configure a client-only system, the configuration process creates principals in the Registry database and entries in CDS to give the system (and the client processes running on it) identities that can be authenticated. All of this happens automatically; you don't have to do anything. As with server system configurations, the client-only configuration process sets things up only for the machine and its resident client processes; no security or other access control arrangements are set up for the users of the client-only system. See Chapter 13 for information on setting up user access in a new cell.

# 12.2.4   Configuring DFS

Unlike the core DCE services, which provide the basic technologies that make it possible for a cell to function, DFS is a *bona fide* distributed application that takes full advantage of DCE. In many ways, the core DCE services can be likened to a brand new 16-lane superhighway. Right now, DFS is one of the only cars on the road.

DFS' Local File System (LFS) offers you a lot more than traditional file systems that reside on single computers. It provides automated fileset updating, replication, and backup, and it can distribute binary information (such as configuration scripts) to specific groups of DFS machines. DFS also takes full advantage of DCE Security and even extends its capabilities through the use of administrative domains. (Some of our discussion is speculative. The DFS component is not available as of this writing.)

To achieve all of this, DFS employs several flavors of DFS servers and database machines (Chapter 8). Let's take a quick look at how many machines of each type you'll need in a full-blown DFS implementation.

### Server Functions on DFS Machines

Dividing your DFS server systems into administrative domains, especially in larger cells, can make DFS a lot easier to manage. For each DFS administrative domain you set up in your cell, you'll need to configure one system control machine and at least one file server. The system control machine should be the first DFS machine you configure in a new domain.

For your cell, you'll need at least one fileset location server and one backup database machine. You'll also need one binary distribution machine for each CPU/OS type of which multiple DFS servers exist. As a precaution against tampering, you may want to locate the machines you configure to store the master copies of the fileset location database and the backup database in a secure room. To conserve hardware resources, you can configure your binary distribution machines also as system control machines.

Don't panic! These recommendations reflect the ultimate goals for a fully developed DFS deployment. You don't need to immediately devote half a dozen (or more) machines to start using DFS. If you've got only one machine to devote to DFS, install and configure the software for all DFS server functions on that machine. You can relocate a particular function or group of functions to other machines later.

# 12.2.5   Configuring GDS

The criteria for selecting a GDS server machine are much the same as those on which you based the selection of your initial CDS server machine. You want to choose a reliable system, with good connectivity to your network and sufficient disk capacity to handle the GDS information you intend to store locally. We expect that most of you who decide to configure GDS will do so initially to store X.400 mail addresses, and perhaps also to store the names of foreign cells with which your cell will communicate. If you're planning to store a large number of mail addresses, be sure to locate your GDS server on a machine with a lot of disk space. The number of foreign cells out there for you to talk to, for the time being at least, is likely to be rather small and the amount of disk space you'll need to store them will be minimal.

Unlike other DCE services, you don't have to specifically configure GDS client software on any machines. Software known as the Global Directory Agent (GDA) provides the conduit between the CDS and GDS. The GDA process (**gdad**) runs on all CDS server systems. If you can get to a CDS server, you can get to GDS. Since you'll probably be starting with one GDS server to support your entire cell, you should locate the server somewhere near the topological center of your network.

Although you may be able to get along with one GDS server in your cell, you should consider configuring at least one additional GDS server to safeguard against a potential single point of failure. If you replicate all of your GDS information on two machines, a system failure on one of them won't interrupt GDS service.

# 13

# *Setting Up Security in a New Cell*

DCE's greatest advantage is that it allows users on one computer to use resources on another computer. Whether these resources are files, programs, or special hardware like printers, they're likely to be valuable resources that need protection. Unfettered access to your cell's resources can pose security risks for the resources being used, especially if the intentions of the remote user are hostile. And even trusted users can inadvertently alter or lose data through casual access. The DCE Security service provides the capabilities you need to clearly identify users and control their access to the resources they need.

Although DCE security is a complex subject on which we could easily fill an entire volume, we'll devote just this chapter to putting DCE security into a manageable perspective. We'll explain the security arrangements created by DCE as a result of cell initialization. We'll look at access controls on the three core services (CDS, Security, and DTS) as well as how the configuration process sets up access controls on DFS and GDS. This should give you a pretty good idea of who is granted permission to do what at the point immediately after you've initialized your cell. We'll also offer some guidelines about how you might want to change the default access control schemes for each of the services you have configured.

## 13.1  Default Access Controls Created by Cell Initialization

Without getting too deep into the gory details, it's probably a good idea to present some background information on default DCE access controls so that the advice that follows later in the chapter will make more sense. Let's start by looking at what happens when you initialize your cell.

Nearly all of the security information created by cell initialization is for DCE's own use internally. First, cell initialization creates the initial CDS hierarchy of directories and then populates it with the minimal entries DCE needs to operate. Cell initialization also creates principal and group accounts in the Registry database, defining identities for the standard DCE servers and clients so they can authenticate each other. All of these accounts, and there are many of them, are created automatically, including accounts for new client-only systems when they are configured into the cell. This takes care of the core server machines and the DCE server and client processes that run on them.

### 13.1.1 The cell_admin Principal Has Unlimited Access to Everything

During your cell's initialization, the DCE configuration process defines an individual principal called **cell_admin**. If you log in to DCE as **cell_admin**, you can perform any operation you want in CDS, DTS, Security, and DFS, as well as perform server management operations on all DCE server and client systems. The **cell_admin** account is roughly equivalent to **root** on an individual UNIX-based system. Immediately after cell initialization, **cell_admin** is the only user account defined in the Registry database. All other users and processes that access the cell must do so as unauthenticated principals.

### 13.1.2 DCE Authorization Groups Get Control of Specific Services

To facilitate managing and troubleshooting DCE services, cell initialization creates a lot of DCE authorization groups in the Registry database. These groups provide a way to assemble DCE administrators into single units to which you can grant a specific set of permissions to each of the DCE services.

For example, the cell configuration process creates an authorization group named **cds-admin** to which it grants full access to the initial CDS hierarchy. This access will propagate to all new CDS directories (and their contents) as they are created.

Another authorization group, **sec-admin**, enables its members to perform any management operation on the Registry database. Similar groups are also created for DTS (**dts-admin**) and DFS (**dfs-admin**).

Because these groups possess full access to the DCE services with which they are associated, their members can intervene, whenever necessary, to solve problems for DCE users who have fewer permissions. When you remove a user from an authorization group, that user loses all the access currently granted to the group.

Immediately after their creation, DCE authorization groups contain only one principal name: **cell_admin**. At some point, you'll need to add the registered principal names of other individuals in your organization who you want to help administer and troubleshoot your DCE services.

## 13.1.3  Initial Access Controls on DCE Core Services

By default, the DCE configuration process creates ACL entries on the CDS root directory. The permissions granted by these ACL entries automatically propagate to every entry in the initial CDS hierarchy and to all future CDS directories and their contents. This results in the following general CDS access control scheme immediately after you initialize your cell.

The **cell_admin** principal gets full access to the CDS hierarchy and all its future contents. The **cds-admin** group (which at this point contains only the **cell_admin** principal) gets full access. The principal defined for the new CDS server (**host/hostname/cds-server**) also gets full access. Users whose identities cannot be verified in the Registry database (unauthenticated users) get read permission and can only look up CDS names and read the values of the attributes associated with them. Depending on whose version of DCE you purchase, the initial security arrangement on CDS may be slightly more or less restrictive. Most vendors will probably preserve this *world read* approach to CDS for unauthenticated users.

The cell initialization process also sets up some initial access controls on the Registry database. These are roughly equivalent to those created on the CDS directory hierarchy. Cell initialization defines a server principal for the new security server, and grants the server adequate permissions to certain security-related CDS entries. The **sec-admin** authorization group (of which the **cell_admin** principal is a member) is granted full access to the Registry database. Unauthenticated users get only read permission.

As in CDS, the **cell_admin** principal has full access to everything stored in the Registry.

The initial access controls on DTS are basically the same as those set up on CDS and the Registry database. In DTS, however, the main idea is to control access to the time server processes themselves, rather than to a hierarchy of names, or to accounts, passwords, and principals. Cell initialization defines a machine principal for the first DTS server in the Registry database and grants the new server adequate permissions to certain DTS-related CDS entries. The **dts-admin** authorization group (of which the **cell_admin** principal is a member) is granted full access to perform any management operation on any DTS server or client. Users who fall into the unauthenticated category get only read access to a new DTS server.

## 13.1.4   Initial Access Controls on DFS

Unlike CDS, Security, and DTS, the cell initialization process (since it does not necessarily include DFS configuration) applies access controls mostly to the **/.:/fs** junction entry in CDS. This entry represents the dividing line between the CDS and DFS.

Whenever you configure your first DFS server, the configuration process defines a machine principal for the new server in the Registry database and grants the principal adequate permissions to certain DFS-related entries in CDS. The **dfs-admin** authorization group (of which the **cell_admin** principal is a member) is granted full access to DFS. All other users, even those who can be authenticated, appear to enjoy no permissions at all to DFS immediately after its configuration.

## 13.1.5   Initial Access Controls on GDS

GDS (X.500) is the only DCE component that does not use DCE ACLs to control access to its resources. Rather, it employs its own ACL mechanisms to control who is allowed to create, delete, read, and modify GDS objects and their attributes. The access control list of the default schema has no access rights when GDS is configured. All users, including those who cannot be authenticated, are permitted read and write access to all attributes in the schema.

## 13.1.6   Summary

Cell initialization automatically defines all DCE core server and client machines as principals in the Registry and grants them all the permissions they need to conduct their affairs. At this point, the only human user principal defined in the Registry is **cell_admin**. The **cell_admin** principal is added to all the other authorization groups created by the initialization process (**cds-admin**, **sec-admin**, **dts-admin**, and so on.). As a result, **cell_admin** has full access to the entire cell. Immediately after cell initialization, no other users have DCE accounts, none is defined as a principal in the Registry, and none can be authenticated.

Users who are unknown to the Registry cannot be authenticated. But, because DCE services initially permit world read access to unauthenticated principals, the user population is free to browse around the CDS hierarchy, the Registry database, DTS, and DFS, and to monitor the operations of these DCE services.

# 13.2 Modifying Default Security Policies of DCE Services

If you don't care for these default security arrangements, the best time to do something about it is immediately after you've initialized your cell. Among the tasks you should perform, or at least consider, include:

- Changing the default access control policy for CDS, Security, and DTS

- Defining accounts/principals in the Registry

- Adding principals to DCE authorization groups

- Creating your own authorization groups

- Taking advantage of ACL entry propagation

Immediately after you initialize your cell and *before* you begin creating new CDS directories, setting up accounts or defining principals in the Registry, or creating DFS directories and filesets, you should consider what changes you want to make to the initial access control schemes described in Section 13.1. You should try to strike some kind of balance between your need for security and your desire for convenience.

Regardless of how you modify the default access for cell users, you should never modify any of the ACL entries created in CDS on behalf of your standard DCE servers and clients. These systems and the DCE processes running on them get what they need for access to the cell automatically as they are configured and you risk serious operational problems in the cell if you start messing around with these default permissions.

Instead, you need to decide how you want to restrict access to the cell for your user population. You'll see what we mean as you read on.

# 13.3 Three Example Security Scenarios

The following three example scenarios help to demonstrate the broad range of security policies that you can enforce using DCE authentication together with DCE authorization. Let's begin by looking at a low-security environment.

## 13.3.1 Scenario One: Low Security

If you leave things as they are, *anyone* logged in to a DCE client machine connected to your network can search through your cell at will. If, in addition to **read** permission, you were also to grant **write** permission on behalf of unauthenticated users, everyone in the network could create and edit directories, entries, and files. Obviously, this is not a very secure arrangement, but it is very convenient. Since, at this early stage, practically no one is defined in the Registry, you don't have to worry about administering accounts and principals or maintaining a lot of ACLs. And, because everyone and anyone effectively has **read** and **write** permission to the entire cell, they can work unhampered by a lot of access controls. Most DCE developers agree, even in this low-security case, that you should reserve the more powerful permissions such as **delete**, **control**, and **administer** for the **cell_admin** principal or for the other users who you do define in the Registry and include as members in one or more of the other DCE authorization groups. Remember, only users who can be authenticated are allowed membership in authorization groups.

This is a nice arrangement, especially if you've set up your cell as a test environment in which to develop and prototype distributed applications. Most of DCE, in fact, was developed in this fashion—with essentially no security restrictions on CDS entries.

Remember that by allowing unauthenticated users access to the cell, you do not forfeit security between and among DCE services. DCE clients and servers must still authenticate themselves to each other before they can exchange information, and the data they transmit remains fully protected. It's only users on client systems who don't need to be authenticated in this scenario.

In a small cell, dedicated to a relatively small number of developers who are engaged in a common effort, this low user-security approach can work well—as long as you're sure you can trust everybody (and we do mean *everybody*) on your network that has access to a DCE client or server system.

You shouldn't have much trouble regulating who gets to put up DCE client software on a machine and, since the configuration process itself registers all DCE machines in the Registry database, it's practically impossible for a DCE client to operate *incognito*. A simple scan of the Registry will tell you how many machines on your network are participating in your cell. As far as human operators are concerned, your normal security measures, such as requiring users to regularly change their passwords, should fill most of the gap left by the DCE Security features you're bypassing.

If you change your mind about leaving your cell so wide open, you can easily reverse your decision. Just start creating accounts and defining principals for your users. Then, reestablish the maximum permissions you grant on behalf of unauthenticated users. If you originally granted them **read/write** permission, you can cut them back to **read** only, or cut them off entirely.

## 13.3.2  Scenario Two: Medium Security

The only way to take full advantage of DCE Security is to define all users of your cell as principals in the Registry database. Once you've got a user population that can be authenticated, you can further restrict or terminate the default access originally enjoyed by unauthenticated users. Rather than lumping all potential users together into the unauthenticated category, you've now got the opportunity to grant a different level of access to users who can be authenticated compared to those who cannot.

You can make even more precise security distinctions between categories of cell users. DCE Security employs special ACL entry types that allow you to distinguish between different classes of principals and grant different sets of permissions on their behalf. For example, you could grant authenticated users from your own cell **read** and **write** permission to a particular DCE service, grant **read** permission only to authenticated users from foreign cells, and deny any access at all to the service for all users who cannot be authenticated. You can enforce a different policy for each of the DCE services.

In Version 1.0 of DCE, you have to register users one at a time. Currently, there is no way to register multiple users simultaneously. In future versions, a DCE command called **passwd_import** will solve this problem (at least on UNIX-based systems) by making it possible for you to register all users on a system based on the existing **etc/passwd** file on the system.

### Adding Members to the DCE Authorization Groups

If you haven't done so already, now is a good time to add members to the DCE authorization groups we mentioned earlier (Section 13.1) to delegate some of the management and troubleshooting responsibility for your DCE services. It's up to you to decide who you want to add to which groups. If you don't add anybody, the **cell_admin** principal remains as the only member in any of them. This constitutes quite a security risk. If you're the only user who knows the **cell_admin** password and you're injured in a bungee-jumping accident (or otherwise sustain a sudden loss of memory), you and the rest of the user population may be locked out of large portions of your cell. Even if you've granted most users world **read** and **write** permission to the cell, that's not enough access to manage it.

There are a couple of minor restrictions in DCE Version 1.0 that you should keep in mind when you add members to authorization groups. First, only individual principals can be included in an authorization group; you cannot include any group as a member in another group. Second, intercell membership in authorization groups is not currently permitted. All principals that you include in a group must belong to the same cell in which the group is defined. These restrictions are likely to be eliminated in future DCE releases.

## Creating Your Own Authorization Groups

In addition to using the canned DCE groups, creating your own authorization groups provides a convenient and flexible way to control access to particular CDS directories, DFS directories and filesets, or other subsets of information in your cell. You can combine users into authorization groups according to organization, job classification, wage class, security status, and so on, and then grant each group a specific set of permissions to specific cell resources.

Many DCE administrators will no doubt manage the lower levels of CDS (and probably DFS too) the same way they've managed more traditional file systems. Below a certain level in the CDS and DFS directory hierarchies, some users will be permitted to create and manage their own directories. Authorization groups can really help you out here. In CDS, for example, if you've created directories to support your sales, promotional, and manufacturing groups (**/.:/sales**, **/.:/promo**, and **/.:/manu**), you can create and populate corresponding authorization groups (**sales-admin**, **promo-admin**, and **manu-admin**) to manage them. By granting these groups full access to their own directories, you can dramatically reduce your central CDS management overhead. You could also create additional authorization groups for the users of these directories (**sales-users**, **promo-users**, and **manu-users**) and grant them whatever level of access you decide is appropriate.

### Taking Advantage of ACL Entry Propagation

When you grant access to CDS and DFS directories, you can indicate that the permissions you assign also apply to the directory's future contents and all subdirectories (and their contents) that you may later create. In fact, this is the primary mechanism through which the **cell_admin** principal gets full access to these services.

Whenever you create a new directory, the permissions you've already granted on behalf of a principal to the parent directory of the new directory can be inherited by the new directory. You can set things up so that the same thing happens for all the names or files that are later created in the directory. If you take advantage of this Security feature, you can avoid the need to create a lot of ACLs every time you create a new CDS or DFS directory or add to its contents.

## 13.3.3 Scenario Three: Clamping Your Cell Shut

The precise access control that you can achieve with DCE authentication and authorization is impressive. If the nature of your business requires high security, you can definitely achieve it with DCE Security.

For example, you can set things up so that only authenticated users defined in your own cell have access to any of the cell's resources. You can deny access to users from foreign cells, regardless of whether they can be authenticated. If you (and your user population) can tolerate the inconvenience, you could entirely abandon the use of authorization groups and require that each user be granted permissions to individual cell resources only by ACL entries that you create specifically for that user.

You can also adjust the interval at which a user's authentication credentials (tickets and secret keys) expire. For example, the default interval for ticket expiration is 10 hours. If you're really concerned about an intruder decrypting this information, you can further minimize the risk by resetting the expiration interval to something measured in minutes instead of hours.

In an typical, medium-security cell, maintaining such a restrictive environment may be impractical. But, if you really need to operate your cell this way, DCE Security can handle it. Just make sure you can handle the intense ACL management you'll face supporting such an environment.

The security model used in DCE is ideal for programmers who want to develop exquisitely secure distributed applications. Server developers pretty much get to define their own ACL management interfaces, their own sets of permissions, and which operations those permissions will allow a user (or the elements within their application programs) to perform in a particular situation. For example, the application server could require every new connection to provide authentication information for the originating process. In addition, the server can enforce a particular set of permissions on each resource offered to its clients.

DCE offers application developers another opportunity for granular security in the way they implement their RPC calls. They can authenticate only upon connection or require authentication on each call. They can also choose whether a particular RPC call is encrypted. And this all in addition to the ACL schemes they set up on the resources used by the application.

## *13.4 A Little Friendly ACL Advice*

As Scenario 3 in the preceding section illustrates, DCE ACLs are powerful. However, managing them can become quite inconvenient. As we pointed out in Section 13.2, for most DCE implementations you should try to strike some kind of balance between security and convenience. The collective wisdom is "Don't overdo it!" Unless the nature of your business or your company's security policies demand restricted access, your goal should be to make access to your cell no more restrictive than necessary.

Few things in life are more frustrating to a software user than trying to execute a command and being informed (through any one of a dozen possible error messages) that they don't have adequate permissions to perform their intended operation. In DCE, this will be especially true for DCE server managers or anyone else responsible for manipulating and troubleshooting DCE services.

If a particular group of DCE users need regular access to certain information or need to perform certain management tasks, you'd be wise to set up security in a way that makes it possible for them to do so. If you're stingy with the permissions, you're likely to have people pounding on your door, constantly demanding that you grant them more access so they can get to the resources they need to do their jobs. If you follow this advice, you'll not only make life easier for your users, you'll also reduce ACL management overhead for yourself and your fellow DCE administrative staff members.

## 13.4.1  How Secure is Secure Enough?

Because CDS contains the information that users and applications need to find everything else in the cell, you should probably start by granting world **read** permission to the CDS hierarchy and all of its contents. If most users in the cell are running applications that need to create their own CDS directories and populate them with their own names, you can also grant world **write** permission to CDS, then restrict access selectively, and only as necessary. You should reserve the more esoteric CDS management tasks (requiring **control**, **administer**, and **delete** permission) for the **cell_admin** principal and members of your **cds-admin** authorization group. Managers of systems with CDS servers (and, consequently, CDS clearinghouses) can be included in the membership of the cell's **cds-admin** group. This permits them to manipulate their server and clearinghouse processes, as well as to create, populate, and delete CDS directories.

You should probably maintain tight security on the Registry database. The general user population doesn't need to (and shouldn't be permitted to) scan or tamper with the contents of the Registry database. Except for your Security administrators, it's really nobody's business who's a member of which authorization groups or how many users are registered in the database at any given time. You may occasionally find it convenient to grant an individual user limited, temporary, permission to browse through the Registry database, but otherwise, the database should remain the sole concern of the **cell_admin** principal and the members of your cell's **sec-admin** authorization group.

For DTS, world **read** is probably acceptable. There's no harm in allowing users to watch DTS clerk and server counters clicking by. Save DTS management operations for the **cell_admin** principal and members of the **dts-admin** authorization group.

For DFS, what you do depends on the directories and filesets you need to protect. This is not so different from what you've done in the past to protect files in nondistributed file systems. Some files, such as open notes conferences, you'll want set to world **read** and **write**. Other files, such as electronic bulletin boards or instructional files, you'll want set only to world **read**. For most files, you'll want to grant **read** and **write** permissions based specifically on what's in the file and which users need access to it.

As with all the other DCE services, you should reserve administrative operations—such as DFS server creation, fileset management, and backup database management—to **cell_admin**, members of the **dfs-admin** authorization group, or the users you include in your administrative lists.

# 14

# *Distributing and Replicating Core DCE Services*

In this chapter, we'll look at several of the benefits you can enjoy by distributing your DCE core services. We'll also lay out some guidelines to help you decide where to locate servers throughout your network. The ability to replicate and distribute DCE services and information provides many benefits:

- **Availability.** If data and services reside in at least two different locations, they are more likely to be available, even in the event of a localized system or network failure.

- **Efficiency.** Users and applications can find information more efficiently because data can be stored close to where it is used most often.

- **Load sharing.** Because the same information exists in more than one place, multiple systems can share the load of finding and retrieving data.

- **Expandability**. New information and services can easily be accommodated as your cell grows and more applications use DCE.

## *14.1  Distributing the Cell Directory Service*

You create the first CDS server in your cell (and its resident clearinghouse) when you configure CDS during the cell initialization process. Thereafter, you can configure additional CDS servers by rerunning the CDS configuration on other systems.

Even if you maintain a small cell that provides services to only a handful of users, you should configure at least one additional CDS server on another stable system whose connectivity to your network is reliable. By maintaining the entire CDS hierarchy on two servers (two clearinghouses), you create a real-time backup of all your CDS data. In addition, if one of the CDS server systems fails, users and applications can still retrieve the information they need from the other server.

We should point out that a temporary lapse in CDS service won't necessarily bring your cell to its knees. This is because the CDS clerks cache the results of all successful name and address lookups as they go along. CDS clerks effectively "remember" what worked the last time around. When another request for the same information comes in, the CDS clerk simply hands the cached information back to the requesting user or application.

Anyway, even small cells should maintain at least two CDS servers and replicate the entire CDS database on both of them. As your cell grows, you will find it advantageous to configure additional servers to further distribute CDS information around the network.

There's no fixed ceiling to the number of CDS servers you can create in a cell. There are, however, some practical reasons why you don't want to overdo it. First, a lot of CDS servers means a lot of CDS server managers (and licenses). From the administrative and disbursements perspective, you may want to keep the number of CDS servers down. Second, if you're storing the same CDS data on most of your CDS servers, then the skulking process (the process by which updates to CDS data are transmitted to all clearinghouses where it is stored) will take longer to complete and is more likely not to complete successfully. To skulk a CDS directory requires each of the clearinghouses that stores a replica of the directory to be running and reachable at the time the skulk is initiated. If you've got replicas of the cell root directory stored in, let's say 100 different clearinghouses, all 100 systems must be up and available, and their resident CDS server and clearinghouse processes must all be running for the skulk to complete successfully.

## 14.1.1   Where Should You Locate Your CDS Servers?

You should try to locate CDS servers near the people and applications that use the information they serve. To some extent, this can depend on where your cell users are and how your cell is configured topologically. For example, if your cell is contained entirely on a single LAN within the confines of your corporate headquarters, you can replicate your CDS database on two clearinghouses and locate them anywhere in the building. (To safeguard against a potential power surge taking out both machines, you should avoid plugging the machines into the same electrical outlet.)

If your cell spans two LANs, you should locate one CDS server on each LAN and replicate the entire CDS database on both of them. CDS clients and servers can communicate between LANs and across WAN links, but response times will be faster if you locate a server on each LAN.

Regardless of where you locate them, once you're using more than two CDS servers, you no longer have to be so concerned about replicating the entire CDS database on each one. Instead, you can be more selective about what (which CDS directories) you replicate on each server. Before we go any further, let's review some information about CDS directory replicas.

Each physical copy of a CDS directory, including the original, is called a replica. When you create a replica of a directory, you replicate all of the CDS names stored in it as well. Two types of CDS replicas can exist: master replicas and read-only replicas.

The master replica is the only replica of a CDS directory that can be directly modified. CDS can create, change, and delete information in a master replica. As a result, a master replica incurs more overhead than read-only replicas, which CDS updates periodically with changes made to the master replica.

A read-only replica is a replica in which users can look up information, but are not permitted to create new information or modify existing information. You should create read-only replicas in clearinghouses whose users need to access the directory, but do not need (or are not permitted) to update its contents.

These characteristics of CDS directory replicas come into play when you use multiple CDS servers. Assume your cell supports your company's three main offices: the administrative headquarters in New York, the manufacturing center in Philadelphia, and the marketing group in Boston. You've configured one CDS server at each site.

On the server in New York, you could store the master replicas of the directories in the initial CDS hierarchy created when you initialized your cell. You should create read-only replicas of these directories on the servers in Philadelphia and Boston. The master replicas of any directories created and used primarily by the New York administrators should be stored on the New York server. You should create read-only replicas of these directories at either or both of the other sites.

The master replicas of CDS directories used at the manufacturing site should be stored on the server in Philadelphia. You should create read-only replicas of these directories at either or both of the other two sites.

The same goes for directories created and used most frequently by the sales folks in Boston. Their master replicas should be stored on the Boston server and read-only replicas should be created at either or both of the other sites.

The main point of this scenario is that you don't have to replicate everything everywhere. You can store bits and pieces of your CDS hierarchy on CDS servers strategically located throughout your cell and make the information conveniently available to the users who need to get to it.

# 14.2 Distributing the Security Service

At this writing, replication of DCE Security services is not yet a reality. The mechanism to allow replication of Security services and, in particular, the Registry database, is still under development. Security replication is scheduled for delivery in Version 1.0.2 of OSF's DCE offering.

Although we don't have a lot of solid facts to go on, we can explore some of the decisions you'll eventually need to make when security replication does become available. Although much of our discussion is speculative, it's likely you'll have to think about most of what we have to say here, regardless of how security replication is eventually implemented.

Having said that, let's briefly review some of the reasons why DCE users want to be able to replicate and distribute the DCE Security service. They are really the same reasons as those embodied in the list at the beginning of this chapter for the other core services.

If you employ multiple security servers, on which your entire Registry database is replicated, your cell can continue to function, even if one (or all but one) of the security servers becomes unavailable.

In a secure cell, every machine, process, and person can be authenticated. This means that, at least on an initial transaction, some DCE component in the communications chain has to contact the security service and receive a response before the transaction can proceed. In a small cell that supports a relatively small number of users, all of whom are located on the same LAN, one security server can probably do the job. But in a cell that spans multiple LANs and is dispersed over many remote sites, multiple security servers located at the major population centers is a much better strategy.

In a small cell, one security server can probably handle the load. In a large cell supporting thousands of servers, clerks, users, and applications, a single security server is likely to get swamped by the sheer volume of traffic---especially when everybody logs in to DCE in the morning. Multiple security servers will solve this problem by sharing the work.

If your cell grows to include user groups on other LANs, you easily locate additional security servers on those LANs to provide local authentication.

For what it's worth, we'll speculate about how security replication might work. First of all, it's likely to be a *master versus read-only* replica arrangement. There's no way to know yet whether you'll be able to mix master replicas and read-only replicas on the same Security server. For that matter, we don't know whether you'll have to replicate the entire Registry database on each Security server or be able to farm out specific portions of it. Because the Registry database is flat rather than hierarchical in structure, it's unclear how you could replicate portions of it at different locations. But if you can, you'll be able to replicate subsets of the security database near the users whose account and private key information are contained in those subsets. This also means that you can locate particular master replicas near the security administrators who manage them.

The means for updating security information across multiple servers is also a mystery at this point. Unlike CDS, where you can usually afford to wait as long as 24 hours or more for an update to propagate to every replica of a directory, such a time lag in security updating would seem to create a security hole big enough to accommodate a Buick. You want updates to propagate to all security servers as quickly as possible. This need for immediate updating may limit the number of Security servers you can have in your cell and still preserve the integrity of the Registry database.

Regardless of how security replication is finally implemented, you can expect to be dealing with multiple Security servers in the near future. The machine selection criteria and location within your network is identical to that suggested for your initial security server. You want a reliable machine with good connectivity to the network, a lot of computing power, and a lot of disk space. If you're already keeping your one security server machine under lock and key, you should probably do the same for any additional security servers you configure.

# 14.3 Distributing the Time Service

Unlike CDS servers, which can store different sets of information and be positioned within your network to provide convenient access for a particular group of users, DTS servers, no matter how many of them you configure, exist to provide only one thing to the entire cell: synchronized time. DTS client software is configured on all server and client-only systems in your cell and the clocks on all systems are regulated by DTS.

Because the need for time synchronization is cellwide, you need to make sure that your DTS servers are accessible to all systems participating in your cell. You can get by temporarily with the one DTS server you configured during your cell's initialization, but as soon as possible thereafter, you should create additional DTS servers. The more DTS servers you configure, the more reliable the time values in your cell will be.

DTS servers come in three flavors: Local, Global, and Courier. Local servers synchronize with other local servers on the same LAN. Global servers provide time synchronization across multiple LANs. Courier servers are really Local servers specifically assigned the task of synchronizing with one or more Global servers at regular intervals. See Chapter 7 for more information on the roles of DTS servers.

If your cell exists entirely within the limits of a single LAN, you should configure at least three DTS Local servers. It doesn't seem to matter too much exactly where on the LAN you locate them, as long as all other systems can get to them.

If your cell spans multiple LANs, you'll need to configure Global and Courier servers in addition to Local servers. There are many possible DTS server configurations available in a multiple LAN implementation. Perhaps the most advantageous is to configure three DTS servers—one Local, one Global, and one Courier—on each LAN.

As with all other DCE servers, you should locate DTS servers on machines that stay up and stay connected to the rest of the network. Remember that you don't want anything in the transmission path between your DTS servers that will create an unreasonable time lag in communication. It's up to you to determine what's unreasonable. Just remember that the longer the delay between transmittal and receipt of time values, the greater the inaccuracy will be.

Unless you're using an external time-provider (to provide the cell with *Coordinated Universal Time (UTC)*, you should also try to configure DTS servers on systems that have accurate clocks and that do not experience a lot of interrupts from other devices.

# PART III

## Appendices

# A

# *DCE Client/Server Examples*

Here are the C code and UNIX commands for the sample client/server application (Section 9.2.1). Remember that this code is meant to be a toy for you to play with, not a complete tutorial on DCE client/server coding. To create a robust, production-ready application (Section 9.2.2), you need more information about the DCE Directory Service, RPC, Security, and Threads.

Here's what you'll find in this appendix:

- A bare-bones client

- A threaded application prototype

- A bare-bones application with authentication

- A threaded application with mutexes, error-checking, and support for server-group registration.

- A sample makefile

The filenames that we used to put these applications together are shown in Table A-1.

The **makefile.hello** file builds all of the programs mentioned in this appendix. Any other filenames are for files already located on your system (for instance, C libraries) or produced in the course of processing the files listed previously (for instance, the IDL compiler creates the **hello_world.h** file).

In the examples, the prompts C> and S> designate the system prompt on the client and server host.

*Table A-1  Sample Programs*

| Files | Descriptions |
|---|---|
| **Bare-bones Client** | |
| hello_world.idl | Interface file (same for all builds) |
| fetch_string_basic.c | Client |
| get_hello_world.c | Server routine (nearly same for all builds) |
| hw_server_init.c | Server initialization (nearly same for all builds) |
| **Threaded Program** | |
| hello_world.idl | Interface file |
| fetch_string.c | Client |
| get_hello_world.c | Server routine |
| hw_server_init.c | Server initialization |
| **Security Program** | |
| hello_world.idl | Interface |
| hello_world_security.acf | Attribute Configuration File |
| fetch_string_security.c | Client |
| get_hello_world_security.c | Server routine |
| hw_server_init_security.c | Server initialization |
| **Error-checking and Mutex Program** | |
| hello_world.idl | Interface |
| fetch_string_complete.c | Client |
| get_hello_world_complete.c | Server routine |
| hw_server_init_complete.c | Server initialization |
| check_status.h | Error-checking macro code |

Before you execute any of the code, you need to set an environment variable on the client's host, as follows:

```
C> setenv RPC_DEFAULT_ENTRY /.:/{server's CDS name}
```

For more information on compiling and linking, see the sample makefile (Section A.5).

## A.1 Bare-Bones Client Code

Before examining code for the more complex applications, take a look at this stripped-down client code to get a basic idea about what we're trying to accomplish. We want the client to make a remote call and to write the fetched data ("hello world") to the terminal screen. That's all!

*Example A-1:  Client code prototype: fetch_string_basic.c*

```
/* File name:   fetch_string_basic.c                          */
/* Purpose:     Rough cut at client code, including only the remote */
/*              call.                                          */
#include <stdio.h>
#include "hello_world.h"
/* Global data */
string_type     returned_string;      /* "string_type" in hello_world.h */
main()
{
    printf ("Client: I'm fetching the message from the server.\n");
    get_hello_world(returned_string);
    printf("From Server:  %s\n", returned_string);
}
/*                                                            */
/*   SECURITY:                                                */
/*   FYI  The security client will add a routine, here.       */
/*                                                            */
```

## A.2 A Simple Threaded Version of the Application

This section contains the code described in Chapter 9.

*Example A-2:  The interface file: hello_world.idl*

```
/*  File name:   hello_world.idl                              */
/*  Purpose:     The interface for the application, containing */
/*               global declarations and type declarations.    */
[
uuid(AAB038A0-3709-11CB-BFC4-08002B0F4644),
version(1.0)
]
interface hello_world
{
/* Data Declarations */
/* Space required for the string  "hello world, call #{integer}" */
const long              MAX_STRING = 28;

typedef [string] char   string_type[MAX_STRING+1];  /* Extra byte for */
                                                    /* NULL char */
```

*Example A-2: The interface file: hello_world.idl (continued)*

```
/* Operations */
void get_hello_world(
     [out] string_type return_string        /* string returned */
     );
}
```

*Example A-3: Threaded client code: fetch_string.c*

```
/* File name:      fetch_string.c                                          */
/* Purpose:        This is the application client code.  It creates a */
/*                 thread to make a remote call, creates another      */
/*                 thread to provide feedback to the user, and upon   */
/*                 termination of the RPC displays the string         */
/*                 from the server.                                   */
❶ #include <stdio.h>
  #include <pthread.h>
  #include "hello_world.h"
❷ #static int        fetch_string();
  static void        print_message();
  main()
  {
      string_type      returned_string;
      pthread_t        thread_for_rpc;        /* type defined in pthread.h */
      pthread_t        thread_for_messages; /* type defined in pthread.h */
      printf("Client: I'm fetching the message from the server.\n");
❸     pthread_create(
            &thread_for_rpc,
            pthread_attr_default,
            (pthread_startroutine_t) fetch_string,
            (pthread_addr_t) returned_string
      );
      pthread_create(
            &thread_for_messages,
            pthread_attr_default,
            (pthread_startroutine_t)print_message,
            (pthread_addr_t)NULL
      );

      /* Wait for RPC call to complete */
❹     pthread_join(thread_for_rpc, NULL);
      /* Cancel thread providing user feed back */
      pthread_cancel(thread_for_messages);
      /* Display the string returned from the server */
      printf("\nFrom Server:  %s\n", returned_string);
  }
  /* Routine that performs an RPC call */
  static fetch_string(returned_string)
  string_type  returned_string;
  {
      get_hello_world(returned_string);  /* remote call */
```

*Example A-3: Threaded client code: fetch_string.c (continued)*

```
    return 1:
}
/* Routine that performs other work during remote call */
static void print_message()
{
    printf("Waiting"); fflush(stdout):
    while(1){
        printf ("."); fflush(stdout):
        sleep(1):
❺       pthread_yield():
    }
}
```

❶  Include the **pthreads.h** file for C run-time library jacket routines and for data-type declarations.

❷  This client uses two subroutines in two threads: one to make a remote call (`fetch_string`) and one to communicate status to the user (`print_message`).

❸  To create a thread, call **pthread_create**, and pass the name of the created thread (`thread_for_rpc` and `thread_for_messages`), thread attributes, the name of the subroutine that will execute in the thread, and a pointer to an argument list for the subroutine. Thread creation and subroutine execution begin with this call.

❹  The call to **pthread_join** causes the main routine to pause and wait for the termination of another thread (the one making the remote call). After this call, the remote call is complete, and the main routine can cancel the `thread_for_messages` thread.

❺  The call to **pthread_yield** tells the Threads Scheduler that the calling thread (`thread_for_messages`) is willing to block for a while to let another thread execute.

*Example A-4: Nonreentrant remote procedure: get_hello_world.c*

```
/* File name:    get_hello_world.c                  */
/* Purpose:      Returns a string to a client.      */
/*               Cannot be used in a multithreaded   */
/*               server due to unsynchronized access */
/*               to shared data (calls_processed).   */

#include <pthread.h>                /* Includes jackets for C RTL */
#include <stdio.h>
#include "hello_world.h"
/* Shared data that should be protected */
static int calls_processed = 0;     /* Counts client-call total  */
void get_hello_world(return_string)
    string_type return_string:
```

*Example A-4: Nonreentrant remote procedure: get_hello_world.c (continued)*

```
{
    sprintf((char*)return_string, "hello world, call #%d.",
    calls_processed++);
}
```

*Example A-5: Single-threaded server initialization code:*
*hw_server_init.c*

```
/* File name:    hw_server_init.c         */
/* Purpose:      Initializes the server.  */
#include <pthread.h>
#include <stdio.h>
#include <ctype.h>
#include "hello_world.h"
#define STRINGLEN 80
main()
{
    unsigned32                              status;
    rpc_binding_vector_t        *binding_vector;
    char                    entry_name[STRINGLEN];
    char                    hostname[STRINGLEN];

    /* Register the interface */
    rpc_server_register_if(
        hello_world_v1_0_s_ifspec,
        NULL,
        NULL,
        &status
    );

    /* Register protocol sequences */
    rpc_server_use_all_protseqs(
        rpc_c_protseq_max_reqs_default,
        &status
    );

    /* Get binding information for server */
    rpc_server_inq_bindings(&binding_vector, &status);

    /* Export entry to name space. */
❶   strcpy(entry_name, "/.:/hello_svr_");
    gethostname(hostname, STRINGLEN);
    strcat(entry_name, hostname);

❷   rpc_ns_binding_export(
        rpc_c_ns_syntax_default,
        (unsigned_char_t *)entry_name,
        hello_world_v1_0_s_ifspec,
        binding_vector,
        NULL,
```

*Example A-5: Single-threaded server initialization code:*
*hw_server_init.c   (continued)*

```
   &status
);
/* Register with endpoint database (rpcd database)  */
rpc_ep_register(
   hello_world_v1_0_s_ifspec,
   binding_vector,
   NULL,
   (unsigned_char_t *)"Hello World Interface",
   &status
);

rpc_binding_vector_free(
   &binding_vector,
   &status
);

/* Wait for RPC calls to arrive. Allow only one client   */
/* call to be serviced at a time.                        */
rpc_server_listen(1, &status);
}
```

❶ The method we use to attach a machine's name to the CDS entry name is nonportable. The **gethostname** routine is a commonly used UNIX call. You can either use a system-dependent method of doing this, or you can devise some other way—such as setting environment variables—to define a variable to be a CDS name.

❷ This call to **rpc_ns_binding_export** uses an automatic binding method by placing an entry for the server into CDS.

# A.3  A Bare-Bones Application with Authentication

This version of the application includes a small amount of security called **mutual authentication**, or creating a **secure binding**. This means that the client and the server are authenticated and can be sure of each other's identity. The process involves a somewhat complex set of events that are mostly hidden from you: they occur within the client and server stubs, the RPC run-time library on both hosts, and the Security Server.

Mutual authentication, in a real-life application, is just the beginning of the work done by a server to guarantee the proper access to the proper people. In our simple example, we don't actually check for particular user names or compare the client's access rights against an access control list. So all we're confirming is that the client and server are legitimate in the eyes of the Security service.

This is a small achievement, but more significant than it might appear. For instance, since the server has the identity that it's supposed to have, this means that it's the same server that registered the binding information in CDS; it hasn't been killed off and replaced with an imposter.

Normally, when the client has the identity it's supposed to have, this means that the user logged into DCE and is not just a snooper. The client program simply takes on the identity and access rights of the user. In our example, to simplify administration, we have created a special principal just for our Hello World client. Therefore, the server can't find out who is running the client, but it can be assured that the client's process is known to the Security service.

Two decisions that a real-life server can make, usually in an ACL manager, are whether to reject all unauthenticated calls outright, or whether to use information contained in the authentication exchange for authorization decisions.

In the example in this appendix, the client requires authentication information from the server when the connection is made. Our client's security work is finished during the initial connection; we do not require any additional proof of identity from the server. During each remote call, the server checks whether the client provided authentication information and rejects calls from clients who tried to bypass this level of security. Thus, if a client without the proper level of security made repeated calls during a connection, we make sure that the server would reject every one.

With the programming example in this section, in addition to authentication (verifying identities), we have taken our first baby steps into authorization. It is beyond the scope of this book to do any fine-grained authorization, such as differentiating between different principals or checking a principal's access rights against an ACL. That would require a number of **sec_** calls from the Security API.

To enable mutual authentication, the programmer just needs to call three Security routines. (Our sample code also uses implicit and string binding, which require additional calls.) The cell administrator needs to enter some straightforward commands that provide context information to the DCE Security Service.

Let's spell out one possible way to do the cell administrator's work, enabling mutual authentication:

1. Use the tool **rgy_edit** to add the principal name for the server to the Security database. (A sample **rgy_edit** session follows this list.)

2. On the client's host, set the environment variable RPC_DEFAULT_ENTRY to be the name of the CDS entry that will help the client find an

appropriate server. This CDS name can be a server (as in the sample code in this appendix), a group, or a profile entry.

3.  On both the client and server hosts, set the environment variable SERVER_PRINCIPAL to be the server's principal name.

4.  While logged into the server UNIX system as **root**, use the **ktadd** command within **rgy_edit** to set up the server's key table entry. (Since this step establishes a password for the key-table entry that may or may not be the same as the principal's password in the security registry, you may want to use the **-r** option to apply the same password to both areas.)

5.  On the server host, run the server program.

6.  Log into the client host and perform a **dce_login** as the client principal.

7.  Run the client program.

This example establishes a separate principal for the client. It's possible to run the client code under a user principal, if you choose. It's also possible to place the key-table entry in a directory other than root. However, that would require additional coding; we chose the path of least resistance.

This is a sample **rgy_edit** session to provide a "look and feel" for the previous list. At many prompts, you can press the carriage return to accept a default. These prompts appear here without any user input following them. An **rgy_edit** session on your system may not be identical to the one shown here, but it should be very similar.

```
node_name> dce_login cell_admin -dce-
exec .cshrc ... wait ...
node_name> rgy_edit
Current site is: registry server at /.../gareng
rgy_edit=> add domain p
Domain changed to: principal
rgy_edit=> add
Add Principal=> Enter name: gerry
Enter UNIX number: (auto assign)
Enter full name: () Gerry Fisher
Enter object creation quota: (unlimited)
Add Principal=> Enter name:
rgy_edit=> domain a
Domain changed to: account
rgy_edit=> add
Add Account=> Enter account id [pname]: gerry
Enter account group [gname]: none
Enter account organization [oname]: none
Enter password:      (Choose a valid password and type it in; it will not be echoed)
Retype password:     (Do what the nice security service says)
Enter your password: (Use your own DCE password here)
Enter misc info: () Gerry Fisher's server account
Enter home directory: (/)
```

```
Enter shell: () /bin/csh
Password valid [y/n]? (y)
Enter expiration date [yy/mm/dd or 'none']: (none)
Allow account to be server principal [y/n]? (y)
Allow account to be client principal [y/n]? (y)
Account valid for login [y/n]? (y)
Allow account to obtain post-dated certificates [y/n]? (n)
Allow account to obtain forwardable certificates [y/n]? (y)
Allow certificates to this account to be issued via TGT \
authentication [y/n]? (y)
Allow account to obtain renewable certificates [y/n]? (y)
Allow account to obtain proxiable certificates [y/n]? (n)
Allow account to obtain duplicate session keys [y/n]? (n)
Good since date [yy/mm/dd]: (1993/03/09.16:00)
Create/Change auth policy for this acct [y/n]? (n)
Add Account=> Enter account id [pname]:
rgy_edit=> ktadd -p gerry -pw behappy
rgy_edit=> exit
bye.
```

This script adds the principal **gerry** to the security database. You should run the server from this account. Before you run your client, make sure that you do so from an account for which a DCE principal has been added to the DCE Security data base.

All you need to know about mutual authentication is that a lot of cross checking takes place that's hidden from the programmer, and that the exchange makes information available so that the server can make execution choices.

For those who enjoy a little bit of pain, here is a more-detailed description of the authentication process between the client and server:

1. After **dce_login**, the client process possesses a privileged ticket-granting ticket (PTGT) and a session key. This ticket and key allow the client to talk to the Security Server.

2. When the client makes its first remote call, the client's run-time library tries to obtain a ticket to authenticate itself to the application's server. It obtains that ticket by sending a request to the Security Server, and the request contains the PTGT and proof that the client run-time library knows the session key. The Security Service sends back the ticket to the requested server and a conversation key that allows the ticket to be used by the client.

3. The client run-time library sends the server ticket and proof that it knows the conversation key to the requested server.

4. The server sends back evidence that it has successfully decrypted the conversation key (which was contained in the encrypted portion of the ticket sent by the client run-time library).

When the client and server obtain the proper keys from the DCE Security Service, in effect, they "prove" their identity and successfully complete the exchanges of encrypted information. If the client sends false authentication information in a call, the call will effectively contain garbage, and the RPC run-time library will reject it before the application even has a chance to evaluate any information. If all goes well, these exchanges are transparent to the application programmer.

The remaining part of this section shows you the minimal code that you need to enable mutual authentication. If you want the server to check the authentication information, perhaps to make authorization choices, you should write an ACL manager as a separate body of code. Each server routine can call the ACL manager in its first line of code, and abort execution if the proper authentication or authorization information isn't present.

**rpc_c_protect_level_connect** is just one of several protection levels. This level performs lots of authentication work up front—at the time the client first binds to the server—and then uses the same encrypted authentication data for any subsequent calls while the binding stays in effect.

If you need more frequent authentication (for instance, on every call), DCE makes several extended forms of security available. The RPC run-time library on each host varies the encrypted authentication data slightly for every remote call and reperforms its comparison. This ensures that the client and server are still using the same conversation key. If you choose, you can also have the encrypted data vary at the transfer of each packet of information. It depends on the level of overhead you want to incur for increased security.

*Example A-6: ACF file for Security: hello_world_security.acf*

```
/*  File name:   hello_world_security.acf          */
/*  Purpose:     Alters the application so that it  */
/*               uses implicit binding.  Security   */
/*               requires this to establish         */
/*               authentication.                    */
[
implicit_handle(handle_t hello_handle)
]
interface hello_world
{
}
```

At the time of this writing, you need to use implicit or explicit binding to choose a security level other than the default (no security). The DCE implementers plan on enabling applications with automatic binding to choose security levels in a future DCE release. However, right now, we need to compile and link this ACF file with our application to set a security level. This code establishes hello_handle as the application's implicit binding handle.

## Example A-7:  *Client code with security: fetch_string_security.c*

```
/* File name:  fetch_string_security.c                        */
/* Purpose:    Rough cut at client code, including only the remote */
/*             call.  This client uses string binding to request    */
/*             that authentication be applied to the binding.       */
#include <stdio.h>
#include "hello_world.h"
/* Global data */
string_type            returned_string;  /* "string_type" in hello_world.h */
short        create_secure_binding;
main()
{
❶    if (create_secure_binding()){ exit(); }
     printf ("Client: I'm fetching the message from the server.\n");
     get_hello_world(returned_string);
     printf("From Server:  %s\n", returned_string);
}
/*  This routine tells RPC to authenticate on connection. */
short create_secure_binding()
{
   unsigned char               *string_binding;
   char                        entry_name[40];
   long                  entry_name_syntax = 3;
❷  rpc_ns_handle_t              import_context;  /*  Types in rpc.h */
   error_status_t                   status;
/* Create import context.    */
❸  rpc_ns_binding_import_begin(
      entry_name_syntax,
      NULL,
      hello_world_v1_0_c_ifspec,
      NULL,
      &import_context,
      &status
   );
/* Return a binding handle for a server.    */
   rpc_ns_binding_import_next(
      import_context,
      &hello_handle,          /* from ACF  */
      &status
   );
/* Destroy import context.    */
   rpc_ns_binding_import_done(
      &import_context,
      &status
   );
/* Convert binding to a string.  */
   rpc_binding_to_string_binding(
      hello_handle,
      &string_binding,
      &status
   );
   printf("Binding handle is %s\n", string_binding);
/* Bind to a server.    */
```

*Example A-7: Client code with security: fetch_string_security.c (continued)*

```
rpc_binding_from_string_binding(
    string_binding,
    &hello_handle,
    &status
);
/* Set up binding for authentication.    */
rpc_binding_set_auth_info(
    hello_handle,
    getenv("SERVER_PRINCIPAL"),
    rpc_c_protect_level_connect,
    rpc_c_authn_secret,
    NULL,
    rpc_c_authz_name,
    &status
);
return(0);
}
```

❹ rpc_c_protect_level_connect,
❺ rpc_c_authn_secret,
❻ NULL,
❼ rpc_c_authz_name,

❶ This code causes the main program to exit if the call to **cre-ate_secure_binding** fails. The **create_secure_binding** routine tells the RPC runtime library to authenticate upon connection.

❷ The IDL compiler includes **rpc.h** in your application's **.h** file.

❸ To establish authentication, you need to use string bindings. To use string bindings, import the binding context, then import the binding itself, and finally clean up by releasing the import context. Once you have the binding handle, you can convert it to a string and read it.

❹ The **rpc_c_protect_level_connect** argument specifies that the RPC runtime library and Security work together to mutually authenticate the client and server at the time of connection (9.1.7).

❺ The **rpc_c_authn_secret** argument specifies that the binding will be a secret-key technology. Key technologies are either public (unsupported at the time of this writing) or secret (the key is stored and administered by DCE Security).

❻ This argument can be used to specify information specific to the particular process in which the client runs.

❼ If you are authenticating, you must specify an authorization value to this parameter other than "none," even though this application does not use authorization. We chose the **rpc_c_authz_name** argument, because that would be the type of authorization we would most likely use when authenticating upon connection. This value indicates that the server can perform authorization by supplying the client's principal name to the ACL manager to check for privileges.

*Example A-8: Authentication in the server initialization code:*
*hw_server_init_security.c*

```
/* File name:   hw_server_init_security.c                */
/* Purpose:     Initializes the server with authentication.    */
/*              This code is exactly the same as hw_server_init.c, */
/*              except that you need to add this call after the   */
/*              call to rpc_ep_register().                 */
   .
   .
   .
/* Register key-technology information.  */
❶  rpc_server_register_auth_info(
      getenv("SERVER_PRINCIPAL"),
      rpc_c_authn_secret,
      NULL,
      NULL,
      &status
   );
   .
   .
   .
```

❶ The call to **rpc_server_register_auth_info** establishes that the server will use a private key and that it will be storing the key in the Security Server's key table.

*Example A-9: Secure remote procedure:*
*get_hello_world_security.c*

```
/* File name:   get_hello_world_security.c    */
/* Purpose:     Returns a string to a client     */
/*              Cannot be used in a multithreaded */
/*              server due to unsynchronized      */
/*              access to shared data.            */
#include <pthread.h>              /* Includes jackets for C RTL */
#include <stdio.h>
#include "hello_world.h"
/* Shared data that should be protected */
static int calls_processed = 0;
void get_hello_world(return_string)
    string_type return_string;
{
/* Tip: for production-ready code, remove these    */
/*     declarations and the inquiry routine, and   */
/*     place them in an ACL manager routine.        */
/*     Then call the ACL manager as the first       */
/*     statement in every server routine.           */
   rpc_authz_handle_t                      privs;
   unsigned_char_p_t     server_princ_name = NULL;
   unsigned32                      protect_level;
```

*Example A-9: Secure remote procedure:*
         *get_hello_world_security.c  (continued)*

```
unsigned32                          authn_svc;
unsigned32                          authz_svc;
unsigned32                             status;

/*  What protection level is the client using?   */
   rpc_binding_inq_auth_client( hello_handle,
                                &privs,
                                &server_princ_name,
                                &protect_level,
                                &authn_svc,
                                &authz_svc,
                                &status);

/* If the client isn't using correct authorization, */
/* then the application rejects it.                  */
   if ((status == rpc_s_binding_has_no_auth) ||
       (authn_svc == rpc_c_authn_none)       ||
       (protect_level == rpc_c_protect_level_connect)){
         sprintf((char*) return_string, "Go away!");
   }
   else{
      sprintf((char*)return_string, "hello world, call #%d.",
              calls_processed++);
   }
}
```

# A.4  The Application with Error Checking, Mutexes, and Server-Group Registration

This application is the threaded application with proper error checking and mutexes. (When using the CHECK_STATUS macro, specify arguments for an input status, a comment, and an action to take.) The server routine is reentrant. We have thrown in one more step toward generalizing the application: we register the server in a CDS group by calling the **rpc_ns_group_mbr_add** routine. When you run this server on multiple hosts, the client can request it by the group name and can be assured of reaching at least one server in the group (as long as all of their hosts are up and running).

*Example A-10:  Complete client code: get_hello_world_complete*

```
/* File name:    get_hello_world_complete.c             */
/* Purpose:      Returns a string to a client.          */
/*               Utilizes a mutex to support            */
/*               multithreaded access to shared data    */
/*               (calls_processed).                      */
```

*Example A-10:  Complete client code: get_hello_world_complete  (continued)*

```
#include <pthread.h>    /* Includes jackets for C RTL */
#include <stdio.h>
#include "hello_world.h"
#include "check_status.h"
/* Server Shared data */
extern int            calls_processed;
extern pthread_mutex_t  mutex_for_calls_processed;
void get_hello_world(return_string)
    string_type return_string;
{
    int status;                  /* pthread status value    */
    int local_calls_processed;  /* Copy of shared data value */

    /*  Lock mutex before accessing global server data */
    status = pthread_mutex_lock(&mutex_for_calls_processed);
    CHECK_STATUS(status,"Mutex lock failed:", ABORT);

    /* Make local copy of value, so we can free the mutex quickly */
    local_calls_processed = calls_processed++;

    /* Unlock mutex so other threads can access it */
    status = pthread_mutex_unlock(&mutex_for_calls_processed);
    CHECK_STATUS(status,"Mutex unlock failed:", ABORT);

    sprintf((char*)return_string, "hello world, call #%d",
        local_calls_processed);
}
```

*Example A-11:  Complete client code: fetch_string_complete.c*

```
/* File name:      fetch_string_complete.c                */
/* Purpose:        This is the complete client code.  It's */
/*                 fetch_string.c with error checking.      */
#include <stdio.h>
#include <pthread.h>
#include "hello_world.h"
#include "check_status.h"
static int             fetch_string();
static void            print_message();
main()
{
    string_type        returned_string;
    pthread_t          thread_for_rpc;       /* type defined in pthread.h */
    pthread_t          thread_for_messages;  /* type defined in pthread.h */
    int                rpc_thread_status;    /* Status from RPC thread    */
    int                status;               /* pthread status code       */
    printf("Client: I'm fetching the message from the server.\n");
    status = pthread_create(
          &thread_for_rpc,
          pthread_attr_default,
```

*Example A-11: Complete client code: fetch_string_complete.c  (continued)*

```
            (pthread_startroutine_t)fetch_string,
            (pthread_addr_t)returned_string
    );
    CHECK_STATUS(status,"Thread create failed:", ABORT);
    status = pthread_create(
            &thread_for_messages,
            pthread_attr_default,
            (pthread_startroutine_t)print_message,
            (pthread_addr_t)NULL
    );
    CHECK_STATUS(status,"Thread create failed:", ABORT);
    /* Wait for RPC call to complete */
    status = pthread_join(thread_for_rpc, (pthread_addr_t)&rpc_thread_status);
    CHECK_STATUS(status,"Thread join failed:", ABORT);
    /* Cancel thread providing user feed back */
    status = pthread_cancel(thread_for_messages);
    CHECK_STATUS(status,"Thread cancel failed:", ABORT);
    /* Display the string returned from the server */
    if (rpc_thread_status == 1)
        printf("\nFrom Server: %s\n", returned_string);
    else
        printf("\nRPC call failed.\n");
}
/* Routine that performs the remote call */
static fetch_string(returned_string)
    string_type     returned_string;
{
    get_hello_world(returned_string);  /* remote call */
    return 1;
}
/* Routine that performs other work during remote call */
static void print_message()
{
    struct timespec     delay;              /* type defined in pthread.h */
    int status;
    memset(&delay, 0, sizeof(delay));
    delay.tv_sec = 2;

    printf ("Waiting");  fflush(stdout);
    while (1) {
        printf (".");  fflush(stdout);
        status = pthread_delay_np(&delay);
        CHECK_STATUS(status,"delay failed:", ABORT);
    }
}
```

*Example A-12:  Multithreaded server's initialiation file:*
                *hw_server_init_complete.c*

```
/* File name:     hw_server_init_complete.c                    */
/* Purpose:       Multithreaded server initialization, with    */
/*                error checking.                               */
#include <pthread.h>
#include <stdio.h>
#include <ctype.h>
#include "hello_world.h"
#include "check_status.h"
#define STRINGLEN 80
/* Server global data */
/* Number of calls processed by the server thus far */
int calls_processed = 0;
/* Mutex to protect the calls_processed variable */
pthread_mutex_t        mutex_for_calls_processed;
main()
{
    unsigned32                            status;
    rpc_binding_vector_t        *binding_vector;
    char                  entry_name[STRINGLEN];
    char           .      group_name[STRINGLEN];
    char                   hostname[STRINGLEN];

    /* Initialize mutex for the calls processed counter */
    status = pthread_mutex_init(
             &mutex_for_calls_processed,
             pthread_mutexattr_default
          );
    CHECK_STATUS(status,"Mutex init failed:", ABORT);
    /* Register interface */
    rpc_server_register_if(
       hello_world_v1_0_s_ifspec,
       NULL,
       NULL,
       &status
    );
    CHECK_STATUS(status,"Server registration failed:", ABORT);

    /* Register protocol sequences */
    rpc_server_use_all_protseqs(rpc_c_protseq_max_reqs_default, &status);
    CHECK_STATUS(status,"Protocol registration failed ", ABORT);

    /* Get binding information for server */
    rpc_server_inq_bindings(&binding_vector, &status);
    CHECK_STATUS(status,"Server inq bindings failed:", ABORT);
    /* Devise an entry name using the host name */
    strcpy(entry_name, "/.:/hello_svr_");
    gethostname(hostname, STRINGLEN);
    strcat(entry_name, hostname);
    /* Export server information to the namespace */
    rpc_ns_binding_export(
```

*Example A-12: Multithreaded server's initialiation file:*
*hw_server_init_complete.c (continued)*

```
    rpc_c_ns_syntax_default,
    (unsigned_char_t *)entry_name,
    hello_world_v1_0_s_ifspec,
    binding_vector,
    NULL,
    &status
);
CHECK_STATUS(status,"Export failed:", ABORT);
/* Add entry to name service hello world group */
/* This allows clients to search through a list of appropriate */
/* servers. */
strcpy(group_name, "/.:/hello_group");
rpc_ns_group_mbr_add(
    rpc_c_ns_syntax_default,
    (unsigned_char_t *)group_name,
    rpc_c_ns_syntax_default,
    (unsigned_char_t *)entry_name,
    &status
);
CHECK_STATUS(status,"Group add failed:", ABORT);
/* Register with endpoint database (rpcd database) */
rpc_ep_register(
    hello_world_v1_0_s_ifspec,
    binding_vector,
    NULL,
    (unsigned_char_t *)"Hello World Interface",
    &status
);
CHECK_STATUS(status,"Server ep registration failed:", ABORT);
/* Free binding handles */
rpc_binding_vector_free(&binding_vector, &status);
CHECK_STATUS(status,"Binding free failed:", ABORT);

/* Create up to 4 threads to serve client requests */
rpc_server_listen(4, &status);
}
```

*Example A-13: Error-checking code: check_status.h*

```
/* File name:     check_status.h                              */
/* Purpose:       To provide error checking to the application. */

#include <stdio.h>
#include <dce/dce_error.h>  /* required for dce_error_inq_text() use */
#include <dce/pthread.h>    /* required if using threads */
#include <dce/rpcexc.h>     /* required if using exceptions */
#define RESUME  0
#define ABORT   1
static int                                   error_stat;
```

*Example A-13:  Error-checking code: check_status.h  (continued)*

```
static unsigned char error_string[dce_c_error_string_len];
void exit();
#define CHECK_STATUS(input_status, comment, action)\
{\
    if(input_status != rpc_s_ok)        \
    {\
        dce_error_inq_text (input_status, error_string, &error_stat); \
        fprintf(stderr,"%s %s\n", comment, error_string); \
        if (action==ABORT)\
        {\
            exit(1);\
        }\
    }\
}
```

# A.5   A Sample Make File

The writers of this book used this makefile to develop the bare-bones, the
threaded, and the error-checking/mutex code.

*Example A-14:  Sample Make File*

```
#  File name:    makefile.hello
#. Purpose:      Build the sample applications

#  Environment variables for libraries and for debugging.
LIBS    = -ldce -lcma -li -ldnet
CDEBUG  = -g
CFLAGS  = -I. $(CDEBUG)

#  By default, the file builds the sample application, both
#     the client and server portions.
default : hello_client hello_server

#  For the sample client.
hello_client : fetch_string.o hello_world_cstub.o
        $(CC) $(CFLAGS) -o hello_client \
            fetch_string.o hello_world_cstub.o $(LIBS)

#  For the sample server.
hello_server : hw_server_init.o get_hello_world.o hello_world_sstub.o
        $(CC) $(CFLAGS) -o hello_server \
            hw_server_init.o get_hello_world.o hello_world_sstub.o $(LIBS)

# Dependancies on hello_world.h
fetch_string.c hw_server_init.c : hello_world.h

hello_world_cstub.o hello_world_sstub.o hello_world.h : hello_world.idl
        idl hello_world.idl

#  For cleaning up the directory
```

*Example A-14:  Sample Make File  (continued)*

```
clean:
        rm -f hello_client hello_server *.o hello_*stub.c \
           hello_world.h *.dat

#  For the client prototype

hello_client_basic : fetch_string_basic.o hello_world_cstub.o
        $(CC) $(CFLAGS) -o hello_client_basic \
            fetch_string_basic.o hello_world_cstub.o $(LIBS)

fetch_string_basic.c : hello_world.h

#  For the client with security.
hello_client_security : fetch_string_security.o hello_world_cstub.o
        $(CC) $(CFLAGS) -o hello_client_security \
            fetch_string_security.o hello_world_cstub.o $(LIBS)

#  For the server with security.
hello_server_security : hw_server_init_security.o \
            get_hello_world_security.o hello_world_sstub.o
        $(CC) $(CFLAGS) -o hello_server_security \
            hw_server_init_security.o get_hello_world_security.o \
                hello_world_sstub.o $(LIBS)

# Dependancies on hello_world.h
fetch_string_secrity.c hw_server_init_security.c \
            get_hello_world_security : hello_world.h

#  For the complete example
#
fetch_string_complete.c hw_server_init_complete.c : hello_world.h

hello_client_complete : fetch_string_complete.o get_hello_world_complete.o \
            hello_world_cstub.o
        $(CC) $(CFLAGS) -o hello_client_complete \
            fetch_string_complete.o hello_world_cstub.o $(LIBS)
hello_server_complete : hw_server_init_complete.o \
            get_hello_world_complete.o \
            hello_world_sstub.o
        $(CC) $(CFLAGS) -o hello_server_complete \
            hw_server_init_complete.o get_hello_world_complete.o \
                hello_world_sstub.o $(LIBS)
```

To build the skeleton client code (Section sAbarebones), invoke these commands:

```
C> make  -f  makefile.hello  hello_client_basic
```

To build the threaded application (Section A.2), invoke these commands:

```
C> make  -f  makefile.hello  hello_client
S> make  -f  makefile.hello  hello_server
```

Before building the application with authentication, you need to rename the **hello_world_security.acf** file to be **hello_world.acf**. (The IDL compiler automatically compiles an **.acf** file that has the same name as the **.idl** file [**hello_world**].) When you are finished building this application, rename the file back to **hello_world_security.acf**, so that it won't be mistakenly used for subsequent builds.

To build the application with authentication (Section A.3), invoke these commands:

```
C> make  -f  makefile.hello  hello_client_security
S> make  -f  makefile.hello  hello_server_security
```

To build the complete application (Section sAapplerror), invoke these commands:

```
C> make  -f  makefile.hello  hello_client_complete
S> make  -f  makefile.hello  hello_server_complete
```

# B

# *Common DCE Questions ... and Some Answers*

We regret that we don't have the opportunity to answer your questions in person. So we've done the next best thing: we wrote down all the questions we had or heard while writing this book, answered them, and placed them in this appendix for you. We probably didn't cover every possible question, but, hopefully, we've eliminated a dozen or so from your list.

These questions and answers are organized according to job category: planners' and purchasers' questions (general questions), network-administrator questions, and application-programmer questions.

## *B.1 "I was just wondering ... "*

### *How do I buy DCE? Do I buy it from OSF?*

You cannot buy DCE from OSF, because OSF is not in the business of selling software. You buy DCE from OSF licensees, who package and sell products.

The Open Software Foundation (OSF) is a consortium of companies that work together to develop software in the open systems market. OSF decides to implement a technology and invites its members to submit applications to develop the software. The chosen company or companies develop the software—with OSF providing leadership—and provide the technology to OSF. In turn, OSF provides the source code (for software and documentation) to all companies who license the DCE software. The member companies port the code to their platforms, package the software, sell the product, and provide royalties to OSF. OSF then provides a percentage of the money to those companies that developed the software.

The OSF DCE software was developed from submissions by Digital Equipment Corporation (CDS, DTS, portions of RPC, and Threads), Hewlett-Packard Company (portions of RPC, Security, Diskless Support), International Business Machines Corporation (software integration), Siemens Nixdorf Informationssysteme AG (GDS, XDS), and Transarc Corporation (DFS and LFS).

There is also an impressive list of companies and groups that have pledged to support DCE. This lists includes IBM, Hewlett-Packard, Sun Microsystems, Digital, Hitachi, and the Unix Software Laboratory (USL).

## Can I use DCE Directory Service names in electronic mail or in my system's command for login?

It depends on the level of support for DCE within the vendor's operating system. It is certainly possible for operating system commands and utilities to recognize DCE names. As a minimum level of support, most operating systems will accept a DCE name when someone logs in.

## What determines which machine I'm logged in to?

DCE does not specify a strict process by which a user logs in. DCE's only requirement is that, at some time, the user must obtain credentials from the Security server to use DCE services.

At least one implementer has decided to integrate the local login process with the DCE login authentication process. When someone logs in to a system, the system uses the password given to the local system to establish DCE credentials. Remember that this is one possible implementation. A vendor could require the user to authenticate as a second action, once the user is logged in to the local system.

There are cell-environment details that determine how seamless the "virtual machine" is, the goal being that a user should be able to log in from any machine in the cell. For instance, one option that requires a lot of overhead is to create user accounts on every machine for every user in a cell. Another option is to provide a default account on each machine, for use by people logging in to a machine other than the one they usually use. Using DFS and DCE applications, you can work from the default account much in the same way you can from your own office.

There is still a human interface issue in regard to the local user environments. What if a user logs in to a machine running an unfamiliar operating system? Even though the files and applications can be made available across machines in a cell, some basic knowledge of the local operating system is still required to log in, to invoke applications, to print, and so forth. This problem can be solved by using a windowing system, such as Motif, that runs on many types of machines within the cell. Another solution is to provide the same basic utilities across machines: common ways to log in, to execute distributed applications, to print files, to send Mail, and so forth.

## *I've invested in many applications, like word-processing and database software. How can I use this software in a distributed environment?*

Although the DCE layers on top of your operating system, it allows users and application programs to use the operating system environment exactly as they had done before the installation of DCE. (Threads can actually be incorporated into your operating system or can be layered on top.) So your word-processing and database software will continue to run exactly as it had previously.

If you want your applications to become distributed applications that use DCE, then someone must rewrite either the operating system (to recognize DCE names passed to it by the application) or the application. For example, an application that used to access files on a single system can access files across the network using CDS and DFS, but the application or operating system must be modified to make calls to these DCE components.

## *Just how many name services are there in DCE, anyway?*

There is one name service, called the DCE Directory Service, which has a cell-local component, two global components, and an agent that determines which global component to use to resolve the name. Matters are complicated further in that the two global components have three alternative labels, and there is an application programming interface.

The DCE Directory Service has two major components, called the Cell Directory Service (CDS) for naming within a cell and the Global Directory Service (GDS) for naming outside the scope of cells. GDS is based on the X.500 directory services standard (ISO 9594 and CCITT X.500).

The DCE Directory Service also recognizes another type of global name: a Domain Name System (DNS, or BIND) name. DCE supports the version of DNS based on Internet Request for Comments (RFC 1034 and 1035).

When CDS determines that a name is not in its own cell, it passes the name to a Global Directory Agent (GDA). The GDA locates the appropriate naming environment (GDS or DNS) and uses it to resolve the reference.

To access the DCE Directory Service from an application program, use the X/Open Directory Services application programming interface, which is based on the 1988 CCITT X.500 Series of Recommendations and the ISO 9594 standard.

So, the DCE Directory Service is the name service. It contains CDS, the GDA, and GDS (X.500), and it interacts with DNS (BIND) and the XDS API.

## Can a DCE cell and non-DCE software communicate using X.500 or DNS naming protocols?

DCE cannot currently share services with non-DCE systems using different protocols, like NFS or NIS. OSF and the software implementers are looking into supporting external X.500 and Domain Name System (DNS) requests into DCE cells, but no decisions have been made.

Since X.500 and DNS are standards recognized outside of DCE, a DCE application should be able to access an entry stored in these global directories. For instance, you can log in remotely with a DNS host name from a machine in a DCE cell. However, remember that the only DCE-supported use of X.500 and BIND is to connect the CDS hierarchies of two different DCE cells.

## What is the difference between a clerk and a client? Are they the same?

A clerk is a client with a limited function. A client usually fetches information from a server, processes it, and applies it to some task. A clerk is a client whose sole purpose is to fetch information from a server and pass it off to another user or application. For example, the CDS clerk's sole purpose is to provide name information to other applications or to users. It performs other tasks, such as caching information, but only to serve its main purpose of delivering information.

## Just what is a daemon? And how is it different from a server or a clerk?

A daemon is running process that is not connected to a terminal. So any server or clerk that runs on a machine in the background, waiting for a user or code to connect to it, is a daemon. Most servers are daemons. Whether a client is a daemon depends on the application design. (Does the client need to be directly connected to a terminal? Does the client perform a task that very few users need?)

Sometimes an application can make special use of daemons outside the scope of a client and server. For example, the RPC Daemon is a process that provides the process endpoint of a server to clients. The CDS Advertiser is also a specialized daemon. Again, whether you need a specialized daemon for an application you're writing depends on design issues.

*If the operating system doesn't support multiple processing streams within a process context, how do you implement Threads as a "layered product"?*

This is an implementation detail determined by the DCE vendor and by the operating system. For instance, some operating systems simulate some of the Thread-scheduling duties using signals or some type of system interrupt.

The rule of thumb is that when Threads is a layered implementation, you should use it only in applications that are not time critical, because computing time will be significantly slower. With layered-Threads scheduling, all of the threads in a given process have to share the time allocated to that process by the operating system. Furthermore, the real-time scheduling policies are effective only within the process. The operating system still carries out its normal time-sharing, and can therefore suspend the whole process in order to run other processes.

# B.2 "I'm a system administrator, and I was wondering ..."

### *How big is a cell? How many nodes should it contain?*

DCE cells are designed to accommodate from 1 node to an infinite number. However, let's deal with reality. The performance degradation—regardless of the circumstances of your computing situation—will be unbearable once you surpass approximately 10,000 users (which translates to hundreds of machines).

You need to factor in various criteria to form a guestimate for an appropriate cell size, because there aren't enough DCE cells currently in existence to speak from experience. For instance, as discussed previously (Section 11.1), you need to analyze the needs of the users in the cell, the security requirements, the administrative requirements, the non-DCE-related computing overhead, and the number of distributed applications layered on DCE to determine how many nodes a cell must comprise to suit your particular requirements.

### *Do we need to buy new machines to effectively install and use DCE?*

Theoretically, you don't. You need only one system, the software, and a network connection. However, the power of your cell may be affected by the amount of compute power you have in it. For example, depending on the load that it is carrying (which in turn depends on the application requirements of the system), you will probably want a separate machine for DCE-component servers. If a machine carries a significant non-DCE load, you way want to place DCE component servers on separate machines. The extent to which your programmers use DCE to create their own client-server programs may also create a need for more hardware, because the number of servers in your cell increases.

## *What is the minimum that I have to do to create a DCE cell?*

Install and configure a CDS server, a DTS server, and a Security server. Elsewhere on the LAN, install and configure a CDS clerk, a DTS clerk, and a Security clerk on each system that will participate in the cell. During the configuration of each client system, DCE adds information to CDS (adds a name for the node to the cell's database) and Security (adds the node and its users as principals in the Registry database, propagates ACL entries for new principals, and so forth).

## *Do I need to log in as superuser to install and configure DCE?*

Yes and no. You need superuser privilege to install DCE.

To configure DCE, your UNIX account does not have to have superuser privileges (or the equivalent privileges on other operating systems). However, you must log in to an account called **cell_admin**, which has superuser-like permission.

It's difficult to talk about the specifics of configuration for two reasons. First, cell-wide administration differs slightly from component administration. For instance, if you need to configure only DTS servers, you can log in to the **dts_admin** account, you can assign the **dts_admin** identity to one or more principals, or you can give a principal a subset of administration privileges. This enables groups of people, working from their own accounts, to have privileges to perform administration of a given component. (At the time of this writing, there is no way to associate the **cell_admin** identity with different principals; to perform cell-wide administration, you must log in to the **cell_admin** account.)

The second issue that makes it difficult to discuss this topic is that the DCE implementors provided the product developers with more flexibility in the administration area. The DCE administration concepts and commands are the same, but some defaults and operating system hooks will vary from product to product.

## *Can admin identities be associated with more than one principal?*

Yes. It can even be associated with a group, so you can enable or disable access to a set of users together.

### Do I need to install and use the Distributed File Service?

By design, you use only the pieces of DCE that you need. So, no, you don't need to use DFS. However, we recommend that you do.

Some people are recommending that, since DFS has not been around as long as the other DCE components (it didn't make it into OSF DCE Version 1.0), you shouldn't install and use it. On the other hand, most people say that DFS is the most useful service to DCE end users, that everyone wants to be able to access files on other machines as if they resided on local disks.

### Do I need to install and use Diskless Support?

You don't have to install and use Diskless Support. But again, we predict that, once it reaches a robust state, you will want to use it. The fastest growing area in software networking involves PCs, machines with limited disk resources. Allowing your PC users to tap into the power of DCE will greatly increase productivity.

### Are the authentication server and privilege server and security server the same thing, or are they different bodies of code?

These are all names for the same process, which is **secd**, short for "Security daemon." There are three logical pieces to the security: PasswdEtc., the privilege "server," and the authentication "server." PasswdEtc. manages user accounts. The privilege server maintains group information. And the authentication server, which is also called the Kerberos KDC—Key Distribution Center—authenticates principals. One given incarnation of **secd** runs on one host system.

## B.3 "I'm an application programmer, and I have a friend who was just wondering . . ."

### Can I write DCE application programs in languages other than C? Please?

We don't recommend that you do, but you can. However, it may cost you more than you are willing to pay (Section 9.3). If you are going to venture into this swamp, you must choose a language that supports reentrant functions, design your IDL declarations so that they map to languages in your data type, translate required **.h** files to your language, call remote procedures using C calling conventions (because the stub code follows those conventions), and deal with the myriad of thread reentrancy issues involved (especially with previously written code).

## *When using C, can I use any C compiler? How can any C compiler recognize the IDL-portable data types?*

Yes, you can use any ANSI C compiler. (The implementers say that you can use most pre-ANSI C compilers, too.) The portable data types are simply typedefs that use ANSI C data types.

## *What type of code can constitute a thread? Can a loop body be a thread, or does it have to be one complete routine?*

The Threads designers intended that programmers execute a routine and all its nested subroutines in a thread. The routine that creates a thread accepts a single entry point or instruction address. If you want to stray from their original design intention by using an instruction address that doesn't map onto a routine, then you are in uncharted and unsupported territory, my friend. Best of luck to you.

## *If I have an interface name and version number, why do I also need a UUID?*

You need a UUID to be unique across cells. Someone in another cell may have used your interface name and version number for another application.

## *If I move my application from one DCE cell to another, will I have a UUID collision problem?*

No, because the UUIDs are structured so that no two cells generate the same identification strings. A UUID is actually a combination of a network address and a timestamp. If you've registered your cell with the DNS or GDS naming authorities (see Appendix D), then your UUID will be unique.

## *I know how to register my RPC interface. But can I deregister it, freeing that identification string for some other application interface?*

You can, but we recommend that you don't worry about it. There are plenty of UUIDs to go around, and this includes running lots of test client-server programs that you will delete once you get used to RPC and Threads programming. If you attempt to reuse UUIDs, there is a danger that you will have two bodies of code from two separate applications trying to talk to one another.

## *How do I automatically activate my server when the host is booted?*

It depends on your system. You want to execute your server initialization program as a daemon, a running process that is not connected to a terminal. In general you place the activation of your server in a script that runs at boot time.

### *Can I write my own jackets for nonreentrant code?*

Yes, you can. Have your application call the jacket routine whenever you want to execute the nonreentrant code. Your jacket routine can use either local mutexes or one global mutex to protect the global data of that routine.

## *Will RPC ever "time out" on me? And what happens if the host node containing my application's server goes down?*

There are occasions when a server will be unavailable (the host system could be down or the network may be experiencing problems). If this happens, your client code should have a provision for recovering from a communications failure. For example, you can use the explicit binding method, string bindings, and CDS group entries to search through a list of servers for a given application, using another server when a preferred one is down (Section A.4).

# C

# *External Time Providers and Services*

Over time, the DTS servers in a cell will drift from the Coordinated Universal Time (UTC). As mentioned in Section 7.3, an external time provider can supply an accurate measure of UTC to the servers, which in turn adjust time within the cell.

The DTS servers can receive a measure of UTC from a hardware hook up (for instance, from a WWV short-wave radio receiver, a satellite receiver, or a modem) or from a software source that's connected to their cell (NTP, which is a distributed time service on TCP/IP). To enable communication between a DTS server and an external time provider, you need to write some code using the DTS time-provider interface. This code is unique to the type of external time provider you use, and it runs in a process separate from the DTS server. To get a feel for using the time-provider interface, take a look at the code examples and descriptions provided with OSF DCE implementations.

We've gathered some contact information about time providers and placed it in this appendix for you. There are several sources of UTC time, including telephone, radio, and satellite

## C.1   *Telephone Services*

Telephone time-provider services require the time-provider software to dial a centralized UTC time source through a modem. Modem speeds and line delays can affect the accuracy of the time returned.

Telephone time-provider services are usually provided by standards agencies. For example, in the United States this service is offered by the National Institute of Standards and Technology (NIST), with its Automated Computer Time Service (ACTS), and by the U.S. Naval Observatory, with its Automated Data Service (ADS). There is often a per-call fee for the service in addition to the cost of the modem software. For telephone time-provider services in other countries, contact the applicable standards organization listed in Table C-1.

# C.2  Radio Broadcasts

Commercial radio receivers that monitor time and frequency broadcasts can return time values back through the time-provider interface to a DTS server. Standards organizations usually operate radio stations that broadcast time and frequency signals. In the United States, NIST operates the following time and frequency stations:

**WWV**       Transmits at 2.5, 5, 10, 15 MHz to North America and South America.

**WWVB**      Transmits at 60 KHz primarily to the United States, providing high-quality frequency information because atmospheric propagation effects are relatively minor.

**WWVH**      Transmits at 2.5, 5, 10, 15 MHz to Alaska, Hawaii, Australia, New Zealand, Japan, and Southeast Asia.

The following stations are available in Europe:

**MSF**       Broadcasts from England at 60 KHz.

**DCF77**     Broadcasts from Germany at 77.5 KHz.

In addition to the stations listed above, more than 30 radio stations worldwide provide UTC time. See the partial list in Table C-1 to contact the national standards organization in your country for further information.

*Table C-1  UTC Radio Stations and Managing Authorities*

| Call Letters | Authority |
| --- | --- |
| ATA | National Physical Laboratory<br>Dr. K.S. Krishnan Rd.<br>New Delhi, - 110012, India |
| BPM | Shaanxi Astronomical Observatory<br>Chinese Academy of Sciences<br>P.O. Box 18 - Lintong<br>Shaanxi, China |

*Table C-1  UTC Radio Stations and Managing Authorities (continued)*

| Call Letters | Authority |
| --- | --- |
| BSF | Telecommunication Laboratories<br>Directorate General of Telecommunications<br>Ministry of Communications<br>P.O. Box 71 - Chung-Li<br>32099 Taiwan, R.O.C. |
| CHU | National Research Council<br>Institute for National Measurement Standards -<br>Time Standards<br>Ottawa, Ontario, Canada  K1A OR6 |
| DCF77 | Physikalisch-Technische<br>Bundesanstalt, Lab.  Zeiteinheit<br>Bundesallee 100<br>W - 3300 Braunschweig<br>Federal Republic of Germany |
| EBC | Real Instituto y Observatorio<br>de la Armada - San Fernando<br>Cadiz, Spain |
| HBG | Service horaire HBG<br>Observatoire Cantonal<br>CH - 2000 Neuchatel, Switzerland |
| HLA | Time and Frequency Laboratory<br>Korea Standards Research Institute<br>P.O. Box 3, Taedok Science Town<br>Taejon 305-606, Republic of Korea |
| IBF | Istituto Elettrotecnico Nazionale<br>Galileo Ferraris<br>Strada delle Cacce, 91<br>10135 - Torino, Italy |
| JJY<br>JG2AS | Standards and Measurements Div.<br>Communications Research Laboratory<br>2-1, Nukui-kitamachi 4-chome<br>Koganei-shi, Tokyo<br>184 Japan |
| LOL | Director, Observatorio Naval<br>Av. Espana 2099<br>1107 - Buenos Aires, Republica Argentina |
| MSF | National Physical Laboratory<br>Division of Electrical Science<br>Teddington, Middlesex TW11 OLW<br>United Kingdom |

*Table C-1 UTC Radio Stations and Managing Authorities (continued)*

| Call Letters | Authority |
|---|---|
| PPE<br>PPR | Departemento Servico da hora<br>Observatorio Nacional (CNPq)<br>Rua General Bruce, 586<br>20921 Rio de Janeiro - RJ, Brazil |
| TDF | Centre National d'Etudes des<br>Telecommunications - PAB - STC<br>Etalons de frequence et de temps<br>196 Ave. Henri Ravera<br>92220 - Bagneux, France |
| WWV<br>WWVB<br>WWVH | Time and Frequency Division<br>National Institute of Standards and Technology<br>325 Broadway<br>Boulder, Colorado 80303, U.S.A |
| YVTO | Direccion de Hidrografia y Navegacion<br>Observatorio Cagigal<br>Apartado Postal No. 6745<br>Caracas, Venezuela |

Table C-2 presents a list of DCE-supported radio receivers.

*Table C-2 Radio Receiver Manufacturers*

| Model | Manufacturer |
|---|---|
| GCW-1001 | Heathkit<br>Heath Company<br>Benton Harbor, MI 49022<br>U.S.A.<br>Tel. 616-982-3200 |
| 6020 | Hopf Elektronik, Gmbh<br>Postfach 1847<br>D-5880 Luedenscheid<br>Federal Republic of Germany<br>Tel. 49-(0)2351-45038 |
| OEM-10 | PSTI (See Traconex) |

*Table C-2  Radio Receiver Manufacturers (continued)*

| Model | Manufacturer |
|-------|--------------|
| 8170 | Spectracom Corp.<br>101 Despatch Drive<br>Rochester, NY 14445<br>U.S.A.<br>Tel. 716-381-4827 |
| 1020 | Traconex Corp.<br>3510 Bassett St.<br>Santa Clara, CA 95054<br>U.S.A.<br>Tel. 408-727-0260 |

# C.3  Satellites

Satellites have worldwide availability; they can provide relatively precise times if their delays are known and compensated for. See the following list for satellite sources of UTC:

**GOES**    Geostationary Operational Environmental Satellite is a satellite network operated by the U.S. National Oceanic and Atmospheric Administration (NOAA). Coverage is limited to the Western Hemisphere.

**GPS**    Global Positioning System is a satellite system operated by the U.S. Department of Defense (DoD). GPS is available worldwide.

**TRANSIT**    U.S. Navy satellite system is available worldwide.

# D

# *Registering a Name: GDS and DNS*

Since DCE cells and their resources do not operate in a DCE vacuum, chances are great that you are going to have to interact with people outside your DCE cell, and outsiders are going to have to interact with you. Before you configure your cell, get a globally unique cell name from the GDS or DNS global naming authorities. Then, your cell will be known to the outside world. We recommend that you obtain a global name for your cell, even if you have no immediate plans to use a Global Directory Service, because you may wish to do so in the future. We've gathered information on registering a cell name, and we provide it here for you.

## *D.1   Obtaining a Unique GDS Cell Name*

To obtain a unique GDS cell name, contact the administrator in charge of the portion of the DIT under which you want to name your cell.

For example, in the United States, the American National Standards Institute (ANSI) delegates X.500 names subordinate to the entry (/C=US). Suppose you are an employee of ABC, a U.S. corporation interested in participating in a worldwide X.500 directory. If you want to configure a single cell whose name is (/C=US/O=ABC), you would contact ANSI to reserve ABC as a unique organization name. After you have an official organization name, if you want to configure multiple cells and name them based on organization units, you would contact a naming authority within your company to establish a cell entry such as (/C=US/O=ABC/OU=Sales).

Send X.500 name registration requests to the following address:

American National Standards Institute
1430 Broadway
New York, NY 10018
Telephone: (212) 642-4976

The person making the request to ANSI is responsible for ensuring that your organization does not send more than one request for an organization name. Once you receive your organization name, we recommend that your organization set up a central administrative authority to manage names subordinate to the unique name.

# D.2  Obtaining a Unique DNS Cell Name

To obtain a unique DNS name, contact the administrator in charge of the subtree under which you want to name your cell. Send registration requests to the NIC at the following Internet address, telephone numbers, or mailing address between the hours of 7:00 a.m. and 7:00 p.m. Eastern Standard Time:

**HOSTMASTER@NIC.DDN.MIL**

(800) 365-3642 or (703) 802-4535

Government Systems, Inc.
Attention: Network Information Center (NIC)
4200 Park Meadow Drive
Chantilly, VA  22021

# *Index*

# Programming

# UNIX, C and MULTI-PLATFORM

*Books from O'Reilly & Associates, Inc.*

Fall/Winter 1995-96

## C Programming Libraries

### Practical C++ Programming

*By Steve Oualline*
*1st Edition September 1995*
*584 pages, ISBN 1-56592-139-9*

Fast becoming the standard language of commercial software development, C++ is an update of the C programming language, adding object-oriented features that are very helpful for today's larger graphical applications.

*Practical C++ Programming* is a complete introduction to the C++ language for the beginning programmer, and also for C programmers transitioning to C++. Unlike most other C++ books, this book emphasizes a practical, real-world approach, including how to debug, how to make your code understandable to others, and how to understand other people's code. Topics covered include good programming style, C++ syntax (what to use and what not to use), C++ class design, debugging and optimization, and common programming mistakes. At the end of each chapter are a number of exercises you can use to make sure you've grasped the concepts. Solutions to most are provided.

*Practical C++ Programming* describes standard C++ features that are supported by all UNIX C++ compilers (including *gcc*), DOS/Windows and NT compilers (including Microsoft Visual C++), and Macintosh compilers.

### C++: The Core Language

*By Gregory Satir & Doug Brown*
*1st Edition October 1995*
*228 pages, ISBN 1-56592-116-X*

A first book for C programmers transitioning to C++, an object-oriented enhancement of the C programming language. Designed to get readers up to speed quickly, this book thoroughly explains the important concepts and features and gives brief overviews of the rest of the language. Covers features common to all C++ compilers, including those on UNIX, Windows NT, Windows, DOS, and Macs.

### Porting UNIX Software

*By Greg Lehey*
*1st Edition November 1995*
*480 pages (est.), ISBN 1-56592-126-7*

This book deals with the whole life cycle of porting, from setting up a source tree on your system to correcting platform differences and even testing the executable after it's built. It exhaustively discusses the differences between versions of UNIX and the areas where porters tend to have problems. The assumption made in this book is that you just want to get a package working on your system; you don't want to become an expert in the details of your hardware or operating system (much less an expert in the system used by the person who wrote the package!).

FOR INFORMATION: **800-998-9938**, 707-829-0515; **INFO@ORA.COM**; **HTTP://WWW.ORA.COM/**

### Programming with Pthreads

By Bradford Nichols
1st Edition February 1996 (est.)
350 pages (est.), ISBN 1-56592-115-1

The idea behind POSIX threads is to have multiple tasks running concurrently within the same program. They can share a single CPU as processes do, or take advantage of multiple CPUs when available. In either case, they provide a clean way to divide the tasks of a program while sharing data. This book features realistic examples, a look behind the scenes at the implementation and performance issues, and chapters on special topics such as DCE, real-time, and multiprocessing.

### POSIX.4

By Bill Gallmeister
1st Edition January 1995
570 pages, ISBN 1-56592-074-0

A general introduction to real-time programming and real-time issues, this book covers the POSIX.4 standard and how to use it to solve "real-world" problems. If you're at all interested in real-time applications—which include just about everything from telemetry to transaction processing—this book is for you. An essential reference.

### POSIX Programmer's Guide

By Donald Lewine
1st Edition April 1991
640 pages, ISBN 0-937175-73-0

Most UNIX systems today are POSIX compliant because the federal government requires it for its purchases. Given the manufacturer's documentation, however, it can be difficult to distinguish system-specific features from those features defined by POSIX. The *POSIX Programmer's Guide*, intended as an explanation of the POSIX standard and as a reference for the POSIX.1 programming library, helps you write more portable programs.

### Practical C Programming

By Steve Oualline
2nd Edition January 1993
396 pages, ISBN 1-56592-035-X

C programming is more than just getting the syntax right. Style and debugging also play a tremendous part in creating programs that run well. *Practical C Programming* teaches you not only the mechanics of programming, but also how to create programs that are easy to read, maintain, and debug. There are lots of introductory C books, but this is the Nutshell Handbook®! In this edition, programs conform to ANSI C.

### Using C on the UNIX System

By Dave Curry
1st Edition January 1989
250 pages, ISBN 0-937175-23-4

This is the book for intermediate to experienced C programmers who want to become UNIX system programmers. It explains system calls and special library routines available on the UNIX system. It is impossible to write UNIX utilities of any sophistication without understanding the material in this book.

### Programming with curses

By John Strang
1st Edition 1986
76 pages, ISBN 0-937175-02-1

Curses is a UNIX library of functions for controlling a terminal's display screen from a C program. This handbook helps you make use of the curses library. Describes the original Berkeley version of curses.

### Understanding and Using COFF

By Gintaras R. Gircys
1st Edition November 1988
196 pages, ISBN 0-937175-31-5

COFF—Common Object File Format—is the formal definition for the structure of machine code files in the UNIX System V environment. All machine code files are COFF files. This handbook explains COFF data structure and its manipulation.

# C Programming Tools

## Microsoft RPC Programming Guide

By John Shirley & Ward Rosenberry,
Digital Equipment Corporation
1st Edition March 1995
254 pages, ISBN 1-56592-070-8

Remote Procedure Call (RPC) is the glue that holds together MS-DOS, Windows 3.x, and Windows NT. It is a client-server technology—a way of making programs on two different systems work together like one. The advantage of RPC is that you can link two systems together using simple C calls, as in a single-system program.

Like many aspects of Microsoft programming, RPC forms a small world of its own, with conventions and terms that can be confusing. This book is an introduction to Microsoft RPC concepts combined with a step-by-step guide to programming RPC calls in C. Topics include server registration, interface definitions, arrays and pointers, context handles, and basic administration procedures. This edition covers version 2.0 of Microsoft RPC. Four complete examples are included.

## Power Programming with RPC

By John Bloomer
1st Edition February 1992
522 pages, ISBN 0-937175-77-3

RPC, or remote procedure calling, is the ability to distribute the execution of functions on remote computers. Written from a programmer's perspective, this book shows what you can do with RPCs, like Sun RPC, the de facto standard on UNIX systems. It covers related programming topics for Sun and other UNIX systems and teaches through examples.

## lex & yacc

By John Levine, Tony Mason & Doug Brown
2nd Edition October 1992
366 pages, ISBN 1-56592-000-7

Shows programmers how to use two UNIX utilities, *lex* and *yacc*, in program development. The second edition contains completely revised tutorial sections for novice users and reference sections for advanced users. This edition is twice the size of the first, has an expanded index, and covers Bison and Flex.

## Applying RCS and SCCS

By Don Bolinger & Tan Bronson
1st Edition September 1995
528 pages, ISBN 1-56592-117-8

*Applying RCS and SCCS* is a thorough introduction to these two systems, viewed as tools for project management. This book takes the reader from basic source control of a single file, through working with multiple releases of a software project, to coordinating multiple developers. It also presents TCCS, a representative "front-end" that addresses problems RCS and SCCS can't handle alone, such as managing groups of files, developing for multiple platforms, and linking public and private development areas.

## Programming with GNU Software

By Mike Loukides
1st Edition TBA 1996 (est.)
250 pages (est.), ISBN 1-56592-112-7

This book and CD combination is a complete package for programmers who are new to UNIX or who would like to make better use of the system. The tools come from Cygnus Support, Inc., a well-known company that provides support for free software. Contents include GNU Emacs, *gcc*, C and C++ libraries, *gdb*, RCS, GNATS, and *make*. The book provides an introduction to all these tools for a C programmer.

## UNIX Systems Programming for SVR4

By Dave Curry
1st Edition December 1995 (est.)
600 pages (est.), ISBN 1-56592-163-1

Presents a comprehensive look at the nitty gritty details on how UNIX interacts with applications. If you're writing an application from scratch, or if you're porting an application to any System V.4 platform, you need this book. It thoroughly explains all UNIX system calls and library routines related to systems programming, working with I/O, files and directories, processing multiple input streams, file and record locking, and memory-mapped files.

## Software Portability with imake

*By Paul DuBois*
*1st Edition July 1993*
*390 pages, ISBN 1-56592-055-4*

*imake* is a utility that works with *make* to enable code to be compiled and installed on different UNIX machines. *imake* makes possible the wide portability of the X Window System code and is widely considered an X tool, but it's also useful for any software project that needs to be ported to many UNIX systems.

This Nutshell Handbook®—the only book available on *imake*—is ideal for X and UNIX programmers who want their software to be portable. The book is divided into two sections. The first section is a general explanation of *imake*, X configuration files, and how to write and debug an *Imakefile*. The second section describes how to write configuration files and presents a configuration file architecture that allows development of coexisting sets of configuration files. Several sample sets of configuration files are described and are available free over the Net.

## Managing Projects with make

*By Andrew Oram & Steve Talbott*
*2nd Edition October 1991*
*152 pages, ISBN 0-937175-90-0*

*make* is one of UNIX's greatest contributions to software development, and this book offers the clearest description of *make* ever written. It describes all the basic features of *make* and provides guidelines on meeting the needs of large, modern projects. Also contains a description of free products that contain major enhancements to *make*.

## Checking C Programs with lint

*By Ian F. Darwin*
*1st Edition October 1988*
*84 pages, ISBN 0-937175-30-7*

The *lint* program is one of the best tools for finding portability problems and certain types of coding errors in C programs. This handbook introduces you to *lint*, guides you through running it on your programs, and helps you interpret *lint's* output.

## Fortran/Scientific Computing

### Migrating to Fortran 90

*By James F. Kerrigan*
*1st Edition November 1993*
*389 pages, ISBN 1-56592-049-X*

This book is a practical guide to Fortran 90 for the current Fortran programmer. It provides a complete overview of the new features that Fortran 90 has brought to the Fortran standard, with examples and suggestions for use. Topics include array sections, modules, file handling, allocatable arrays and pointers, and numeric precision.

"This is a book that all Fortran programmers eager to take advantage of the excellent features of Fortran 90 will want to have on their desk." —*FORTRAN Journal*

### High Performance Computing

*By Kevin Dowd*
*1st Edition June 1993*
*398 pages, ISBN 1-56592-032-5*

Even if you never touch a line of code, *High Performance Computing* will help you make sense of the newest generation of workstations. A must for anyone who needs to worry about computer performance, this book covers everything, from the basics of modern workstation architecture, to structuring benchmarks, to squeezing more performance out of critical applications. It also explains what a good compiler can do—and what you have to do yourself. The author also discusses techniques for improving memory access patterns and taking advantage of parallelism.

Another valuable section of the book discusses the benchmarking process, or how to evaluate a computer's performance. Kevin Dowd discusses several of the "standard" industry benchmarks, explaining what they measure and what they don't. He also explains how to set up your own benchmark: how to structure the code, how to measure the results, and how to interpret them.

# Database

## ORACLE Performance Tuning

*By Peter Corrigan & Mark Gurry*
*1st Edition September 1993*
*642 pages, ISBN 1-56592-048-1*

The Oracle relational database management system is the most popular database system in use today. Oracle offers tremendous power and flexibility, but at some cost. Demands for fast response, particularly in online transaction processing systems, make performance a major issue. With more organizations downsizing and adopting client-server and distributed database approaches, performance tuning has become all the more vital. Whether you're a manager, a designer, a programmer, or an administrator, there's a lot you can do on your own to dramatically increase the performance of your existing Oracle system. Whether you are running RDBMS Version 6 or Version 7, you may find that this book can save you the cost of a new machine; at the very least, it will save you a lot of headaches.

"This book is one of the best books on Oracle that I have ever read.... [It] discloses many Oracle Tips that DBA's and Developers have locked in their brains and in their planners.... I recommend this book for any person who works with Oracle, from managers to developers. In fact, I have to keep [it] under lock and key, because of the popularity of it." —Mike Gangler

## ORACLE PL/SQL Programming

*By Steven Feuerstein*
*1st Edition September 1995*
*916 pages, Includes diskette, ISBN 1-56592-142-9*

PL/SQL is a procedural language that is being used more and more with Oracle, particularly in client-server applications. This book fills a huge gap in the Oracle market by providing developers with a single, comprehensive guide to building applications with PL/SQL—and building them the right way. It's packed with strategies, code architectures, tips, techniques, and fully realized code. Includes a disk containing many examples of PL/SQL programs.

# Multi-Platform Programming

## DCE Security Programming

*By Wei Hu*
*1st Edition July 1995*
*386 pages, ISBN 1-56592-134-8*

Security is critical in network applications since an outsider can so easily gain network access and pose as a trusted user. Here lies one of the greatest strengths of the Distributed Computing Environment (DCE) from the Open Software Foundation (OSF). DCE offers the most complete, flexible, and well-integrated network security package in the industry. The only problem is learning how to program it.

This book covers DCE security requirements, how the system fits together, what is required of the programmer, and how to figure out what needs protecting in an application. It will help you plan an application and lay the groundwork for Access Control Lists (ACLs), as well as use the calls that come with the DCE security interfaces. Using a sample application, increasingly sophisticated types of security are discussed, including storage of ACLs on disk and the job of writing an ACL manager. This book focuses on version 1.0 of DCE. However, issues in version 1.1 are also discussed so you can migrate to that interface.

## Guide to Writing DCE Applications

*By John Shirley, Wei Hu & David Magid*
*2nd Edition May 1994*
*462 pages, ISBN 1-56592-045-7*

A hands-on programming guide to OSF's Distributed Computing Environment (DCE) for first-time DCE application programmers. This book is designed to help new DCE users make the transition from conventional, nondistributed applications programming to distributed DCE programming.
In addition to basic RPC (remote procedure calls), this edition covers object UUIDs and basic security (authentication and authorization). Also includes practical programming examples.

"This book will be useful as a ready reference by the side of the novice DCE programmer." —;login

## Distributing Applications Across DCE and Windows NT

By Ward Rosenberry & Jim Teague
1st Edition November 1993
302 pages, ISBN 1-56592-047-3

This book links together two exciting technologies in distributed computing by showing how to develop an application that simultaneously runs on DCE and Microsoft systems through remote procedure calls (RPC). Covers the writing of portable applications and the complete differences between RPC support in the two environments.

## Understanding DCE

By Ward Rosenberry, David Kenney & Gerry Fisher
1st Edition October 1992
266 pages, ISBN 1-56592-005-8

A technical and conceptual overview of OSF's Distributed Computing Environment (DCE) for programmers, technical managers, and marketing and sales people. Unlike many O'Reilly & Associates books, Understanding DCE has no hands-on programming elements. Instead, the book focuses on how DCE can be used to accomplish typical programming tasks and provides explanations to help the reader understand all the parts of DCE.

## Multi-Platform Code Management

By Kevin Jameson
1st Edition August 1994
354 pages, Includes two diskettes, ISBN 1-56592-059-7

For any programming team that is struggling with build and maintenance problems, this book—and its accompanying software (available for 15 platforms, including MS-DOS and various UNIX systems)—can save dozens of errors and hours of effort. A "one-stop-shopping" solution for code management proplems, this book shows you how to structure a large project and keep your files and builds under control over many releases and platforms. Includes two diskettes that provide a complete system for managing source files and builds.

## Encyclopedia of Graphics File Formats

By James D. Murray & William vanRyper
1st Edition July 1994
928 pages, Includes CD-ROM
ISBN 1-56592-058-9

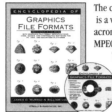

The computer graphics world is a veritable alphabet soup of acronyms; BMP, DXF, EPS, GIF, MPEG, PCX, PIC, RIFF, RTF, TGA, and TIFF are only a few of the many different formats in which graphics images can be stored. The Encyclopedia of Graphics File Formats is the definitive work on file formats—the book that will become a classic for graphics programmers and everyone else who deals with the low-level technical details of graphics files. It includes technical information on nearly 100 file formats, as well as chapters on graphics and file format basics, bitmap and vector files, metafiles, scene description, animation and multimedia formats, and file compression methods. Best of all, this book comes with a CD-ROM that collects many hard-to-find resources. We've assembled original vendor file format specification documents, along with test images and code examples, and a variety of software packages for MS-DOS, Windows, OS/2, UNIX, and the Macintosh that will let you convert, view, and manipulate graphics files and images.

## Understanding Japanese Information Processing

By Ken Lunde
1st Edition September 1993
470 pages, ISBN 1-56592-043-0

Understanding Japanese Information Processing provides detailed information on all aspects of handling Japanese text on computer systems. It brings all of the relevant information together in a single book and covers everything from the origins of modern-day Japanese to the latest information on specific emerging computer encoding standards. Appendices provide additional reference material, such as a code conversion table, character set tables, mapping tables, an extensive list of software sources, a glossary, and more.

# *At Your Fingertips—*
# A COMPLETE GUIDE TO O'REILLY'S ONLINE SERVICES

O'Reilly & Associates offers extensive product and customer service information online. We invite you to come and explore our little neck-of-the-woods.

## For product information and insight into new technologies, visit the O'Reilly Resource Center

Most comprehensive among our online offerings is the O'Reilly Resource Center. You'll find detailed information on all O'Reilly products, including titles, prices, tables of contents, indexes, author bios, software contents, and reviews. You can also view images of all our products. In addition, watch for informative articles that provide perspective on the technologies we write about. Interviews, excerpts, and bibliographies are also included.

After browsing online, it's easy to order, too, with GNN Direct or by sending email to **order@ora.com**. The O'Reilly Resource Center shows you how. Here's how to visit us online:

### ☞*Via the World Wide Web*

If you are connected to the Internet, point your Web browser (e.g., `mosaic`, `netscape`, or `lynx`) to:

`http://www.ora.com/`

For the plaintext version, `telnet` to:
`www.ora.com` (login: `oraweb`)

### ☞*Via Gopher*

If you have a Gopher program, our Gopher server has information in a menu format that some people prefer to the Web.

Connect your `gopher` to: `gopher.ora.com`

Or, point your Web browser to:
`gopher://gopher.ora.com/`

Or, you can `telnet` to: `gopher.ora.com`
(login: `gopher`)

## A convenient way to stay informed: email mailing lists

An easy way to learn of the latest projects and products from O'Reilly & Associates is to subscribe to our mailing lists. We have email announcements and discussions on various topics, for example "ora-news," our electronic news service. Subscribers receive email as soon as the information breaks.

### ☞*To join a mailing list:*

Send email to:

**listproc@online.ora.com**

Leave the message "subject" empty if possible.

If you know the name of the mailing list you want to subscribe to, put the following information on the first line of your message: `subscribe` "listname" "your name" `of` "your company."

For example: `subscribe ora-news`
`Kris Webber of Fine Enterprises`

If you don't know the name of the mailing list, listproc will send you a listing of all the mailing lists. Put this word on the first line of the body: `lists`

To find out more about a particular list, send a message with this word as the first line of the body: `info` "listname"

For more information and help, send this message:
`help`

For specific help, email to:
**listmaster@online.ora.com**

## The complete O'Reilly catalog is now available via email

You can now receive a text-only version of our complete catalog via email. It contains detailed information about all our products, so it's mighty big: over 200 kbytes, or 200,000 characters.

To get the whole catalog in one message, send an empty email message to: **catalog@online.ora.com**

If your email system can't handle large messages, you can get the catalog split into smaller messages. Send email to: **catalog-split@online.ora.com**

To receive a print catalog, send your snail mail address to: **catalog@ora.com**

## Check out Web Review, our new publication on the Web

Web Review is our new magazine that offers fresh insights into the Web. The editorial mission of Web Review is to answer the question: How and where do you BEST spend your time online? Each issue contains reviews that look at the most interesting and creative sites on the Web. Visit us at **http://gnn.com/wr/**

Web Review is the product of the recently formed Songline Studios, a venture between O'Reilly and America Online.

## Get the files you want with FTP

We have an archive of example files from our books, the covers of our books, and much more available by anonymous FTP.

`ftp` to:

`ftp.ora.com` (login: `anonymous` – use your email address as the password.)

Or, if you have a WWW browser, point it to:

`ftp://ftp.ora.com/`

## FTPMAIL

The ftpmail service connects to O'Reilly's FTP server and sends the results (the files you want) by email. This service is for people who can't use FTP—but who can use email.

For help and examples, send an email message to:

`ftpmail@online.ora.com`

(In the message body, put the single word: `help`)

## Helpful information is just an email message away

Many customer services are provided via email. Here are a few of the most popular and useful:

**info@online.ora.com**
> For a list of O'Reilly's online customer services.

**info@ora.com**
> For general questions and information.

**bookquestions@ora.com**
> For technical questions, or corrections, concerning book contents.

**order@ora.com**
> To order books online and for ordering questions.

**catalog@online.ora.com**
> To receive an online copy of our catalog.

**catalog@ora.com**
> To receive a free copy of *ora.com*, our combination magazine and catalog. Please include your snail mail address.

**international@ora.com**
> Comments or questions about international ordering or distribution.

**xresource@ora.com**
> To order or inquire about *The X Resource* journal.

**proposals@ora.com**
> To submit book proposals.

**info@gnn.com**
> To receive information about America Online's GNN (Global Network Navigator).™

## O'Reilly & Associates, Inc.

**103A Morris Street, Sebastopol, CA 95472**

Inquiries: **707-829-0515, 800-998-9938**

Credit card orders: **800-889-8969**
(Weekdays 6 A.M.- 5 P.M. PST)

FAX: **707-829-0104**

# O'Reilly & Associates—
# LISTING OF TITLES

## INTERNET

CGI Scriptin on the World Wide Web (Winter '95-96 est.)

Connecting to the Internet: An O'Reilly Buyer's Guide

Getting Connected (Winter '95-96 est.)

The Mosaic Handbook for Microsoft Windows

The Mosaic Handbook for the Macintosh

The Mosaic Handbook for the X Window System

Smileys

The USENET Handbook

The Whole Internet User's Guide & Catalog

The Whole Internet for Windows 95

Web Design for Designers (Winter '95-96 est.)

The World Wide Web Journal (Winter '95-96 est.)

## SOFTWARE

Internet In A Box™

WebSite™

## WHAT YOU NEED TO KNOW SERIES

Using Email Effectively

Marketing on the Internet (Winter '95-96 est.)

When You Can't Find Your System Administrator

## HEALTH, CAREER & BUSINESS

Building a Successful Software Business

The Computer User's Survival Guide (Fall '95 est.)

Dictionary of Computer Terms (Winter '95-96 est.)

The Future Does Not Compute

Love Your Job!

TWI Day Calendar - 1996

## USING UNIX

### BASICS

Learning GNU Emacs

Learning the bash Shell

Learning the Korn Shell

Learning the UNIX Operating System

Learning the vi Editor

MH & xmh: Email for Users & Programmers

SCO UNIX in a Nutshell

UNIX in a Nutshell: System V Edition

Using and Managing UUCP (Winter '95-96 est.)

Using csh and tcsh

### ADVANCED

Exploring Expect

The Frame Handbook

Learning Perl

Making TeX Work

Programming perl

Running Linux

Running Linux Companion CD-ROM (Winter '95-96 est.)

sed & awk

UNIX Power Tools (with CD-ROM)

## SYSTEM ADMINISTRATION

Building Internet Firewalls

Computer Crime: A Crimefighter's Handbook

Computer Security Basics

DNS and BIND

Essential System Administration

Linux Network Administrator's Guide

Managing Internet Information Services

Managing NFS and NIS

Managing UUCP and Usenet

Networking Personal Computers with TCP/IP

Practical UNIX Security

PGP: Pretty Good Privacy

sendmail

System Performance Tuning

TCP/IP Network Administration

termcap & terminfo

Volume 8 : X Window System Administrator's Guide

The X Companion CD for R6

## PROGRAMMING

Applying RCS and SCCS

C++: The Core Language

Checking C Programs with lint

DCE Security Programming

Distributing Applications Across DCE and Windows NT

Encyclopedia of Graphics File Formats

Guide to Writing DCE Applications

High Performance Computing

lex & yacc

Managing Projects with make

Microsoft RPC Programming Guide

Migrating to Fortran 90

Multi-Platform Code Management

ORACLE Performance Tuning

ORACLE PL/SQL Programming

Porting UNIX Software

POSIX Programmer's Guide

POSIX.4: Programming for the Real World

Power Programming with RPC

Practical C Programming

Practical C++ Programming

Programming with curses

Programming with GNU Software (Winter '95-96 est.)

Programming with Pthreads (Winter '95-96 est.)

Software Portability with imake

Understanding and Using COFF

Understanding DCE

Understanding Japanese Information Processing

Using C on the UNIX System

## BERKELEY 4.4 SOFTWARE DISTRIBUTION

4.4BSD System Manager's Manual

4.4BSD User's Reference Manual

4.4BSD User's Supp. Documents

4.4BSD Programmer's Reference Manual

4.4BSD Programmer's Supplementary Documents

4.4BSD-Lite CD Companion

4.4BSD-Lite CD Companion: International Version

## X WINDOW SYSTEM

Volume 0: X Protocol Reference Manual

Volume 1: Xlib Programming Manual

Volume 2: Xlib Reference Manual:

Volume 3: X Window System User's Guide

Volume. 3M: X Window System User's Guide, Motif Ed

Volume. 4: X Toolkit Intrinsics Programming Manual

Volume 4M: X Toolkit Intrinsics Programming Manual, Motif Ed.

Volume 5: X Toolkit Intrinsics Reference Manual

Volume 6A: Motif Programming Manual

Volume 6B: Motif Reference Manual

Volume 6C: Motif Tools

Volume 8 : X Window System Administrator's Guide

PEXlib Programming Manual

PEXlib Reference Manual

PHIGS Programming Manual

PHIGS Reference Manual

Programmer's Supplement for Release 6

The X Companion CD for R6

X User Tools (with CD-ROM)

The X Window System in a Nutshell

## THE X RESOURCE

*A QUARTERLY WORKING JOURNAL FOR X PROGRAMMERS*

The X Resource: Issues 0 through 15

## TRAVEL

Travelers' Tales France

Travelers' Tales Hong Kong (12/95 est.)

Travelers' Tales India

Travelers' Tales Mexico

Travelers' Tales Spain

Travelers' Tales Thailand

Travelers' Tales: A Woman's World

# O'Reilly & Associates—
# INTERNATIONAL DISTRIBUTORS

Customers outside North America can now order O'Reilly & Associates books through the following distributors.
They offer our international customers faster order processing, more bookstores, increased representation at tradeshows worldwide, and the high-quality, responsive service our customers have come to expect.

## EUROPE, MIDDLE EAST, AND AFRICA
*(except Germany, Switzerland, and Austria)*

**INQUIRIES**
International Thomson Publishing Europe
Berkshire House
168-173 High Holborn
London WC1V 7AA, United Kingdom
Telephone: 44-71-497-1422
Fax: 44-71-497-1426
Email: itpint@itps.co.uk

**ORDERS**
International Thomson Publishing Services, Ltd.
Cheriton House, North Way
Andover, Hampshire SP10 5BE, United Kingdom
Telephone: 44-264-342-832 (UK orders)
Telephone: 44-264-342-806 (outside UK)
Fax: 44-264-364418 (UK orders)
Fax: 44-264-342761 (outside UK)

## GERMANY, SWITZERLAND, AND AUSTRIA

International Thomson Publishing GmbH
O'Reilly-International Thomson Verlag
Königswinterer Straße 418
53227 Bonn, Germany
Telephone: 49-228-97024 0
Fax: 49-228-441342
Email: anfragen@ora.de

## ASIA *(except Japan)*
**INQUIRIES**
International Thomson Publishing Asia
221 Henderson Road
#08-03 Henderson Industrial Park
Singapore 0315
Telephone: 65-272-6496
Fax: 65-272-6498

**ORDERS**
Telephone: 65-268-7867
Fax: 65-268-6727

## JAPAN

O'Reilly & Associates, Inc.
103A Morris Street
Sebastopol, CA 95472 U.S.A.
Telephone: 707-829-0515
Telephone: 800-998-9938 (U.S. & Canada)
Fax: 707-829-0104
Email: order@ora.com

## AUSTRALIA

WoodsLane Pty. Ltd.
7/5 Vuko Place, Warriewood NSW 2102
P.O. Box 935, Mona Vale NSW 2103
Australia
Telephone: 02-970-5111
Fax: 02-970-5002
Email: woods@tmx.mhs.oz.au

## NEW ZEALAND

WoodsLane New Zealand Ltd.
21 Cooks Street (P.O. Box 575)
Wanganui, New Zealand
Telephone: 64-6-347-6543
Fax: 64-6-345-4840
Email: woods@tmx.mhs.oz.au

## THE AMERICAS

O'Reilly & Associates, Inc.
103A Morris Street
Sebastopol, CA 95472 U.S.A.
Telephone: 707-829-0515
Telephone: 800-998-9938 (U.S. & Canada)
Fax: 707-829-0104
Email: order@ora.com

# Here's a page we encourage readers to tear out...

## O'REILLY WOULD LIKE TO HEAR FROM YOU

*Please send me the following:*

❏ *ora.com*

O'Reilly's magazine/catalog, containing behind-the-scenes articles and interviews on the technology we write about, and a complete listing of O'Reilly books and products.

Which book did this card come from?

_____

Where did you buy this book?
   ❏ Bookstore    ❏ Direct from O'Reilly
   ❏ Bundled with hardware/software    ❏ Class/seminar

Your job description:   ❏ SysAdmin    ❏ Programmer
   ❏ Other_____

Describe your operating system: _____

_____

*Please print legibly*

Name _____ Company/Organization Name _____

Address _____

City _____ State _____ Zip/Postal Code _____ Country _____

Telephone _____ Internet or other email address (specify network) _____

Nineteenth century wood engraving
of the rhesas monkey from the O'Reilly
& Associates Nutshell Handbook®
*Exploring Expect.*

POST CARD

O'Reilly & Associates, Inc., 103A Morris Street, Sebastopol, CA 95472-9902

PLACE
STAMP
HERE

NO POSTAGE
NECESSARY IF
MAILED IN THE
UNITED STATES

# BUSINESS REPLY MAIL

FIRST CLASS MAIL   PERMIT NO. 80   SEBASTOPOL, CA

*Postage will be paid by addressee*

### O'Reilly & Associates, Inc.
103A Morris Street
Sebastopol, CA 95472-9902

||I||I||I|I|I||I||II||I||I|I|I|II|I||I||I||II||II||I||I|I||I|

**04418784**